A TREASURY
OF JEWISH
ANECDOTES

A TREASURY OF JEWISH ANECDOTES

Lawrence J. Epstein

JASON ARONSON INC.
Northvale, New Jersey
London

Copyright © 1989 by Lawrence J. Epstein

10 9 8 7 6 5 4 3 2

Library of Congress Cataloging-in-Publication Data

Epstein, Lawrence J. (Lawrence Jeffrey)
    A treasury of Jewish anecdotes / Lawrence J. Epstein.
      p. cm.
    Bibliography: p.
    Includes index.
    ISBN 0-87668-890-3
    1. Jews—Anecdotes. I. Title.
DS115.E6 1989
920'.0092924—dc19   89-393
                                                        CIP

Manufactured in the United States of America. Jason Aronson Inc. offers books and cassettes. For information and catalog write to Jason Aronson Inc., 230 Livingston Street, Northvale, New Jersey 07647.

*This book is to honor
the blessed memory of my father,
Frederick Epstein,
and the loving kindness of my mother,
Lillian Scheinert Epstein.*

CONTENTS

ACKNOWLEDGMENTS

A book such as this almost needs a companion volume simply to acknowledge all those who have helped in its development. I am a literary middle-man passing on the reworked stories of others. The ultimate acknowledgments must be given to the subjects of the anecdotes, to those whose efforts were important or witty or interesting enough to have been remembered. Obviously, also, these anecdotes are available only because someone was there to pass them on until they reached this book. The book's debt to others is extraordinary.

Arthur Kurzweil is the first person who deserves mention. Arthur not only listened to but helped shape the idea for the book, with remarkably insightful editorial guidance. He provided consistent support and encouragement in a way that authors welcome but too rarely receive.

Anecdotes in this book have been graciously provided to me by the following: Professor Robert Alter, the well-known literary critic; Professor Emil Fackenheim, the renowned Jewish philosopher; Dr. Robert Gordis, the editor of *Judaism*; Dr. Norman Lamm, president of Yeshiva University; the late Nathan Perlmutter of the Anti-Defamation League of B'nai B'rith, who had information forwarded to me just weeks before his death; Dr. Emanuel Rackman, chancellor of Bar-Ilan University in Israel; and Simon Wiesenthal, the foremost hunter of Nazi war criminals. Anecdotes were also provided by Stan Barkan, of Cross-Cultural Communications; Zeldon Cohen; Nettie Cohen-Cole; Rabbi Adam Fisher of Temple Isaiah in Stony Brook, New York; Monroe H. Freedman, law professor at Hofstra University; Dr. Paul Gastwirth; Hugo Jelinowicz; Irina Mass of Temple Ansche Chesed in New York; Phil Miller, librarian at Hebrew Union College-Jewish Institute of Religion in New York; Rabbi Samuel Silver of Temple Sinai in Delray Beach, Florida; Mrs. D. Silverman; Sam Sokolow; and Ethel Zelen.

I turned for advice in searching for anecdotes to the following: Rafi Danziger, of the American Jewish Congress, who has an intimate grasp of Jewish history and current affairs; Robert Milch, a gifted author and editor who opened his library to me; Dr. Carl Rheins, co-editor of *The Jewish Almanac*, who, as always, was willing to share his extensive knowledge; Lynn Singer, executive director of the Long Island Committee for Soviet Jewry, who provided insights about Soviet Jews; Rabbi Tuvia Teldon, who provided guidance in searching out anecdotes related to Hasidism; and Laura Wiletsky, whose experience in public relations prompted some good suggestions. Valuable advice also came from Dr. Mark Bernheim, of Miami University in Ohio, and Leo Rosten, author of *The Joys of Yiddish* and other works.

It would have been impossible to write this book without bibliographic advice. I would particularly like to thank Nathan Kaganoff, of the American Jewish Historical Society; Dr. Jacob Rader Marcus, director of the American Jewish Archives; Peggy K. Pearlstein, of the Hebraic section, African and Middle Eastern Division, of the Library of Congress; and Esther Togman, director of the Zionist Archives and Library.

Special mention must be given to the librarians and staff at Suffolk County Community College. They were unfailingly enthusiastic and helpful. Numerous requests for interlibrary loans were met not only with cheerful willingness but with offers to do as much as was needed. Books came in from all over the country. Carole Gambrell, Peter Kaufman, Shirley Levitt, Patricia Hogan, John Longo, Marge Olson, and Dominic Provenzano were some of those at the Suffolk College library who were there to help.

Suffolk County Community College has always been extraordinarily supportive. The college granted me a sabbatical, which I used to complete this book. My colleagues there have been generous in their encouragement of my writing.

My rabbi, Moshe Edelman of the North Shore Jewish Center in Port Jefferson Station, New York, always provides staunch and much-needed support for my Jewish endeavors.

I cannot imagine writing without the help of close friends. Friends who provided solace and advice, who took me to lunch and were always there to listen, include Mike Fitzpatrick, Steve Israel, Steve Klipstein, and Norman Rabinowitz. Richard Gambrell has provided bibliographical and indexing help for all my books. His advise is always valuable. Douglas Rathgeb listened to every problem I encountered and joined in every moment of joy. Doug and I visited many bookstores and libraries searching for needed works. He always provided words of wisdom and a clear-headed analysis.

My family was, as always, unfailing in their support. My father, Fred Epstein, passed away while I was working on this book. He consistently encouraged my writing, and I hope this effort honors his memory. My mother, Lillian Scheinert Epstein, was particularly enthusiastic about the book and provided many suggestions for subjects. Her knowledge of Yiddish theater and motion pictures made my work much easier. My late mother-in-law, Goldie Goldman Selib, was always tremendously supportive of my efforts. My brother, Richard Epstein, helped me gather materials in a wide variety of libraries, patiently listened, and offered significant advice.

Finally, the support provided by my wife, Sharon, made this work possible. She listens, always gives dependable advice, and provides help in endless ways.

Our children, Michael, Elana, Rachel, and Lisa, were always willing to cooperate and always eager to help. They fill my life with the wonder and joy of being a parent.

INTRODUCTION

This book is a collection of anecdotes about prominent and interesting Jewish people from biblical times to the present. An anecdote is a story with a point. The story is a brief account of a biographical incident. It is usually about a famous person and often reveals a little-known aspect of the person's life. An anecdote is sometimes humorous, sometimes poignant, sometimes thought-provoking, and sometimes just interesting. An anecdote's ending is often a surprise. Reading a good anecdote is like receiving an unexpected gift. There is a sensation akin to the sudden insight derived from a work of literature, described by Edmund Wilson as a shock of recognition. An anecdote's point evokes a somewhat milder reaction, perhaps a tap of recognition.

The purposes of an anecdote are to arouse, to inculcate a moral lesson, to illuminate the character of its subject and the times in which the subject lived, and to encourage further study of the subject's life and thoughts. Anecdotes are the seasoning of history and the dramatic snapshots of an individual's life. Anecdotes illustrate the fact that a life can provide a symbol of itself in a simple and unique but ironically typical moment. Anecdotes humanize individuals and turn abstract concepts into concrete ones. They can make complex ideas immediately clear.

Anecdotes can also provide the context for witty or wise or historically significant quotations—quotations that on their own might not sound very witty or wise or historically significant. Genuine quotations can stand on their own, without context; they are not real anecdotes. Similarly, anecdotes can be compared to invented jokes and humorous stories. Sometimes the words *anecdote* and *joke* are used interchangeably. In 1897, for instance, Sigmund Freud wrote in a letter that he was making a collection of Jewish anecdotes—by which he meant jokes about Jews. But the two are separate kinds of literary creations. Jokes and humorous stories aim to provoke laughter but are not purported to be true. Anecdotes can provoke laughter, but the laughter emerges from a real human encounter, not an invented one.

An anecdote does have the connotation of describing a light and trivial incident, but this is not necessarily so. Some anecdotes *are* humorous, but even in such anecdotes the humor is not an end in itself but a prod to make us see some deeper meaning in an experience. More serious anecdotes can be about the turning points in an individual's life or even about turning points in history. Using a single incident as a jumping-off point, a good anecdote leads us to an understanding of a character and of history, and, at its best, leads us to wisdom.

A caveat must be entered here. Most anecdotes are based on fact, but because they are often oral accounts, they are prone to being exaggerated with each retelling. Some ungenerous people might even accuse them of being untrue. In fact, some anecdotes were invented for the purposes of humor or publicity, and even today the dictionary definition of the word is broad enough to encompass such fictional accounts. The anecdotes presented in this book are factual to the extent that fact can be determined. In questionable circumstances it is hoped that the reader will bear in mind the oft-expressed view that even if a particular story isn't true, it ought to be. Anecdote collections are not so much works of scholarship as they are works of a special kind of literature.

Anecdotes have their place in Jewish literature. Some anecdotes provide information about Jews who were or are famous. Their fame evokes our curiosity about them, about their lives, their accomplishments, their influences, and their indebtedness to their Jewishness. Sometimes, in the very best anecdotes, there is more than a laugh, and even more than an insight into a famous person or a historical event; there is, in addition, a kernel of truth revealed about Judaism itself, about how the heritage of Judaism weaves its way into the being of its people.

Anecdotes have been part of Jewish life from its inception. Oral stories passed from one generation to the next have included many anecdotes. I could have included many more biblical anecdotes than I did; their exclusion is due only to their familiarity and to the need to reserve space for some lesser-known anecdotes. The great biblical figures, the patriarchs and matriarchs, the judges and kings and prophets, the wise and the wicked, stirred Jewish imaginations. Legends and stories about them, so abundant in postbiblical literature, attest to Jewish interest in biblical ancestors and their exploits.

Anecdotes are not yet a distinctive category of Jewish literature; rather, they are embedded in biographical stories. They form their own subgenre halfway between gossip and wisdom literature. Anecdotes can be a valuable addition to Jewish literature. The sheer diversity of Jewish history, the story of a people across the centuries, across continents, across linguistic borders and religious beliefs, across customs and traditions, makes it difficult to encompass. Anecdotes, because of their relative brevity, can begin to encompass that diversity. They form the appetizer for the main course of Jewish learning. They can provide an introductory overview of the sweep of Jewish life.

One self-imposed limitation of this book is that its subjects are restricted to Jews, although the principle of inclusion under the general term *Jewish* is extraordinarily broad. Subjects who were born Jews, regardless of any changes later in life, subjects who adopted Judaism as a religion, and subjects widely regarded as Jewish but whose Jewishness is arguable under Jewish law will be included. This principle has been stretched in one case—that of Raoul Wallenberg—because of his unique achievements and some claims of distant Jewish ancestry. By limiting the book to Jewish subjects, I do not mean to imply that non-Jews have not made valuable or important contributions to Jewish life. There are important Jewish anecdotes involving non-Jews that deserve to be remembered.

Indeed, there are many important Jews who made vital contributions to Jewish life but who are not included in this volume. Beyond that, there are even more anecdotes about the individuals mentioned that I could not include. Inevitably, choices had to be made. For instance, there are subjects included in this book who may be famous only to some groups within Jewish life. There are subjects who are not famous but who deserve to be because of their accomplishments. There are, no doubt, significant Jewish anecdotes about "ordinary" people. Maybe the success of Jewish history lies in its being a succession of extraordinary achievements by ordinary people. Such anecdotes deserve to be included when the history of the Jews is written, and some representative ones should be included in a complete collection of Jewish anecdotes. It is more with pleasure than with guilt that I admit that no single volume could contain all the Jewish anecdotes worthy of mention.

The principles of inclusion and exclusion are these: the insight provided by the anecdote into personality and Jewish life and history, variety (that is, trying to ensure that Jews of all views and historical periods are included), and, not least, my own limitations. It would be a foolhardy assertion for any one individual to claim an adequate mastery of all the sources that Jewish literature comprises. I hope that this book will provoke readers to unearth hidden anecdotal gems in Jewish writing. Still, in Rabbi Tarfon's oft-quoted words, "The day is short, the labor is great. The workers are lazy, and the Master is urgent. It is not your duty to complete the work, but neither are you free to desist from it."

This book is organized alphabetically according to the last (or best-known) name of the subject of the anecdote. The Jews who are included here are an extraordinarily diverse lot. In fact, placing their names side by side was jarring. Here was a twentieth-century Zionist next to a philosopher from the Middle Ages and a Hasid. In these pages, Jews of all types mingle. Persons who have little in common rest next to each other, united by their bond of Jewishness. The best image of this diversity came from Arthur Kurzweil, who told me that Elie Wiesel had once described a library in a similar way, as shelves of books whose authors, had they met in life, might not even have talked to each other, but there, in the library, they were side by side.

The anecdotes in this book are of various lengths. Many are the typically brief anecdote that provides the backdrop for a witty or insightful remark. But others are longer, setting the stage for an important event in Jewish history in which a prominent person played a part. These slightly expanded, more serious anecdotes are meant to show the substance and the flexibility of the anecdotal form.

One of the most intriguing questions about anecdotes is their source. Indeed, the word *anecdote* comes from a Greek word meaning "things not given out"—that is, things private or unpublished. Anecdotes originally had an air of secrecy. The search for anecdotes, therefore, is much like a hunt.

The task of finding anecdotes is compounded by another problem. Although I have revised and rewritten every anecdote that appears in this volume, the raw anecdotes themselves were gathered from a variety of sources. The acknowledgments are meant to spell out the particulars of that debt. Still, I hope I have not plundered the efforts of others. I recognize that those who deserve credit for the anecdotes are the subjects of the anecdotes and those who originally passed the stories on to others. It is in the spirit of a reshaper and teller of tales, rather than of an inventor, that I present this book.

I used a variety of sources for these anecdotes. First, there are published collections of anecdotes, scattered within which can be found items about Jews. There are also numerous biographies and autobiographies, which frequently contain anecdotes. Books, newspapers, and magazines were another source; I read many books and periodicals in search of interesting anecdotes. In addition, I requested anecdotes from selected prominent Jews and from the Jewish public. Friends and relatives were also an invaluable source. Some anecdotes were found in many places (only one of which I include in the "Source" section), and some I just heard somewhere.

The purpose of this book is to promote Jewish learning and to pass on the Jewish heritage. Its success will be measured not by the laughter or tears or thoughts it may evoke, but rather by its enhancement of the reader's Jewish experience. I only hope that I have made manifest my own enthusiasm for learning about being Jewish.

AARONSOHN, SARAH (1890–1917)

Zionist heroine, co-founder of NILI, which stands for Netzach Yisrael
Lo Yeshakker, or "the strength of Israel will not lie," an intelligence
group for the British in World War I.

Sarah Aaronsohn gave her life to advance the Zionist cause. She worked with
her brother Aaron and others in NILI, a secret group set up to provide the
British with intelligence information about the Turks.

Sarah was an intelligence agent for several reasons. In 1915 she had been
an eyewitness to the savage treatment of the Armenians by the Turks. In
addition, she was convinced that if during the war the British gained control
over the Jewish areas of settlement and ended Turkish rule (which had begun in
1517), then the British would give the Jews an independent nation and fulfill the
Zionist dream.

The Turks learned of NILI's existence in September 1917. Sarah ordered
the network disbanded, but in order to counter open gossip about her involve-
ment, she refused to leave her home town of Zikhron Ya'akov. This decision not
to flee allowed other network members to reach safety.

Sarah was arrested in her home on October 1, 1917. She was tortured for
four days, but would not reveal any information. The authorities decided to
transfer her to the main prison in Nazareth, where the torture would continue
in an even more brutal way. (The Turkish prison there was famous for putting
boiling eggs under a prisoner's armpits.)

The Turkish soldiers who came for Sarah led her through the streets of her
town. Her hands were chained, and a rope connected her to a soldier in front.
Her long green dress was torn. The few children who gathered around could see
the streaks of blood on her dress and hair. She wore a green kerchief, which she
tied under her chin; it could not hide the blood. People stayed in their houses

1

and stared from behind the shutters. Sarah walked on, almost stumbling, and gazed back and forth, surveying the town. She saw the landmarks of her life, the synagogue, the Hotel Graf, Tomshi's grocery, the clothing store.

The soldiers came to a stop in front of the Aaronsohn home. Sarah gazed at the olive tree. A Turkish soldier removed her rope and chain and began to lead her into the house. She stopped him, asking that she be allowed to see to her wounds and change her clothing in private. The soldier agreed and waited outside with the others. The soldiers began to smoke. They heard the sound of water coming from inside the house.

But Sarah was not washing. She had pressed a secret button on one of the walls to release a hidden panel. She retrieved a revolver from the panel and then went to the bathroom. She turned the water on as she contemplated her act. She feared that additional torture would force her to betray her friends.

One of the soldiers became anxious and entered the house. He knocked on the bathroom door and told Sarah to hurry. She said she'd be ready in a moment.

She then fired a single shot. The bullet paralyzed her, but it would take four days—until October 9—for her to die.

Less than a month after her death, on November 2, the British issued the Balfour Declaration, expressing their sympathy toward Jewish national aspirations. The British Army, with contingents of Jewish soldiers, entered the land in late October. On December 9, exactly two months after Sarah's death, Jerusalem fell into British hands. General Allenby, leader of the victorious British fighters, later stated that NILI had played a crucial part in their victory.

ABELE (1764–1836)
Rabbi of Vilna and talmudic scholar.

An author came to see Rabbi Abele, wishing the rabbi to provide a favorable introduction to the author's commentary on the Book of Job. The rabbi agreed.

Later, the same author came back to the rabbi for still another introduction, this time for a commentary on Proverbs. The rabbi was not impressed by the work, but he did not wish to offend the author, so he simply said that he could not provide his approval by writing the introduction.

"But, Rabbi," said the author, "What made you prefer my commentary on Job to the one on Proverbs?"

The rabbi thought for a moment. "I will tell you if you insist. Job had a million problems, so one more book about him would be only a very slight additional affliction. Solomon, on the other hand, led a happy life. I didn't see why you should make him suffer."

ABRABANEL, ISAAC (1437–1508)
Philosopher, biblical scholar, and
Jewish representative.

Don Isaac Abrabanel tried to prevent Jews from being expelled from Spain. The edict to expel Jews was signed on March 31, 1492, by King Ferdinand. The edict proclaimed that Jews could remain in Spain only if they were baptized. Those who refused to become Christians would have to leave within three months. Unlike previous orders of expulsion, this order came directly from the monarchs, Ferdinand and Isabella, rather than from the Inquisition, which monitored religious conformity. The Jewish attendants at court received no advance notice of the order.

Don Isaac Abrabanel, as the chief spokesman for the Jews, requested an audience with King Ferdinand. Along with two other leaders, Abrabanel spoke passionately and eloquently. He asked for mercy. "Oh King, save your loyal subjects. Why do you act so cruelly toward us? We have prospered in this land, and we would gladly give all we possess for our country." The king was deeply impressed and decided to reconsider the expulsion. The publication of the edict was suspended, at least for a time. Abrabanel used the time to argue and appeal to all those he knew at court.

The king wavered, and Abrabanel knew that a second meeting was called for—one in which moral arguments would be backed by financial inducements. At this meeting, Abrabanel offered 300,000 ducats, the absolute maximum he thought could be raised. The king seemed interested at first, but he was dissuaded from abandoning the eviction edict by Tomas de Torquemada, the grand inquisitor. Torquemada told him, "Judas Iscariot sold his master for thirty pieces of silver. You want to sell him for 300,000 ducats. Here he is—take him and sell him!"

Abrabanel held a third meeting with the king. The king indicated that the decision had not been his alone, but also Queen Isabella's. Although he sensed that Ferdinand was seeking to evade responsibility, Abrabanel spoke to the queen, a ruler who reigned without the benefit of mercy. Don Isaac told Isabella that such efforts as expulsion would not render the Jews extinct. She looked at him and asked, "Do you believe that this comes upon you from us? The Lord put this in the king's heart." The Jewish leaders then asked Isabella if she would try to influence the king to withdraw the order. She replied that she was not allowed to use such influence, even if she wanted to, because "The king's heart is in the hands of the Lord, just as are the rivers. He turns it wherever He wishes."

The edict was made public in Spain between April 29 and May 1. Abrabanel joined some 300,000 other Jews who left. The Golden Age that the Jews had enjoyed in Spain was over.

ABRAHAM *(nineteenth century* B.C.E.*)*
First patriarch of the Jewish people.

(1) There is a story about how Abraham's spiritual journey to a belief in one God began when he was a boy.

Abraham's father, Terah, manufactured and sold idols. One day, Terah left his son in charge of the business. An elderly customer entered the establishment. Young Abraham asked the customer, "How old are you?"

"Quite old," the man answered immediately.

"What?" Abraham exclaimed. "How is it possible that a man with so many years of wisdom would want to worship an object that is only one day old?" The customer grew ashamed of his intention and left the shop.

No other customers bought idols that day. Instead of selling the idols, Abraham took a staff and broke all the idols except the largest one. Abraham placed the staff into the hands of the single remaining idol.

Terah returned and asked what had happened to all the idols. "The biggest god killed all the rest with his staff, which even now he holds," Abraham said, openly mocking pagan beliefs that idols had any genuine power.

(2) In keeping with his religious views, Abraham took particular pride in making his house available to the needy, the hungry, and the homeless. He kept doors on all sides of his house for travelers to enter. Whenever a passing traveler ate and wished to pay for the meal, Abraham would say, "Put the money back in your purse. God will pay me."

Abraham's generosity was known far and wide. It soon became known to Nimrod, who claimed that he was a god, just as powerful as the God that Abraham worshipped. Nimrod decided to play a trick on Abraham.

Nimrod came to Abraham's house with an army of 5,000 men. He asked Abraham if the army could have a meal. Abraham agreed. An entire flock of sheep was prepared, and the army had a feast.

As Nimrod thanked his host and prepared to leave, Abraham presented him with a bill for several thousand shekels.

Nimrod was surprised. "I thought you entertained us free of charge. Don't you tell everybody that God will pay you?"

Abraham stared at him. "But you say that *you* are a god."

Nimrod considered his situation and said, "I admit that I am not a god."

"Then you will have to sign a statement confessing that you are a human and not a god. Otherwise you will have to pay."

Nimrod signed the statement.

(3) Abraham was sitting near his tent when an old man approached. The man was obviously exhausted. Abraham, who was known for his hospitality, rose to

meet the stranger and to welcome him. The stranger was offered a place in the tent to rest. The old traveler declined the offer, however, preferring instead to rest under a nearby tree. Abraham continued to press the offer, wishing to give the man every comfort. Finally the traveler was persuaded to enter the tent.

Abraham gave the man some goat's milk, butter, and cakes. The hungry man gratefully ate all the food. After the meal, Abraham told the stranger that it was time to pray to the Lord.

"But I do not know your God," said the stranger. "I only pray to the idol that my hands have built."

Abraham began to tell the man about God. He tried to convince the man of God's goodness and urged the man to abandon faith in idols. But the man would not listen to Abraham; instead, he remained steadfast in his pagan beliefs. Abraham angrily demanded that the man leave the tent. The man departed without a word.

The incident haunted Abraham. As he thought about the stranger, he slowly came to realize that God had endured the man's disbelief for many years, yet Abraham had not been able to stand it for a single night. Furthermore, Abraham realized, forgiveness could not come from God; it could come only from the wronged traveler.

Abraham ran from the tent. He searched all night, and he finally found the man and begged to be forgiven. After listening carefully to Abraham's words, he offered forgiveness. The traveler had provided Abraham with a crucial ethical lesson about imitating the forgiving aspect of God's nature.

ABRAHAM, REUEL (born c. 1924)
German World War II soldier who converted to Judaism.

Reuel Abraham was a Nazi who became a Jew.

Abraham began life as Karl Heinz Schneider. In his youth, he organized Hitler youth battalions. When he turned 18, he volunteered for combat service with the Luftwaffe in its Stuka squadron, which specialized in dive-bombing.

One day, Schneider was walking through a town in Nazi-occupied Poland. He witnessed some Nazi stormtroopers killing a group of Jews in the courtyard of a synagogue. The synagogue's rabbi died clutching the Torah.

This single experience changed Schneider's life. He began to deliberately neglect his orders. He feigned illness, dropped bombs into lakes or uninhabited areas of the forest, and altered the detonators on his bombs so that they would not explode.

After Germany's surrender, Schneider made a personal vow to perform twenty years of penance. He began to work in the coal mines, anonymously donating two-thirds of his wages to the postwar agencies that aided Jewish war orphans and those who had survived concentration camps. Schneider taught himself Hebrew. He bought a Bible that had been made in Israel. Under an assumed name, he began attending Sabbath services in a synagogue in Frankfort.

After his twenty-year penance had ended, Schneider sold the land that he owned and purchased a farm in the western Galilee region of Israel. Schneider then went to rabbinical authorities in Haifa, seeking to become a Jew. The Supreme Religious Council of Israel investigated his story. Despite his years of service in Hitler's army, his application was accepted. After changing his name, Reuel Abraham grew a beard, obeyed all the commandments of his new religion, and became a citizen of Israel.

ABRAM, MORRIS (1918–   )
Attorney and community leader.

One of Abram's early tasks after he assumed the presidency of the American Jewish Committee (AJC) in 1963 was to meet with the pope and confront the historic charge of deicide against the Jewish people.

While the Second Vatican Council had produced significant documents under Pope John XXIII, efforts continued to eliminate references in church literature to the charge of deicide. Jewish leaders were unsure about how the new pope, Paul VI, would react to their efforts. Abram arranged to have a private, unpublicized meeting with the new pope.

To prepare for the meeting, Abram began to search for some theological and political ammunition. Together with John Slawson (then the AJC's executive vice-president), Abram went to see Francis Cardinal Spellman, the most powerful American Roman Catholic and, equally important, a man who would be speaking to the AJC on April 30, 1964. Abram was ushered into a parlor that looked to him distinctly like a Dublin townhouse at the turn of the century. When the cardinal arrived, Abram asked him to specifically renounce the deicide charge in his speech. The cardinal remained uncommitted; he said that he wasn't sure what the subject of his speech would be.

On the night of the speech, the cardinal called the deicide charge "absurd." US Secretary of State Dean Rusk, sitting on the same dais, heard the cardinal and gave permission to Abram to say that he hoped for a similar statement from the pope.

Abram then met with the pope. The pope began by taking out a piece of paper and reading it. The pope upheld the dignity of the Jewish people in very general terms, but he made no mention of deicide. Abram, unsure of what to do, pursued the issue. He told the pope that the delegation was there specifically to discuss the deicide charge. The pope responded that the matter was under judicial consideration. Abram reminded the pope that millions of people — including the US secretary of state — were hoping that he would issue a declaration. Abram then told the pope about Cardinal Spellman's speech. The pope responded immediately: "Cardinal Spellman has spoken my sentiments."

Abram was astonished. He wasn't quite sure whether or not the pope had just uttered a historic statement. No more was said about deicide. Abram's great fear was that the pope, hearing Spellman's name, had simply agreed with an important colleague. But Abram had given a promise of silence, so he could not reveal the pope's comments.

Abram received a message at his hotel after the meeting: The pope planned to publish his statement. Abram suddenly saw an opportunity. In his return message, Abram said that he now understood that he could make the entire conversation known. A messenger returned soon afterward. The pope said Abram could release the content of their discussion when he returned to the United States.

The AJC released the text. A historic mission had been fulfilled.

ABULAFIA, ABRAHAM *(1240–c. 1291)*
Kabbalist.

In the summer of 1280, Abraham Abulafia went to Rome to convert the pope to Judaism. He wanted to meet Pope Nicholas III on the eve of the Jewish New Year and persuade the leader of the world's Roman Catholics to become a Jew. The pope, then at a summer house, heard of the plan and ordered that Abulafia be burned at the stake.

Abulafia arrived at the outer gate of the papal residence, but he was not arrested. The pope had died of an apoplectic stroke during the preceding night. Abulafia was jailed for 28 days and then released.

ADLER, CYRUS *(1863–1940)*
American scholar and co-founder of major Jewish organizations.

Adler helped in the naming of a Jewish college and thereby kept alive the name of its benefactor.

The well-known Philadelphia lawyer Moses Aaron Dropsie died in July 1905. He left virtually all of his estate so that a college might be founded in Philadelphia and devoted especially to the study of Hebrew and cognate studies.

Admission to the college was to be available to all students, and there was to be no tuition. The governing body and faculty were to be Jewish. Dropsie named several life governors in his will, including Cyrus Adler and Oscar Straus.

The first important discussion was about what to name the college. At first, Adler suggested some sort of general name with the addendum "founded by Moses Aaron Dropsie," arguing that a college would be at a disadvantage if it were named after a particular individual. Straus asked whether Dropsie had any children. Adler replied that he did not. Straus then said, "Well, by God, the college ought to be named after him even if there *is* a disadvantage."

The argument swayed Adler. Dropsie's name would be preserved. Dropsie University became a leading graduate academic institution for Jewish learning.

ADLER, HERMANN (1839–1911)
Chief rabbi of the British Empire.

Rabbi Adler was sitting next to Herbert Cardinal Vaughan at a luncheon one afternoon. The cardinal turned to the rabbi and said, "Now, Dr. Adler, when may I have the pleasure of helping you to some ham?"

"At Your Eminence's wedding," replied the rabbi.

ADLER, JACOB P. (1855–1926)
Leading Yiddish actor and manager.

Adler was widely known for his dramatic talents. His admirers remembered him fondly long after his career ended.

One day in 1940 an old man showed up at the National Theater with a pass. The pass had been signed by Adler, but it was good for December 31, 1919. The man told the theater's manager that Adler had given him the ticket, but he had been unable to use it on the assigned date. Then he had read that Adler's daughter Celia was appearing in a production of *Dos Leben Geit On (Life Goes On)*, remembered the pass, and decided to go.

The manager's respect for the great Yiddish actor was such that he honored the pass and let the old man in to see the show.

AGNON, SHMUEL YOSEF (1888–1970)
Hebrew author who received the Nobel Prize in Literature in 1966.

Agnon saw the value of winning a Nobel Prize most clearly through a Jewish lens. After receiving the prize, Agnon knew that he would have to travel to

Sweden to accept it from the king. The author was pleased by this prospect because, he said, "I have never had the opportunity to say the blessing one makes upon seeing a king."

AHAD HA'AM (1856–1927)
Writer and cultural Zionist who opposed Herzl's political vision,
emphasizing instead that the land of Israel should be a cultural
center for world Jewry. Ahad Ha'am means "one of the people."
It was the pseudonym of Asher Ginzberg.

Even at a very early age, Ahad Ha'am showed the intelligence and independence that were to mark his life.

When young Asher was only 11 years old, he developed the habit of smoking. This obviously caused his parents great concern, so they took him to a well-known physician, Dr. Piogov, who advised Asher that he would have to quit smoking or he would die. The boy agreed to give up smoking but was determined to find a subject of interest to prevent him from thinking about tobacco. He searched his father's library and found an eighteenth-century Hebrew book that contained the basics of algebra and geometry. Asher was particularly taken with algebra—so taken that he was almost as devoted to it as he later became to the study of Hebrew culture. His preoccupation was such that he studied algebra in his Hebrew school, a dereliction of duty abetted by his teacher's persistent habit of sleeping. Worse still, he began to scribble algebraic formulas on the doors and windows at home. His mother's father accused the boy of practicing witchcraft. After that, algebra was no longer allowed.

Poor Asher went back to smoking.

AKIBA (c. 50–135 C.E.)
Rabbi, editor of the Mishna; aided Bar Kochba in the revolt
against the Romans.

(1) Because of his support for Bar Kochba's revolt, Akiba was captured by the Romans, tried, found guilty, and condemned to die.

The Romans carried out the execution order by tearing the flesh from his body while he was still alive. He was lying in indescribable agony when he noticed dawn coming over the hills to the east. Religious law obliged traditional Jews to recite the Sh'ma. Summoning all his strength, Akiba said in a loud, clear voice the very words that the Romans had forbidden: "Hear, O Israel the Lord our God, the Lord is One. And you shall love the Lord thy God with all thine heart, and with all thine soul and with all thine might."

Rufus, a Roman general who had been in charge of the execution, was astonished. He went to the rabbi and asked, "Are you a wizard, or are you utterly insensible to pain?"

"I am neither," Akiba answered, "But all my life I have been waiting for the moment when I might truly fulfill this commandment. I have always loved the Lord with all my might and with all my heart. Now I know that I love him with all my life."

The rabbi started to repeat the verse again, dying as he reached the words "the Lord is One."

(2) Rabbi Akiba was going on a long journey. He traveled on a donkey, carrying a rooster that would awaken him each morning and a candle to see in the dark.

After the very first day of weary travel, he came to an inn but was told that there was no room for him. He accepted this, saying, "All that God does is for the best."

He spent the night in a field near the inn. During the night, both his rooster and his donkey wandered away, and his candle blew out.

The next morning he rose to discover that a gang of robbers had attacked the people staying at the inn.

He thought to himself, "See how narrowly I escaped death!" He realized that if he had stayed at the inn, he would have been attacked, that the donkey's braying or the rooster's crowing or the candle's light might have alerted the robbers to his presence.

He then remembered his earlier words: "All that God does is for the best."

(3) Papus ben Judah saw that Rabbi Akiba continued to teach the Torah in public despite the fact that such a practice had been prohibited by Roman authorities.

"Aren't you afraid of the authorities?" Papus asked.

"I will tell you a parable," Rabbi Akiba answered. "Once while walking beside a river, a fox saw some fish darting back and forth in the stream. The fox asked them from whom they were fleeing. They told him they were fleeing from the nets. The fox suggested they go to the dry land where there were no nets at all and where, the fox assured them, they could live in peace. The fish, knowing foxes to be the most cunning of animals, did not listen to him, believing that if they had cause to fear the place where it was natural for them to live, then they had even more to fear from a place where they would surely die.

"Just so," Rabbi Akiba continued, "is it with us who study the Torah, in which it is written: 'For that is thy life and the length of thy days,' for if we suffer while we study the Torah, how much more shall we suffer if we neglect it."

(4) Rabbi Akiba has always served as a model for those who began studying late in life.

As a young man, Akiba was a poor shepherd working for Calba Shevua, one of Jerusalem's wealthiest citizens. Calba's only daughter, Rachel, fell in love with Akiba, and the two met secretly. Her father finally discovered the nature of the relationship and threatened to disinherit his daughter. He asked Rachel how she could love the son of a convert, a man old enough to be her father, and a man who could neither read nor write. Nevertheless, Rachel continued to follow her heart and married Akiba.

They were married for only a short while when Rachel decided that her husband should study. He resisted her suggestion because the place of study was far from home, and he didn't know how he felt about studying Jewish law. But Rachel persisted in her efforts, and he finally consented.

One day on his journey to the place of study, he stopped to rest at a waterfall. He marveled at how the steady dripping of the water wore away the solid rock. He thought to himself that just as the water wore away the rock, so the Torah would work its way into his still hard heart. And so, at age 40, Akiva learned the Hebrew alphabet and began to study.

(5) Rabbi Akiba knew that although Rabbi Tarfon was quite wealthy, he never gave money to the poor. One day, Rabbi Akiba asked Tarfon, "Rabbi, should I purchase land for you?" Rabbi Tarfon liked the idea and gave Akiba 4,000 pieces of gold. Rabbi Akiba took the money and gave it all to the poor.

Some time later, Rabbi Tarfon asked Akiba where the land was that Akiba had supposedly purchased. Akiba took Tarfon to a house of study and read the psalms with him until they reached a verse proclaiming that whoever gives to the poor has a righteousness that endures forever. Akiba said, "This is the land I bought for you, the land of righteousness."

Rabbi Tarfon did not object. He was finally convinced of the importance of providing for the poor.

(6) While Rabbi Akiba was imprisoned by the Romans, Rabbi Joshua brought him water. One day, Akiba's jailer saw Rabbi Joshua and said, "You brought too much water. Do you intend to use it to dig a hole through the prison?" The jailer poured half the water away.

When Akiba saw how little water remained, he grew sad. "I am old and need water to live." Rabbi Joshua then told him what had happened. Akiba heard the story and said, "Give me the water so I may wash my hands."

Rabbi Joshua was shocked. He knew that washing was a necessary part of the blessing done before eating, but he also knew that if water was used for the blessing, there would be an insufficient amount left to drink. He told this to Akiba, who responded, "It is better to die of thirst than to violate a commandment."

Akiba washed his hands. Only then did he drink the remaining water.

ALEICHEM, SHOLOM (1859–1916)
Yiddish humorist and writer famed for creating the characters upon whom the musical Fiddler on the Roof *was based.*

(1) When Sholom Aleichem came to the United States in 1906, the Yiddish writer became an attraction at a variety of receptions. Mark Twain was the guest of honor at one such reception. Aleichem was introduced to the well-known American humorist as the "Jewish Mark Twain." Twain asked the introducer to translate his response into Yiddish. Twain wanted to be introduced as "the American Sholom Aleichem."

(2) Sholom Aleichem was having dinner one evening with his family when a long-haired, obviously hungry man came into the dining room and told those assembled that he had just composed a great poem on the beauty of sunsets. He wanted Sholom Aleichem to publish it in the literary journal he edited. The man then proceeded to read his self-proclaimed masterpiece.

The humorist simply went on with his meal, eating as he listened, and interrupting the reading with such exclamations as "very good, wonderful." The young poet was delighted with this warm reception.

The poet finished his work and asked Aleichem when the poem would be published.

"I am not going to print it," Aleichem told the now despairing man.

"Didn't you tell me it was very good?"

"Who said your poem was very good?" Aleichem replied. "I was talking about the dinner."

(3) Sholom Aleichem was walking down the street and talking to himself. A friend stopped him and asked if he realized what he had been doing.

"What if I *have* been talking to myself?" Aleichem answered. "When at last I have found a suitably clever person with whom to converse, why do you have to interrupt?"

ALLON, YIGAL (1918–1980)
Israeli statesman and military leader.

Yigal Allon never forgot the day on which he was almost killed.

Yigal Paikovits (his original family name) had just turned 13. His father called him to the grain shed for a private talk. Yigal's father said that his son could now fulfill religious commandments, but there was also another aspect of becoming a man. Young Yigal would get his own weapon. The father took a metal can out from behind the wheat bin, pried open the top, and took out a semiautomatic Browning pistol, which had been carefully wrapped in a woolen cloth. His father said, "This weapon was mine. Now it belongs to you. You must clean it. You know how to use it. There is no license for it, so it must remain here behind the wheat bin." Then his father continued. "Tonight you will guard the remainder of the sorghum harvest in Balut." (*Balut* was an Arab name meaning "oak tree.") The field that Yigal's father wished him to guard was at the northern end of their village's fields.

Just after the sun had set, Yigal began his adventure. It was a long, lonely walk to the field. He arrived there by 8:00. Yigal immediately scouted a suitable location and decided that the best place to sit for his vigil was under the oak tree beside the big rock. He then realized that the spot was not the best: A bullet could ricochet off the rock, and a bird in the tree might make noise and indicate his presence. Still, he felt settled in and decided not to move. Yigal listened to the sounds of the night. This was the first time he had ever been allowed to guard a crop by himself.

Some time after midnight, Yigal heard a caravan passing alongside the field. The boy stayed hidden and watched as the travelers passed. Yigal thought that all was well. At 2:00, however, Yigal noticed three men riding horses. They entered the field, dismounted, and began to collect the harvest in their sacks.

Yigal remembered the words his father had spoken: After letting the thieves do their work for a while, Yigal was to shout a warning in Arabic. If that failed, he was to fire his weapon in the air, taking care not to fire at anyone unless his life was endangered.

Yigal raised his voice and tried to make it sound as manly as he could. He screamed "Andak!" and clicked his pistol, hoping that his very presence and the sound of a weapon would convince the thieves that they should flee without the sorghum.

Instead, the men prepared to fight. They stationed themselves in various places in the field. Yigal pulled the trigger and waited. He didn't know what to do. He realized how grateful he was for the protection provided by the large oak tree under which he sat. Just then, from behind him, came a series of screams in Arabic and several rifle shots aimed at the marauders. This time the thieves did flee, and without the crop. It was Yigal's father. He had wanted to test Yigal, but, as he had done with his older sons, he made sure that he was there in case of trouble.

About sixteen years later, Yigal was at the Israel Defense Forces headquarters. Prime Minister David Ben-Gurion had asked all leaders to Hebraicize their names. Yigal decided, after discussions with his wife, that he would change his family name of Paikovits to Allon, which is Hebrew for "oak."

ALTER, ROBERT (1935–   )
American literary critic.

Professor Alter has supplied the following anecdote.

> When I was starting out as a critic in New York in the early 1960s, I was, I would guess, writing pieces with that tone of weighty authority that only a self-conscious young man could assume. At a reception, I met Isaac Bashevis Singer for the first time. After someone had introduced us, he stared at me for a moment with his sparkling, mischievous eyes and said, "So you're Alter" (pronouncing it as one would in Yiddish, where it means, of course, 'the old one'). "I thought that you were someone much older." Then, after a brief contemplative pause, he added, "I see. Perhaps you are the dybbuk of someone much older."

AMNON (tenth century)
Rabbi and martyr.

Rabbi Amnon defended his faith with his life as he came to a profound understanding of the trials of belief.

Rabbi Amnon lived in the town of Mayence. The rabbi was well known throughout the area for the virtuous way in which he led his life.

The Prince of Mayence heard of the rabbi and wished to see him. The rabbi visited the ruler and spoke to him about religion. The ruler was deeply impressed by the rabbi's piety and determined that such a good man should leave the Jewish faith and join the ruler's faith. The ruler therefore gently argued with Amnon, trying to show how his faith was superior to Judaism. The ruler held out promises to the rabbi that money and fame would be his if only he would convert. Amnon remained steadfast. He responded to each entreaty with a simple "No."

The prince soon dispensed with gentleness. "You are as stiff-necked as all your people! You can be sure that I will quickly end your stubbornness and make you do as I wish."

One day soon after that, the prince confronted the rabbi at the palace. "Accept my faith or you will die."

Rabbi Amnon felt afraid. He said to the prince, "Give me only three days to ponder the matter—then I shall bring you my answer."

"So be it," the prince agreed.

Rabbi Amnon returned to his home. He put on sackcloth and ashes. He prayed, "O God of my fathers, let me not be led into temptation, for my spirit grows faint with fear."

Three days passed, but Rabbi Amnon did not return to the palace. The prince was astonished. "Is the Jew not afraid?" he said to his guards. "He has defied my will. Bring him to me quickly that I may judge him."

The guards quickly seized the rabbi and brought him to the palace. The prince confronted the rabbi, who remained frightened for his life. "Jew, how dare you disobey me? Why have you broken your promise to bring me your answer after three days?"

Rabbi Amnon looked up sadly. "Alas, in a moment of weakness I fell into sin and lied and made false promises. To save my life without defying my faith, I sought the cowardly grace of three days in which to give you my answer. I should have said right away to you, 'Hear O Israel, the Lord our God the Lord is One,' and then perished at your hands."

The prince was angry. "Your feet disobeyed me by not coming to the palace. They shall be severed from your body."

"No," Rabbi Amnon said. "My feet should not be torn, but rather my tongue, for it betrayed my God."

"Your tongue has uttered the truth, and it therefore will not be punished."

The sentence was carried out on Rosh Hashanah. Soon the rabbi began to die of his wounds. He was carried to the synagogue.

Once there, he asked to recite a prayer, U-Nesanneh-Tokef. He died just as he finished the last words of the prayer.

According to Jewish tradition, no one saw how the rabbi's body was taken away, but three days later he appeared in a dream to Rabbi Kalonymus ben Meshulam and made Rabbi Kalonymus learn the prayer so that all the Jewish people would know it.

U-Nesanneh-Tokef is recited in the Musaf service at Rosh Hashanah and Yom Kippur, just before the Kedushah. In the prayer, the high holy days are seen as a time of judgment, as people symbolically pass before God. In the prayer, there is an enumeration of the various possible fates that may befall people, but also an emphasis on God's forgiveness.

AMRAM (third century C.E.)
Rabbi and scholar.

Rabbi Amram learned that the temptations of the body endanger the purity of the soul. He found his own solution to temptation.

Some Jewish women had been captured by non-Jewish traders. The women were to be slaves. They were taken to the town of Nehardea, where the Jews collected enough funds to free the women.

The women were then taken to the home of Rabbi Amram. Many in the town had been concerned because the women were beautiful, and it was thought that it would be difficult to find a safe place for them to stay. Rabbi Amram was considered morally strong and good enough to resist any lustful temptation. Rabbi Amram took the women up to a garret that could be reached only with a ladder. He then had the ladder removed.

Some time during the night, when everyone else was asleep, one of the women stood at the garret window. Rabbi Amram saw her and was overwhelmed by her beauty. He could not understand his own feelings of desire. Almost against his will, he got up and carried the heavy ladder over to the window. Slowly he began to climb the ladder. He had reached half way when he regained control of his feelings. He stood there, midway between ground and window, and screamed, "Fire! Fire!"

The townspeople came running to help the rabbi put out the supposed fire. They then saw that there were no flames, and they got angry at the rabbi, telling him that they were ashamed of him for his actions. He remained calm and told them: "It is far better that you should be ashamed of me in this world than that I should be ashamed of myself in the next world."

ANGEL, MARC (1945–   )
Rabbi, Sephardic leader and author.

Rabbi Angel learned of the severed roots of his own Sephardic tradition in Europe on a visit to Rhodes, the island near Greece. Rabbi Angel had gone there because his father's parents had lived on the island; the Jewish community there had been virtually exterminated by the Nazis.

Rabbi Angel attended services in a local synagogue and then went to visit the Jewish area, the *juderia*. The streets were paved with stones, and the small houses were inhabited by Greeks instead of Jews. At the *calle ancha*, the square at the center of the Jewish quarter, Rabbi Angel saw, not bustling Jews anxious to go about their work, but Scandinavian and German tourists. The street going through the old Jewish section had been renamed *Martyron Evreon*, the street of the Hebrew martyrs.

Rabbi Angel, overcome by the sense of loss, simply whispered "Grandfather, grandmother," and went back to his hotel.

ANIELIEWICZ, MORDECAI (1919–1943)
Leader of the Warsaw ghetto uprising.

Mordecai Anieliewicz remains a potent symbol of Jewish resistance to Nazi tyranny and of the incredible sacrifices made by his generation.

Mordecai was a long-time advocate of armed resistance to the Nazis.

When the Jewish Fighting Organization (the ZOB) was formed in the Warsaw ghetto, it was Anieliewicz who headed it. He led the ghetto uprising in April 1943.

By the first week of May, however, after suffering heavy losses, the Nazis fought back. On May 8, some 120 Jewish resistance fighters were gathered at 18 Mila Street. This was the last large group of Jewish fighters. The entrance to the building was bombed on that day, but the Jews were in a bunker and remained unscathed.

When the Nazis realized this, they began to drill overhead. Anieliewicz sent guards to the bunker's five entrances. For two hours the drilling continued, and then it suddenly stopped. The Jews waited. Just as suddenly there came the call of a traitor, telling the fighters in Yiddish to come out to be sent to do work. The response was clear: Shots were fired. The Nazis sent hand grenades into a tunnel leading to the bunker. A Nazi soldier came into the tunnel. The Jews shot him, and the Nazis pulled back.

The drilling soon resumed. Mordecai made a vow. He had not even expected to live this long. Now he would die here, in this bunker, resisting the Nazis. One final demand for surrender was rejected.

The Nazis then sent gas through a hole they had drilled into the bunker. Some of the fighters began crawling toward the exits, seeking to surrender. But Mordecai and his group did not. They remained behind to discuss their options. One of the fighters, Aryeh Wilner, argued for suicide so as not to be taken alive by the Nazis. Another, Michal Rozenfeld, argued that they should not die by their own hands, but rather die killing Nazis. It was soon clear, however, that escaping and fighting were not viable options. Two choices remained for the fighters: die by suicide or die by gas. Mordecai argued against suicide. He wanted to see whether it would be at all possible to survive the gas. He ordered his fighters to wet pieces of cloth in a puddle under the water tap and cover their faces. But it did not work.

In the end, Mordecai Anieliewicz died. Nearly one hundred of his comrades joined him in death, including Berl Broyde, who had jumped off a train going to Treblinka to return to the ghetto and fight.

Among those who escaped through the sewers was Tsivia Lubetkin. She fought with partisans and eventually moved to the land of Israel in January 1944. There she was among the founders of Kibbutz Lohamei Ha-Getta'ot (the Ghetto Fighters' Kibbutz).

ARENDT, HANNAH (1906–1975)
Political and social theorist.

Hannah Arendt became well known in the Jewish community for her coverage of the trial of Adolf Eichmann in April 1961. Eichmann, of course, had served as a gestapo officer in the Head Office for Reich Security. One part of that office dealt with opponents of the state, among whom Jews were considered to be prominent. It was Eichmann who was in charge of dealing with all Jewish "opponents." In practice, this meant that Eichmann organized the "evacuations" of Jews to the killing camps. The Israeli secret service had seized Eichmann in Buenos Aires and had flown him back to Israel for trial.

As Hannah Arendt covered the trial, she saw Eichmann's responsibility and the need to punish him by hanging. But in her five articles in *The New Yorker* (the articles would form the basis of her book *Eichmann in Jerusalem*), Arendt drew a controversial portrait of the Nazi. She saw Eichmann as sane and proud, but incapable of moral clarity. He was not a monster to her, but an ordinary man. He was an example of, in her famous words, "the banality of evil."

Many critics, fairly or unfairly, saw in her characterization an attempt to justify Eichmann's (and other Nazis') actions.

The articles appeared in February and March of 1963. In July, Professor Arendt was asked to speak before Jewish students at Columbia University. The crowd was enormous; the overflow had to be accommodated on a fire escape outside.

After speaking for an hour, Arendt asked for questions. Members of the audience jumped up and shouted, accusing her of siding with the Nazis. She argued, insisting that she had been misunderstood. Slowly, she felt a turning point; these young students began to realize that she had merely painted a portrait of a man, and that she did not in any way side with Eichmann.

It was after this meeting that, finally, she felt understood.

ASCH, SHOLEM (1880–1957)
Yiddish writer noted for his use of Jewish and non-Jewish sources.

(1) The following anecdote was supplied by Ethel Zelen.

The controversial Yiddish novelist Sholem Asch lived for some years in my home town of Stamford, Connecticut. He was not a very popular figure in the Jewish community at that time because of such novels as *The Nazarene* and *The Apostle*, in which he seemingly accepted Christian theology.

As a young girl, some time in the late 1930s or early 1940s, I recall seeing him on numerous occasions. He would especially frequent "Jewish" Pacific Street, where "appetizing" stores (delicatessens), kosher butchers, and bakeries lined the sidewalks for a block. I would often accompany my mother on her shopping forays to the appetizing store, where Mr. Asch was a fellow customer.

One might have called him an aggressive bargain hunter. What particularly amazed us was the frugality of this celebrity. He would monitor the cutting of a quarter pound of butter from a large slab. I was particularly fascinated by his selection of eggs. He would place several cartons on the scales to find the one that weighed the most. I can still remember the whispers and buzzing about his behavior when he left, and I was so disappointed that this man of letters was so "human."

(2) Asch went to the Sea of Galilee on his first visit to the land of Israel. In particular, he sought out the spot where, according to legend, Jesus had begun his foot journey across the lake. Asch saw an Arab boatman nearby. The writer asked how much it would cost for the boatman to take him across.

"Five dollars," was the reply.

The frugal Asch commented, "Now I understand why Jesus walked."

ASHI (c. 335–428 B.C.E.)
Major Babylonian scholar.

Ashi used his wisdom and love of learning to preserve the Jewish heritage.

Ashi was a wealthy courtier in Babylonia. Queen Ifra-Ormizd was fond of him. Later, her son and grandson became kings. The grandson, Yezdegerd, was especially friendly to Jews, but Ashi realized that after him the Jews might face a harsh ruler. In addition, many Jews had turned away from practicing their religion. Rabbi Ashi decided that only a revived academy at Sura could ensure the survival of Judaism.

Ashi went to the aged queen and charmed her, but she could not understand why he would want to leave the court. He went to her grandson, the king, after she continued to advise him not to leave.

The king asked him why he wanted to go. Ashi thought about how to answer without offending the ruler. "I wish to spend my life studying the Torah. I wish to teach it and also to be an example to my pupils."

The king seemed offended. "Do you mean that you set a bad example for the young by living in my court?"

"The court is for nobles. You, my Sovereign, set the only example. We just mirror your greatness. I wish to be among my people and reflect your justice there."

The king appreciated Ashi's skillful response. He remained angry about Ashi's request, however, so he continued, "If you want to be an example for your pupils, you must live as they live. If you do not, they will say that it is easy to be good when you have wealth to buy what you need. It is a lot harder to be poor."

Ashi immediately knew the king's intent, but he praised the king's wisdom. The king saw his chance. "So if you do leave the court to teach among the poor, you will no doubt wish to give your money away to the royal treasury."

"It is what I most wish," Ashi said.

The king did not stop. "As a teacher you will have no need for your fields, or the forests in which you hunt, or your palaces. They should be given to some noble at the court. That is, if you still wish to leave us."

"You tell me who is the most deserving noble, and I will give him my holdings."

The king paused for a minute. He remembered Ashi's great love for the horse Ashmund. The king spoke again. "All day the teacher is in school. At night the teacher is with books. A teacher cannot properly exercise or take care of a horse. It is for your horses' well-being that you will want to give them to the captain of the guard—that is, if you still intend to leave."

"I will give my horses to someone who can take care of them. Do I have your permission, then, to go to Sura?"

The king could not come up with another challenge. The permission was granted. And the king let Ashi retain his money, his estates, and his horses.

At Sura, Ashi rebuilt the academy. All his money was used for that purpose, and to help needy students. He stayed on to head the academy for sixty years.

Ultimately it was at Sura, under Ashi, that the Talmud was gathered for a later generation to complete.

ASIMOV, ISAAC (1920–   )
American biochemist and author.

Asimov's father looked at one of his son's books and asked, "How did you learn all this, Isaac?"

"From *you*, Pappa."

"From *me*? I don't know any of this."

"You didn't have to, Pappa. You valued learning, and you taught me to value it. All the rest came without trouble."

BAAL SHEM TOV *(Israel ben Eliezer, c. 1700–1760)*
Leader of Hasidism in Eastern Europe.

(1) It was a cantor who taught the Baal Shem Tov to avoid despair.

Before Rosh Hashanah, the Baal Shem Tov came to a new city. He asked the people how the cantor did his job there. The people replied that their cantor was strange: He sang the prayer for their sins in a joyful way. The Baal Shem Tov asked the cantor why he did this, and the cantor replied with a story. He said that even those who sweep the king's courtyard are not sad; rather, they feel privileged to keep the king's house clean. The cantor explained that he served the King of all the world, and he cleaned sins. "Is this not worthy of song?" he asked.

The Baal Shem Tov agreed. "Let man never despair. Sadness is always forbidden" was the lesson he learned and then taught.

(2) As was his custom, the rabbi began a journey into the country soon after the Havdalah service ended the Sabbath. This time he took the large carriage and brought all his closest disciples along. They rode all night and finally, by morning, they arrived in the town of Kozenitz and called on the head of the Jewish community. The townspeople gathered, greatly honored by the Baal Shem Tov's presence. After the morning service, the Baal Shem Tov asked the head of the community to get the bookbinder, Reb Shabsi. The community leader was aghast. "Why do you wish to see him? He is a good man, to be sure, but he is not learned in the Torah. We have great scholars in our town. Surely you'd like to meet one of them instead."

But the Baal Shem Tov insisted. Soon Reb Shabsi and his wife arrived. The Baal Shem Tov said to him, "Shabsi, tell us all that you did last night. Hold back nothing."

Reb Shabsi agreed, asking that the Baal Shem Tov judge his actions. Then Reb Shabsi began his story.

"I have always been a bookbinder. Each Thursday, I would take my earnings and give them to my wife so that she could make all the purchases needed for the Sabbath—challah, fish, meat, wine, and wax candles. On Friday, unfortunately, I discovered that I had no money to give my wife. I did not wish to beg, and so I decided that the only thing I could do was to fast during the Sabbath. My only fear was that my dear wife would tell our neighbors, and they would give us challah. I asked her not to accept anyone's help. I closed my store at 10:00 in the morning and made my way to the synagogue. I remained there, as is my custom, until after the evening service. This night I planned to stay even later than usual so I wouldn't meet a neighbor who had noticed that no Sabbath candle burned in our window.

"My wife cleaned the house during the day. Quite unexpectedly, she found one of my old jackets that had been lost. The jacket had silver buttons with a gold overlay. She sold the buttons and bought candles and food and still had money left over.

"I returned home very late. I was surprised to see candles burning. Then I came into the house and saw the beautiful Sabbath table. So as not to destroy the peace of the Sabbath, I did not say a word to my wife. But my wife could tell how I felt. After our prayers, she told me about the coat. I began to cry. I was so happy, my wife and I began to dance. We danced three times. Tell me, Rabbi, do you think I have sinned?"

Instead of responding, the Baal Shem Tov said, "What is it you wish?"

The bookbinder hesitated. "We are old, Rabbi, but we have not had a child. That is what we want above riches."

According to Hasidic legend, the bookbinder and his wife had a son within the year. They named him Israel, after the Baal Shem Tov, who attended the boy's bris. The boy grew up to be the Preacher of Kozenitz, widely known for his wisdom and his saintliness.

(3) A man complained about his son to the Baal Shem Tov. The man claimed that his son had abandoned God.

"What shall I do?" asked the man of the great teacher.

The Baal Shem Tov replied, "Love him more than ever."

(4) The Baal Shem Tov had a grown daughter named Udel. She was concerned that she was not married, and she came to ask her father how she should know the right man to be her husband. The Baal Shem Tov told her to wait for a sign.

That Simchas Torah, many people came to dance in the Baal Shem Tov's house. In the middle of the wild dancing, one student's shoe came off. The student laughed and sang a popular verse of the day involving a woman putting a shoe on a man's foot. In the song, the woman eventually became the man's wife.

The Baal Shem Tov immediately called out for his daughter. Udel understood as well and looked for the shoe but couldn't find it. She quickly removed her own slippers and gave them to the young student.

Eventually, Udel and the student married.

(5) The Baal Shem Tov engaged in frequent arguments with those whom he considered overattached to books rather than religious experience. Once, he was strolling through a house of prayer. He observed a man, deep in study, mumbling the prayers very quickly. The Baal Shem Tov looked at the man and commented, "This man is so absorbed in what he is learning that he forgets that there is also a God looking over the world."

BAECK, LEO (1873–1956)
Rabbi and theologian.

Rabbi Leo Baeck refused to leave sick and dying concentration camp survivors despite the threat to his own health.

The rabbi was an inmate in the concentration camp at Theresienstadt. The camp was finally liberated in early May of 1945. The Russian army turned the camp guards over to the Jewish inmates, who planned to murder their Nazi guards. Rabbi Baeck argued with the inmates to persuade them not to kill the guards. He finally convinced them by urging them not to lose their own humanity.

One day an American jeep arrived at the camp. A major from the United States army stepped out. His name was Patrick Dolan, and he was carrying orders to take Rabbi Baeck out of the camp and back to meet his family.

But the rabbi refused to leave with the major. Rabbi Baeck explained that he remained the rabbi of all those left behind. Most of the inmates still alive were then at the point of death. A severe epidemic of typhus was widespread in the camp. Only when the rabbi was certain that all the remaining Jews would be taken care of and would, if possible, be transported where they wished to go did he agree to leave.

On July 1, Rabbi Baeck was flown by an American bomber to Paris. On July 5, he was flown by a British military aircraft to London, where, after six years, he was reunited with his daughter, son-in-law, and granddaughter.

BAR KAPPARA (third century C.E.)
Scholar.

Bar Kappara's bravery and humanity once saved the Jews of Caesarea.

Bar Kappara was walking near the city harbor when suddenly he saw a ship sinking. The proconsul of the city was on the ship. He began to swim ashore. Bar Kappara went to his aid, risking his own life to help bring the proconsul to safety. Bar Kappara then took him to his home, fed and clothed him, and gave him 5 selaim because all the proconsul's money and possessions had gone down with the ship.

Some time later, all the Jews of Caesarea were ordered by a court to be sent to prison. Bar Kappara was chosen to plead the case for the Jews. He was given 500 denarii to pay in bribes. When Bar Kappara came to the court, the proconsul was there and recognized the man who had assisted him. The proconsul asked why he was there, and Bar Kappara told him that he had come to plead for the Jews.

The proconsul asked, "Don't you know that nothing is done here without money?"

"I've brought 500 dinarii. Please take them and intercede on our behalf," Bar Kappara said.

The proconsul answered, "Keep your money as security for the 5 selaim you lent to me. You gave me food and drink when I needed them. Because of that, your people will be saved. Go in peace."

BAR KOCHBA (?-135 C.E.)
Leader of the revolt against Roman rule.

Bar Kochba's name has resonated through Jewish history as a symbol of rebellion against foreign rule. Even during his life his greatness was recognized. Rabbi Akiba, for instance, was a great admirer of his.

Rabbi Akiba was profoundly saddened by the conditions of his people. The Romans had conquered the land, destroyed the temple, and sent many Jews into exile. Akiba wandered through the Diaspora urging Jews to return to their homeland. The rabbi began looking for a leader to rise up against Roman tyranny.

One day a man named Simeon bar Kosiba came to see the rabbi. The man said that he wanted to lead his people to freedom. He asked for Akiba's blessing. Akiba renamed the rebel *Bar Kochba* (son of the star—a reference to Numbers 24:17, wherein it is prophesied that a star shall rise to beat off Israel's enemies). Akiba went so far as to wonder whether Bar Kochba was, in fact, the Messiah.

Bar Kochba gathered an army of 24,000 men. According to the Aggadah, Bar Kochba selected only men who were willing to have a finger cut off as a sign of strength and willingness to fight to the death to free the Jewish land from foreign rule. When some rabbis complained about such mutilation, Bar Kochba changed tests. He allowed those who wished to join him to do so if they could unearth a cedar tree.

Some time around the year 132 C.E., the Roman emperor Hadrian ordered the Roman governor of Judea, Tinneius Rufus, to turn Jerusalem into a Roman city renamed Aelia Capitolina, and on the site of the razed temple to build a temple to Jupiter. The governor began to do as he had been ordered.

Bar Kochba began his revolt. His men dug up their swords and the other weapons they had hidden. It has been estimated that his army comprised as many as 400,000 men.

Bar Kochba led his men in attacks against Roman garrisons. The men seized towns. The revolt spread. Jerusalem was taken back for a short while. Bar Kochba and his men, often hiding in caves in the hills, were winning stunning victories. They faced a Roman legion led by Tinneius Rufus, and they won.

In Rome, the original reports of the revolt had been treated with indifference, but as Bar Kochba's army continued to be victorious, the emperor became concerned about the effect of the rebellion on other provinces controlled by Rome. Hadrian then sent in Publius Marcellus, but he, too, was defeated. The emperor then called upon his best general, Julius Severus, and ordered him to take four legions and capture Bar Kochba alive.

Severus devised a plan to cut off food supplies to the Jewish rebels. A drought compounded the problem. Severus began to win back the land that had been taken by Bar Kochba.

Finally, Bar Kochba was in retreat in the fortified city of Bethar. In 134 C.E. the Romans laid siege to the city, preventing all food from entering. Eventually the Jews could not hold out. Some time in August 135, the walls were breached.

Rather than surrender, Bar Kochba and most of his men fought to the death. Most of the remaining Jews in Judea were subsequently murdered.

BARON, SALO (1895–   )
Foremost contemporary historian of Jewish society and religion.

Baron is still at work producing his magisterial work, *A Social and Religious History of the Jews*. Since he is long past the age at which most people continue to labor, he was once asked by the president of Brandeis University how his work habits had changed since his retirement. Baron replied that before he retired, he worked from 7:00 A.M. until 11:00 P.M., but now that he has retired, he works from 6:00 A.M. until midnight.

BARUCH, BERNARD (1870–1965)
American business leader and financier.

Bernard Baruch was one of the most successful and famous of Wall Street financiers. After he had made his first million, he went to tell his father about his accomplishment. Despite the son's enthusiasm, however, the father did not seem impressed by the financial achievement. Exasperated, the young Baruch asked, "I am not even 30 and already I've made a million—and you're not even happy?"

The father looked at him. "No, my son. I am not impressed. What I want to know is—how will you spend the money you have earned?"

BARUCH OF MEDZEBOTH (1757–1811)
Grandson of the Baal Shem Tov.

(1) The rebbe heard about one of his disciples who had taken to reading forbidden books. When Rebbe Baruch learned this, he was saddened, but he reassured himself that the disciple was young and susceptible to influence. The rebbe determined to speak to the man when he next came to prayer. But the disciple did not appear.

The rebbe began to hear new rumors, even more disturbing than the first. It was said that the wayward disciple had stopped praying, stopped living a Jewish life. Rebbe Baruch continued to wait, assuming that his disciple would come to see him, hear the rebbe's rebuke, and then repent. Finally the rebbe decided that he had waited long enough, and he went to see the man.

The rebbe spoke before the other man had a chance. "Listen," the rebbe began, "I understand you. You have passed through fifty gates of knowledge. First, you went through one and saw the knowledge, but that knowledge led you to another gate. You passed through more gates, believing that you were going on a lonely journey away from your faith. Now you stand at the fiftieth gate. If you go through this one, you will be lost. This is the gate away from your people."

"What can I do?" cried the distraught disciple, "Go back to where I started?"

The rebbe shook his head. "It is impossible to go back." The rebbe then waited in silence. Suddenly the disciple began to beg for help, asking for guidance about which direction to take.

"Look, look beyond the fiftieth gate," said the rebbe. "There is the abyss you are headed for, but there is also faith. They are side by side. Take the leap through the gate to faith."

The disciple took that leap and was brought back to his people.

(2) Rebbe Baruch's grandson Yehiel was crying as he entered his grandfather's study. The concerned rebbe asked about the source of the tears.

"I have a friend who cheated me and left me alone to cry."

"Please explain," said the rebbe.

"The two of us were playing hide-and-seek, grandfather. It was my turn to hide, and I did it so well that my friend couldn't find me. Instead of continuing to look, he gave up. That's not fair, is it?"

The rebbe kissed the boy and began to cry. Yehiel asked why he was crying. The rebbe explained. "Like you, Yehiel, God, too, is unhappy. He is hiding and humanity does not look for him. Humanity has stopped its search. That also is not fair."

BEGIN, MENACHEM (1913–   )

Former Israeli prime minister and commander of the Irgun in the struggle for independence.

(1) Menachem Begin was relentless in his pursuit of a Jewish nation. He, far more than leaders of the mainstream Haganah, was willing to engage the British in a military struggle. The British reaction was one of hostility and determination to destroy Begin's group, the Irgun, as well as another underground group, the Lehi.

It was after the explosion of the King David Hotel in Jerusalem (the location of the British headquarters at the time) on July 22, 1946, that the British used all the power they could muster. In August they sent 20,000 troops and tanks to sweep through Tel Aviv, the city that British intelligence believed was the heart of Jewish underground resistance. All approaches to Tel Aviv were securely sealed. A curfew was ordered. A house-by-house search was then undertaken. All adult males went in groups to screening centers, where British intelligence officers checked off each man against a list of names and photographs. Eight hundred people were detained. The British claimed a major victory, but in fact they had really captured only two key leaders, one of whom was Yitzhak Ysernitsky (who would later adopt his underground name— Shamir—and eventually become the Israeli prime minister).

Menachem Begin was the only one of the underground leaders not picked up. He had hidden in a cupboard in his apartment. The cupboard had been built out of sight for very brief stays when a hiding place was needed. The investigators came into the Begin apartment and began to search for the Irgun leader. Begin's wife told them that "Dr. Koenigshoffer" (Begin's assumed name at the time) was in Jerusalem.

The apartment was on a ground floor, and a platoon of soldiers was camped in the garden adjacent to the apartment, directly under the Begins' window where the cupboard was hidden. Because of that, Begin's wife dared not give her husband food or drink or open the cupboard. Soldiers routinely came in for drinks of water, and Mrs. Begin did not know how her small children would react if they knew where their father was hiding. She remained particularly concerned because of the summer heat.

Begin stayed hidden in the cupboard for four days. Finally, the British left. Begin's wife gave the all-clear signal with a broom.

(2) In September of 1940, Begin had also been hiding out, at that time from the Russians. Once, while playing chess with his wife, Begin was interrupted when Russian soldiers suddenly broke into their home and began to drag him away. As the soldiers took him out of the house, he called back to his wife, but only to say that he would concede the match.

(3) Sam Sokolow of Baltimore, Maryland, was on a tour of Israel in 1979. Members of the tour were taken to Prime Minister Begin's home in Jerusalem. When the prime minister came into the living room, he saw that some of the tour members did not have any chairs. Begin said, "I'll go into the kitchen and get some chairs." Some of the group members, stunned that a prime minister would be carrying kitchen chairs for guests, stopped him and went to get the chairs themselves, but they always remembered this example of Begin's famed courtesy.

(4) Begin achieved a reputation for toughness in the peace negotiations at Camp David. His greatness, though, lay in knowing just how far he could go. By September 17, 1978, the thirteenth day of negotiating, it looked as though a final deal was at hand. Broad frameworks had been agreed upon, one about a peace treaty between Israel and Egypt, and another on regional peace in the Middle East.

All sides had agreed that Jerusalem would not even be mentioned in any agreement because control of the holy city was such an emotional issue. The Americans were pushing for an exchange of letters in which Begin, President Carter of the United States, and President Sadat of Egypt would simply summarize their governments' positions. The problem was that the American letter used language spoken by US ambassadors to the United Nations in which the United States did not recognize Israel's annexation of East Jerusalem. Begin let it be known that he could not sign a final agreement in which the United States sent a letter to Sadat refusing that recognition.

The entire agreement now hung in the balance. All sides consulted. Begin held his ground. Carter desperately wanted an agreement. The president finally decided to revise the letter. All mention of the annexation was removed. Still, Carter was not sure what Begin would do.

Then Carter had an idea. Before he took the revised letter to Begin, he decided to follow up on a request Begin had made. The Israeli prime minister had asked the American president to sign some photographs. Begin wished to give the pictures to his grandchildren. Carter asked his secretary to find out each of the grandchildren's names. Carter then inscribed each picture individually.

Armed with the revision and the signed photos, Carter made his way to Begin's cabin. Begin was very grateful, thanking Carter for the pictures and describing each of his grandchildren. The letter was almost an afterthought. Begin took a look at the text, saw that his objections had been considered and that the offending language had been removed, and accepted the letter immediately. Carter saw it as a personal triumph.

BEILIS, MENAHEM (1874–1934)
Subject of an anti-Semitic blood libel in Russia.

The story of Menahem Beilis's ordeal as he confronted Russian anti-Semitism has remained vital as Jews continue to struggle in their relationship with the Soviet Union.

On March 20, 1911, the badly mutilated body of Andrei Yushchinsky was found in a cave near Kiev. The 12-year-old boy's death was widely blamed on the Jews. Even though an investigation indicated that a criminal gang was responsible, the anti-Semites charged that a ritual murder had taken place. (The charge, also known as a blood libel, was that Jews killed non-Jews, particularly Christians, to obtain blood to bake matzoh or for other religious rituals. The blood libel evidently began during the Middle Ages.)

In July of 1911, a lamplighter testified that he had seen the boy playing near a brick kiln. Menahem (Mendel) Beilis was the superintendent of the brick kiln.

Early on the morning of July 21, 1911, fifteen police headed by Colonel Kuliabko, local chief of the Okhrana, the Russian secret police, raided the Beilis home. The police were looking for arms, subversive literature, and, most important, instruments used for torture, so that they would have some positive evidence that a blood ritual had taken place.

Instead they found Beilis, his wife, and his five children. At 3:00 in the morning, Beilis and his oldest son, then a student, were taken to Okhrana headquarters. The boy was released about two days later. Beilis was taken to a city prison, where he would remain for two years and two months before standing trial.

Beilis was acquitted at the trial. In 1920 he moved to the United States.

BELKIND, ISRAEL *(1861–1929)*
A founder of Beit Ya'akov Lekhu ve-Nelkhah (BILU), an early
organization devoted to settling Jews in the land of Israel.

The return to Zion was spurred by young Russian Jewish students fearful of their
future. The students began to organize following the pogroms that took place
after the assassination of Czar Alexander II on March 13, 1881.

January 21, 1882, was set aside to commemorate Jewish victims of the
pogroms. It was a day filled with fasting and praying. The synagogue was
crowded. The unobservant sat next to the Orthodox; all were bewildered,
fearful, and unsure of what to do.

Soon after the evening service ended in Kharkov, Israel Belkind, a
21-year-old student from Mohilev, invited other students to his room to discuss
the direction of their lives and the situation of Russian Jewry. Belkind argued for
uprooting themselves from Russia and moving to the land of Israel. A group was
formed out of the meeting. The group, established to foster emigration, was first
called *Davio* (the Hebrew acronym for "Speak unto the children of Israel that
they go forward"–Exodus 14:15), but the name was later changed to *BILU*, after
the Hebrew initials of a verse in Isaiah (2:5), "O House of Jacob, let us go
forth. . . . " The change was made because "instead of advising the people to go
to Eretz, the land of Israel, we decided to go there ourselves."

The Biluim, eventually numbering 525 people, formed the beginnings of
the First Aliyah, the return to the holy land. Some of them did emigrate and
become important Zionist pioneers. Belkind, for instance, opened the first
modern Hebrew school in Jaffa in 1889.

BELLOW, SAUL *(1915–   )*
American author and winner of the Nobel Prize for literature.

When Saul Bellow met a Hasid, it was a classic encounter between the modern
and the traditional within Jewry.

Bellow was on a British Airways flight to Israel with his wife, Alexandra.
They were seated in a row of three seats, with the third seat occupied by the
Hasid, who appeared very agitated.

The Hasid stared at Bellow, finally asking him whether he spoke Yiddish.
Bellow assured the man that he did. The man then said that he could not sit
next to Bellow's wife; he asked if Bellow could sit between them. Being seated in
the middle was not the author's favorite way to fly, but he obliged.

There were quite a few Hasidim on the plane. Bellow thought that they seemed oblivious to any of the rules of flying, a situation that put the flight personnel on edge. When it was time to order dinner, Bellow knew that unnecessary difficulties could be avoided if he made a point of ordering a kosher dinner. He made this request known, but there were not enough kosher dinners because the airline had not prepared for so many Orthodox travelers. Bellow delayed getting his chicken dinner for three hours; he had wanted to avoid any dispute with the Hasid sitting next to him.

Nevertheless, when the chicken finally did arrive, the Hasid, as expected, recoiled in horror. Again he addressed Bellow in Yiddish, saying that he had to speak and asking whether Bellow would be offended. Bellow said that he didn't think he would.

The Hasid warned Bellow that he might wish to slap him in the face for what he was to say, but then the Hasid asked him how, as a Jew, he could eat the nonkosher chicken. Bellow agreed that the chicken did not look appetizing. The Hasid, obviously pleased, told Bellow that he had kosher beef sandwiches.

He then asked whether Bellow's wife was Jewish. Again wishing to avoid shocking the fellow, Bellow decided to allude as delicately as possible to his wife's non-Jewish status. He told the Hasid that his wife had not been given a Jewish upbringing. This seemed to satisfy the Hasid, who then asked whether Bellow would like one of the kosher beef sandwiches. Bellow cheerfully agreed to the offer, but the Hasid decided to use his bait for a bigger catch. He told Bellow that the sandwich would be given on the sole condition that Bellow promise never to eat nonkosher food again. Bellow said that he could not make that promise, that it was a lot to ask for one sandwich.

The Hasid was not finished, though. He professed having a sacred duty and asked whether Bellow would listen to a proposition. Bellow agreed, and the Hasid laid out his proposal. He offered to send Bellow $15 a week if Bellow would eat only kosher foods.

Bellow expressed his view that this was generous. He asked what the Hasid did for a living and was told that he worked in a sweater factory in New Jersey. The Hasid pushed for an answer. Bellow countered that kosher food was expensive, and the Hasid upped his offer to $25. Bellow said that he could not accept what would clearly require so much sacrifice.

Bellow ate his chicken while the Hasid prayed—perhaps, as Bellow's wife suggested, for the author. The Hasid returned to his seat after the prayer. Bellow resumed the conversation. He told the Hasid that his wife would be lecturing in mathematics at the Hebrew University. The Hasid asked what mathematicians do. In his response, Bellow included the name of Albert Einstein. The Hasid had never heard of the great physicist.

Bellow and the young Hasid saw each other for the last time at the airport's baggage carousel—two figures almost from different historical eras groping to find what it was that made the common Jewish ground between them.

BEN-GURION, DAVID (1886–1973)
First prime minister of Israel, key leader of Israel's pioneer Labor movement.

(1) It was May 14, 1948. David Ben-Gurion was in the Tel Aviv Museum on Rothschild Boulevard. The diminutive leader, uncharacteristically dressed in a jacket and black silk tie, stood at the microphone. A huge portrait of Theodor Herzl, bordered by two large flags, hung directly over Ben-Gurion's head.

Members of what will be the first government of Israel were seated at the table on either side. There were more than 350 people in the room. Most sat less than quietly on the brown wooden chairs. Others stood and filled the aisles and the back of the room.

It was a hot day, made worse by the *hamsun*, the dry desert wind. The windows were open to let in any available air. A huge crowd was outside making great noise. Automobile horns honk.

Ben-Gurion was waiting until 4:00 to read the declaration. But he knew what the huge crowd didn't—that the declaration wasn't there yet. An official was supposed to be delivering it, but he had not yet arrived.

Ben-Gurion's decision to declare the state had been made only two days earlier. Jewish officials managed to come up with $450 for the ceremonies. Otto Wallisch, an artist, was sent out to get all the needed accouterments. He found Herzl's portrait covered with dust in a cellar. The Zionist flags he obtained were equally dusty; these he had had cleaned in a laundry. There had also been some disagreement about what the name of the new nation would be. Ben-Gurion had been adamant. He rejected *Judea* because that was a name for only a small area of the land of Israel. *Zion* was a mountain. He got what he wanted: *Israel*.

Ben-Gurion waited nervously for the declaration to arrive. He could not know that, despite some last-minute feuding over the wording, it was ready. Unfortunately, the official carrying it could not find a taxi. A policeman was called upon for help. The policeman stopped the first car, whose driver was rushing home to hear the Declaration of Independence read over the radio. Instead, the driver took the official to the Tel Aviv Museum. Ben-Gurion was handed the parchment with a minute to spare.

Ben-Gurion, declaration in hand, picked up a walnut gavel. He pounded the gavel on the table top and read the declaration that restored Jewish sovereignty for the first time in almost 2,000 years.

Ben-Gurion then signed a blank parchment, which would later have the declaration printed on it.

The Jewish Philharmonic Orchestra, away from the audience's view, broke into an especially poignant rendition of *Hatikvah*.

Ben-Gurion stepped down, looked at a British reporter, and said, "You see, we did it!"

(2) An important socialist came from France to visit Israel and called on Ben-Gurion. The man, wary of being in a Jewish nation, told the prime minister, "I'd better tell you. I am a socialist first, then a Frenchman, and only then a Jew."

"That's all right," Ben-Gurion said. "Here we read from right to left."

(3) Ben-Gurion was famous for his aversion to formal attire. Once he was about to depart for a dinner party when an aide rushed to him. "Mr. Prime Minister, you can't go to a formal affair without a necktie and with your collar open that way."

Ben-Gurion stared at him. "Why can't I? Winston Churchill told me it was all right."

It was the aide's turn to stare. "Winston Churchill told you it was all right?"

"Absolutely," Ben-Gurion said, and then told the story of this approval. "I was in London, and I attended a formal dinner party dressed just as I am. Churchill said to me, 'That kind of dress is all right in Israel, but not in England.' "

(4) A new automobile company wanted to give Ben-Gurion the very first car manufactured. Many, including Ben-Gurion himself, objected to the free gift, but the company persisted. Finally, a compromise was reached. The prime minister would pay one lira, the Israeli currency at the time.

At the ceremony, Paula, Ben-Gurion's wife, considered the situation. Finally she leaned over and said to her husband, "Ben-Gurion, at that price, buy two."

(5) Ben-Gurion was famous for retiring and then unretiring. Finally, after the ninth time this happened, the Old Man, as he was called, was asked by an American visiting Israel why he resigned so often. The visitor asked, "What is the real significance behind your resigning, anyway?"

Ben-Gurion thought for a minute and then replied, "Why, it has the same significance as those 'Going Out of Business' signs along Seventh Avenue. It is a chance for one to unload some stock one doesn't want, hire new workers, and make a different contract with the union."

(6) Ben-Gurion was serving as prime minister in 1958 when he concluded that golf would be important for the Jewish state. His main reasoning was political. Dwight Eisenhower was the American president. Many important discussions with the president were held on or around a golf course. The very photograph of an Israeli leader playing golf with an American president would, in Ben-Gurion's eyes, enhance Israel's image.

K. Jason Sitewell was chosen to come to Israel, first to design a golf course to attract tourists, and second to teach Ben-Gurion how to play golf. The lessons were to be secret.

Ben-Gurion was then 73 years old and had never been near a golf club in his life. For their first five meetings, Ben-Gurion lectured Sitewell on a variety of arcane subjects—lectures specifically and successfully designed to forestall the scheduled lessons. Finally, one day, the truth emerged.

Ben-Gurion told Sitewell that he planned to resign in the spring of 1959 and never really had any intention to play. Naturally, he was asked why the ruse had taken place. The prime minister said, "I knew that my successor would be Golda Meir. I wanted to create a precedent that would be binding on her . . . and every time I think of Golda playing golf, it makes me feel good all over."

"What makes you think she'll do it?" Sitewell asked.

"She would have no way of refusing—not when all the advisors go to work on her the way they did on me. It might not even be necessary to bring in the advisors. I think I can do it all by myself."

Ben-Gurion then looked at his watch and said, "It is now 10:45 A.M. I telephoned her yesterday and asked her to come to my office at 11:00. I want her to meet you, just so she'll know how serious I am."

As Meir arrived, Ben-Gurion launched into an hour-long discussion of his political plans, of his desire that she succeed him. Then, in the same tone of voice, he raised the subject of the importance of a prime minister learning to play golf.

"That makes good sense," Meir said. She was ready to begin. Ben-Gurion was immensely satisfied with himself.

As it turned out, Meir was as cagey as the Old Man. After arguing with Sitewell over which clubs to use and how to play, Sitewell gently suggested that since she knew so much, she didn't need a teacher. She agreed and asked him to put that in writing. Only much later did Sitewell realize that the clever Meir, who had no more wanted to learn to play golf than Ben-Gurion had, could go to her advisors and tell them that she had wanted to learn, but her instructor had resigned.

(7) After Ben-Gurion left his job as prime minister, he made a private trip to Turkey. He wandered through Istanbul's streets looking for books, as he often did. Finally, he finished and hailed a cab.

"Where to?" the driver wanted to know.

Ben-Gurion responded in the literary Turkish that he had learned before the First World War, when he had studied law in Turkey.

The cab driver was amazed. The two men entered into a long conversation. The cab driver said, "Can you read Turkish of that period?"

"Of course," Ben-Gurion replied.

The driver then took an old Koran out of the glove compartment. The text was in the old-fashioned Arabic script rather than the modern Turkish Latin script. Ben-Gurion spent the rest of the trip reading the Koran aloud to the driver.

When they reached Ben-Gurion's hotel, the Israeli asked how much the fare was.

The driver laughed at him. "Money? No! How could I take money from a foreigner who reads and speaks ancient Turkish better than any Turk?"

BEN-YEHUDA, ELIEZER *(1858–1922)*
The father of modern Hebrew, who wrote a pioneering Hebrew dictionary.

(1) Ben-Yehuda was a student at the Sorbonne in Paris when he reached the conclusion that a national revival of the Jewish people could only be successfully accomplished if it were accompanied by a revival of the Jews' ancient language, Hebrew. Stunned by his own observation, Ben-Yehuda, always a man of action who refused to settle simply for the right idea, decided to experiment. He began speaking Hebrew as he talked with his friends. It soon became apparent to him that there was no adequate vocabulary for many modern ideas and inventions. It was just as obvious, however, that the language itself was vast and beautiful. More important, the Bible (and other traditional literature) was a storehouse of Hebrew words. Thus the great idea of Ben-Yehuda's life came as he tried to speak to his friends: create a Hebrew dictionary, developing new words when necessary, but if at all possible developing them from traditional Hebrew roots.

(2) After Ben-Yehuda's wife, Deborah, told him that she was expecting their first child, the couple stayed up late into the night discussing the child's future. Ben-Yehuda asked Deborah to make a pledge: Their child would be the first in centuries to hear only Hebrew. He not only wanted Deborah to speak exclusively Hebrew to the child, but he wanted every visitor to the house to abide by the Hebrew-only pledge. Ben-Yehuda intended, more forcefully than by only writing and speaking, to set an example, a model to inspire all the Jewish world.

Deborah was depressed by Ben-Yehuda's plea. She had studied Hebrew, but even in Jerusalem, where they lived, only a few people could speak Hebrew.

Finally, though, she took an oath that the child would hear Hebrew only. The oath was kept.

BEN-ZVI, ITZHAK *(1884–1963)*
Second president of Israel.

(1) Itzhak Ben-Zvi became well known for both his humanity and his down-to-earth approach to his office.

He displayed these characteristics on the day he became president. Ben-Zvi returned to his home and found a guard marching back and forth in front of the house. The new president asked what the guard was doing. The young sentry replied that he was serving as an honor guard. This amazed Ben-Zvi, who went into his home.

A few minutes later, Ben-Zvi went outside again and stood in the cold night air of winter. "Look," the president finally said to the guard, "It's cold outside. Come in and have a cup of hot tea." The guard explained that he was not allowed to leave his post. The orders had been very strict. Ben-Zvi went back inside his home. "Make some hot tea, please," he asked his wife. Once again he walked outside. He went up to the soldier and said, "Look, I have an idea. You go in and have a cup of tea. I will stand outside with your gun and take your post."

(2) When Ben-Zvi was president of Israel, he met with Alexander Abramov, the Soviet ambassador, who came to present his credentials. The two soon began to speak more informally to each other. Abramov asked, "When did you leave Russia?"

"In 1901," the president responded.

"Why did you leave?"

"There was no room in Russia for me and Czar Nicholas II."

"Why did you go, though?" the ambassador continued. "You should have held your ground."

Ben-Zvi said, "I had somewhere to go. The czar didn't."

BENJAMIN, JUDAH P. (1811–1884)
American attorney and statesman.

Benjamin is credited with a remark that is strikingly similar to one made by Benjamin Disraeli, though Benjamin gave his remark an American edge, one that reflects the immigrant nature of the country.

The incident took place during a debate that reportedly occurred on the floor of the US Senate (some claim that it took place while Benjamin was campaigning in Louisiana). Benjamin was called "that Jew from Louisiana." Benjamin arose and said, "It is true that I am a Jew, and when my ancestors were receiving their Ten Commandments from the immediate hand of Deity, amid the thunder and lightning on Mount Sinai, the ancestors of the distinguished gentleman who is opposed to me were herding swine in the forests of Scandinavia."

BENNY, JACK *(1894–1975)*
American stage, radio, and television comedian.

Jack Benny's pride in being Jewish was evident in many ways in his life.

Once Benny was preparing for his Sunday program, which would begin at 4:00 P.M. in Los Angeles. Sundown was the beginning of Yom Kippur. Benny would be finished with the program by then, but on the East Coast, because of the time difference, sundown would already have taken place by the program's conclusion. He told an assistant that he "wouldn't want people to think I'm desecrating this holiday by working on it."

The assistant tried to lighten the somber mood by joking that all the Jews on the East Coast would be in synagogue and wouldn't know about it. Benny shook his head. "I wasn't thinking of the Jews. I wouldn't like the Gentiles to think I didn't respect my religion."

BERLIN, NAFTALI TZEV JUDAH *(1817–1893)*
Rabbi.

Rabbi Berlin sought to defend Orthodox traditions against what he viewed as an onslaught of modernism. He often used the familiar story-telling method to underscore his views.

One day, a group of Jewish leaders was gathered in Vilna. Discussion turned to Professor Daniel Chivalson (1819–1911), then a well-known Orientalist. He had also become famous for his defense of Jews, especially against the blood libel of using a Christian child's blood during Passover. Some of the Jewish leaders defended him because of this. But Chivalson was also an apostate, having left Judaism. Therefore, some of the Jewish leaders renounced him.

Rabbi Berlin was among those taking the latter position. The rabbi spoke to the assembled group to make his point: "Let me tell you a story. A religious Jewish woman took seriously ill, and the physician prescribed for her a diet that included bacon. The problem was brought to a local rabbi. He considered the matter and concluded that since it was a matter of life or death, the bacon would be allowed.

"The woman agreed to eat the bacon, but only on condition that it be prepared according to proper rituals. A pig was selected and slaughtered, but the slaughterer discovered a defective lung. The rabbi was asked to examine the lung. He stared at it for a long time. 'Were this the lung of a cow, I would have said that the meat is fit for consumption. However, how can I pronounce a pig kosher?'"

BERNHARDT, SARAH *(1844–1923)*
French actress.

In 1874, Sarah Bernhardt was advised to give up her profession because of poor health. Instead, she returned to the theater as soon as she was able. A friend then asked her what gift he could send. She replied, "They say I am to die, so you may send me a coffin."

When the coffin arrived, the actress kept it with her always. She had a trestle made on which the coffin stood at the end of her bed, so she could see it without effort on awakening.

She was asked why she always kept such an unusual object so close to her. She responded, "To remind me that my body will soon be dust and that my glory alone will live forever."

BERURIAH *(second century C.E.)*
Scholar and wife of Rabbi Meir.

(1) One of the most famous stories from the Talmud concerns the wisdom of Beruriah in dealing with life's most difficult moments.

Beruriah had been caring for her sons during an epidemic. It was a Sabbath day, and Rabbi Meir was in the synagogue.

Both sons died during that day. Because mourning is forbidden on the Sabbath, Beruriah withheld her feelings and put the bodies of her sons in a bed, covered them with a sheet, and locked the door.

Rabbi Meir came back and inquired about his sons. Beruriah told him that they were out visiting friends.

Later, after Havdalah, Beruriah came to her husband seeking advice. "Yesterday somebody left two golden vessels here. He is coming for them today, and I want to know if I should return them to him."

"Certainly," her husband said. "Why do you ask?"

"Come with me," she responded. She took him to the room where their lifeless children lay on the bed.

Rabbi Meir began to cry with sadness.

"Calm yourself," his wife said. "Did you not say that we must return things entrusted to us? The Lord gave them to us, and the Lord has taken them back."

(2) Beruriah's husband, Rabbi Meir, was often bothered by some rowdy men who lived in their neighborhood. He once prayed that they would die. But Beruriah said to him, "Why do you pray for their death. Is it because in the Psalms it says 'Let sinners cease out of the earth'? But the text can be interpreted

to mean that sins should cease out of the world. When the sins cease, the wicked shall not be wicked any more. You should pray that those sinners will repent and not be wicked any more."

Rabbi Meir understood his wife and altered his prayer accordingly.

BIALIK, CHAIM NACHMAN (1873–1934)
Foremost Hebrew poet of his day.

(1) Bialik visited the land of Israel in 1925 and was riding in a *sherut*, or cab, with a man who was involved with the Yiddish theater. The two conversed in earthy Yiddish. The Sephardic driver, tired of hearing a language he didn't know and wishing to make a point that Hebrew should be spoken in the land of Israel, asked the two to speak Hebrew.

"Hebrew!" Bialik exclaimed. "How can we speak Hebrew? There isn't even a word for intercourse!"

(2) Bialik established a publishing house in Tel Aviv that, like most business ventures, had difficult financial beginnings. Bialik borrowed heavily to open his enterprise. He was soon confronted by a real estate speculator who had lent him 100 pounds. Payment of the debt was overdue. Bialik notified the creditor that the money would be forthcoming, but that there would still be a wait, because there were some more important obligations such as rent, salaries, and royalties to his authors.

The creditor was surprised at this last obligation. "Royalties to authors? Why, I am told that you are printing the works of Ibn Gabirol and Ibn Ezra, both of whom, I understand, are dead." (Indeed they were: Ibn Gabirol wrote in the eleventh century; Ibn Ezra, in the twelfth.)

"True," Bialik said, "But don't forget that they have left orphans and widows, and I cannot let them starve."

The real estate man relented. "If that is the case, I will wait. Orphans and widows come first."

(3) Several days prior to Bialik's death, there was open speculation in the press that the aging author would be awarded the Nobel Prize for literature. But the prize was given to another writer. Bialik was asked to react. He said, "I'm very glad I didn't win the prize. Now everybody's my friend and feels sorry for me. My, my, how angry they are on my behalf. 'Now isn't that a scandal,' they say. 'Imagine such a thing—Bialik, the great poet Bialik, doesn't get the Nobel Prize! And—tsk! tsk!—just look who they gave it to! To X, that so-and-so! Why, he can't even hold a candle to Bialik!'

"On the other hand, what if I had been awarded the Nobel Prize? Then, I'm sure, some of the very people who are now so indignant on my account would have said, 'Nu, nu, what's so wonderful about winning the Nobel Prize? Why, even that poet Bialik got one.' "

BLITZER, WOLF (1948–   )
American journalist.

President Anwar Sadat of Egypt once claimed that the idea for his journey to Jerusalem to make peace had come from a journalist.

President Sadat was visiting the United States on April 6, 1977. He held two days of talks with President Jimmy Carter and afterward held a news conference.

Wolf Blitzer, Washington correspondent for *The Jerusalem Post*, was among those attending. Sadat, dressed in a dark pinstriped suit, looked calm and relaxed. He told the assembled reporters that he very much wanted peace between Israel and Egypt, but normal relations depended on Israel's agreeing to a Palestinian Arab state in the West Bank and Gaza Strip. As the news conference was nearing its conclusion, Blitzer raised his hand to ask a question.

The Egyptian ambassador to the United States, Ashraf Ghorbal, called on him immediately. Blitzer wasn't sure whether Ghorbal knew which paper he represented, but he proceeded. First he identified himself and stared directly into Sadat's eyes. Sadat didn't react in any way, so Blitzer continued. "Mr. President, you seem so sincere in your quest for peace. Why don't you do something to demonstrate that to Israel? Perhaps you could open some direct human contact with Israel. Why not allow an exchange of journalists or athletes or scholars?" Blitzer was thinking of the "ping-pong diplomacy" between the United States and China that had taken place a few years earlier and had served to speed the process of normalizing relations. Blitzer believed in the efficacy of direct contact as a way to change perceptions.

Sadat then responded. "Part of the Arab–Israeli conflict is a psychological one. I myself have no objection to this. But, believe me, our people are not yet ready for this, after twenty-nine years of hatred and four wars and bitterness. . . . We must take it gradually."

Blitzer filed his story, which became the lead in the following day's edition of the *Post*. Blitzer then went on with his journalistic work, not thinking very much about the exchange with Sadat.

Then, seven months later, on November 9, 1977, Sadat spoke to the Egyptian parliament. "The Israelis are going to be stunned on hearing this. I am ready to meet with them. . . . I am ready to go to the Knesset to discuss peace with them."

On November 11, Israeli Prime Minister Menachem Begin, in a message to the people of Egypt, accepted Sadat's proposal of a visit, and on November 19 Sadat arrived in Jerusalem.

During the news accounts that followed Sadat's speech to his parliament, much was made of his statement that it had been Blitzer's question that had given the Egyptian president the idea for his journey to Jerusalem.

BOROCHOV, BER (1881–1917)
Socialist Zionist.

Not long before the First World War broke out, Ber Borochov attended a lecture given in Liege, Belgium. The lecturer was Vladimir Lenin, the leader of the Communist movement.

After Lenin had finished speaking, Borochov arose to expound upon and defend his theory that Marxism and Zionism were compatible. Lenin laughed, saying Borochov wandered both "here and there." Lenin said Borochov was trying to sit on two chairs at the same time, and when someone tries to do that, he ends up sitting in the empty space between the two chairs.

BRANDEIS, LOUIS (1856–1941)
First Jewish US Supreme Court justice.

(1) Louis Brandeis was already an eminent jurist when he came to Zionism. His interest in the movement to reestablish a Jewish nation was prompted by a chance visit by a journalist.

In 1910, Jacob de Haas, who had served as English secretary to Zionism's founder, Theodor Herzl, was serving as editor of the Boston *Jewish Advocate.*

In that editorial capacity, de Haas called on Louis Brandeis for an interview about savings-bank life insurance. After the interview, de Haas rose and began to leave. As he was getting ready to go, he asked whether Brandeis was related to Lewis N. Dembitz. Brandeis replied that he was Dembitz's nephew. (Dembitz was a well-known jurist who had helped establish the Jewish Theological Seminary and was an active Zionist.) De Haas remarked that "Dembitz was a noble Jew." Brandeis was taken with the remark and asked de Haas to explain. For the next two hours, de Haas told Brandeis about Theodor Herzl, about how Dembitz was involved in the Zionist movement, and about the movement itself, its program and its hopes. Brandeis asked the editor to send him any materials he had on Zionism.

Brandeis's meeting with de Haas was the jurist's first encounter with

Zionism, a fateful one for him and the movement to which he was to provide so much prestige.

(2) The First World War had many unintended consequences, most of them bad, but some good. One of the good consequences was the opportunity for Brandeis to follow up on the encounter with de Haas and become actively involved in the Zionist movement.

Dr. Arthur Ruppin, who was the chief Zionist official in the land of Israel, had seen the desperate financial situation that the war had brought to the Jewish community in the holy land. To save the Jewish community, $50,000 was needed immediately.

Shmaryahu Levin, then in the United States, called an emergency meeting for August 30, 1914. Brandeis was among those invited. It was expected that the nationally known Brandeis, with his many connections to wealthy and powerful people, would serve in an honorary role on the committee that would be set up to raise funds. It was de Haas who had recommended Brandeis precisely for such a small role.

The meeting was held at the Hotel Marseilles in New York. Brandeis accepted the nomination to lead the committee. He gave a brief speech, announced that an emergency fund was being established, and initiated the fund with a $1,000 donation. Nathan Straus donated $5,000. All had so far gone according to plan.

But Brandeis, by his nature, was not a dabbler. All of a sudden, he told those gathered that he did not yet understand the organizations they represented. He requested that the delegates stay on and tell him.

For the next day and a half, Brandeis got a crash course in the labyrinthian world of American Zionism. He listened patiently, asked questions, and learned a tremendous amount. Slowly, as he learned about how the various organizations were administered, he came to an unavoidable conclusion: American Jewry was very poorly organized.

As he concluded his meetings on August 31, Brandeis sat, shocked. The brilliant Boston lawyer determined at that moment to organize American Zionism into an efficient and effective force.

Neither American Zionism nor Louis Brandeis would ever be the same again.

(3) Brandeis's devotion to Zionism, his enthusiasm for its efforts, was well illustrated by his willingness to donate not just his time and good name but also his money.

Brandeis was visiting the land of Israel in 1934. David Ben-Gurion came to see the distinguished American visitor. Ben-Gurion presented a memorandum to the justice, describing how economically important the port city of Eilat (then called Uman Rashrash) would soon be to the Jewish community.

"It is important that we establish a pioneering Jewish settlement here. But it will not bring a profit, and it might cost $100,000," Ben-Gurion admitted to Brandeis.

Brandeis read the memorandum carefully, took out a pen, and wrote a check. He handed it to Ben-Gurion, saying, "Here is $100,000."

Overwhelmed, Ben-Gurion protested, saying that he had come not for money, but for moral support.

Brandeis insisted. "I want to be the first," he said, "to help stake a claim on this important spot."

BREITBART, ZISHA (1883–1925)
Athlete and strongman.

Zisha Breitbart was widely considered to be the strongest man in the world. He got his start by confronting an anti-Semitic dog.

As a child, Breitbart had dreamed of being another Samson. One day he mentioned his dream to his brother, who questioned his sanity. The brother reminded Zisha that Samson had lived in the land of Israel. Then he asked where Zisha would find Philistines, especially ones who would burn his eyes out. That point stumped young Zisha. He could live without eyes, but he couldn't figure out where he was going to find any Philistines. At any rate, Zisha began letting his hair grow and stopped even sipping wine. He worked very hard in his father's blacksmith shop and waited for the day that would prove he was Samson.

The day finally arrived.

There was an anti-Semite who lived in an alley not far from the Breitbart home. The anti-Semite owned an extremely vicious dog that attacked Jewish children. Zisha decided that he would attack the dog and prove to everyone that he was indeed the Samson of modern times. He gathered some boys and went to the anti-Semite's house. The dog saw them. It began gnashing its teeth and barking. Zisha moved forward. The other small boys stood frozen in fear. Zisha turned to them and, although they were his own age, said, "Children, have no fear. I am with you. I, Samson, will tear this lion apart." Zisha stared at the dog. His imagination had transformed it into a lion. The other boys began to follow him.

The dog suddenly leaped at them. The other boys shouted in terror. Zisha screamed out "Shema Yisrael!" and fought with the dog. The animal endeavored to get its jaws into the boy, but each time it opened its mouth, Zisha hit it hard.

The boy and the beast battled for five minutes until the bleeding animal had to lie still. Its owner, watching from a distance, had intended to witness his dog's bloody triumph over a Jew. Instead, the anti-Semite, seeing the result of the fight, grabbed a gun. The boys all fled, but the dog disappeared, and the anti-Semite never bothered the boys again.

Stories of Zisha's exploit soon filled the neighborhood.

BROD, MAX (1884–1968)
Jewish author and composer.

Max Brod, a close friend of author Franz Kafka, encountered many intellectuals who had assimilated. Brod, who had remained faithful to his religion, always treated those intellectuals with great humanity.

Once, just before the First World War, Brod was in Prague, where he spoke with a Jewish professor at the German university in that city. In reply to a question, the Jewish professor said, "I have abandoned Judaism."

Dr. Brod replied, "You may have abandoned Judaism, but Judaism has not abandoned you."

BUBER, MARTIN (1878–1965)
Philosopher, theologian, Zionist leader.

(1) Many years after he had settled in Jerusalem, Buber was asked "How good is your Hebrew?" The philosopher's answer was "Good enough to lecture in—but not sufficiently good to be obscure."

(2) Martin Buber's development of his philosophy of dialogue rested on a sense of encounter he felt not only with God or other humans, but also with animals. He had been impressed as a child by his father's treatment of all animals—acting toward them as though they were people.

When he was 11 years old, Buber, who was spending his summer on the family farm, grew close to a particular horse. Buber would sneak into the barn and rub the neck of a big dappled horse. The closeness between boy and horse was deeply felt; Buber later thought of the feeling as being in touch with the Other, with a direct feeling of otherness and, in addition, an otherness that let him come close to it. Even in his adulthood, Buber vividly recalled how the horse would raise its head, flick its ears, and then quickly snort, a sound which, to Buber's mind, indicated an understanding. Once, though, as he stroked the horse's mane, Buber suddenly became conscious of his hand. This very consciousness changed the feeling of otherness Buber had felt. Indeed, the next day the horse did not raise its head. The boy understood this as evidence that the special closeness was a thing of the past.

This lesson of the immediacy of otherness and the potential for loss through a conscious understanding of it was one lesson Buber would retain for his entire life.

CAHAN, ABRAHAM *(1860–1951)*
Author, and editor of the Jewish Daily Forward.

Abe Cahan thought of himself as a realist. As an editor, he used to argue that Isaac Bashevis Singer's stories were too full of supernatural demons and hobgoblins. Cahan told the young writer of his distaste for such subject matter because there were no demons or hobgoblins in the United States, and readers didn't want to read about them. But Singer assured the "king of American Yiddish" that if there were demons in Poland, then there were also demons in the United States.

CARMEL, ABRAHAM *(born 1911)*
Ex-priest who converted to Judaism.

Carmel was a Roman Catholic priest. For seven years he practiced his vocation with great care, but a gnawing feeling was emerging in his soul. Some time after the seventh year, he realized he could no longer bring himself to subscribe wholeheartedly to the notion that Jesus was Divine. Such a theological conclusion was, to say the least, embarrassing.

Carmel was spiritually adrift. He searched, almost desperately, for a solution to his dilemma. One day he was reading Professor Josef Klausner's scholarly book *From Jesus to Paul.* One of the themes of the book was that Jesus was a simple Jewish "rabbi" whose teachings had been transformed by the missionary Paul into a dogmatic system with a huge organization. Carmel was stunned as he sat and read. The insight struck him: Paul, not Jesus, had been the true founder of Christianity. Relieved at finding a useful way to understand his religious roots, Carmel began an intense reevaluation of his spiritual beliefs.

Eventually he converted to Judaism and, some years after his conversion, moved to Israel. Later, his health problems forced him to return to the United States, where he became a distinguished Jewish educator.

CARO, JOSEPH (1488–1575)
Religious authority and author of the Shulchan Aruch.

The mystical kabbalists had to deal with all aspects of life, including private sexual experiences and the sexual nature of the relationship between men and women.

One Sabbath night on the 28th of Iyar, Caro was walking with friends in either Adrianople or Nicopolis. They passed a *tekiye*—a Turkish word for a monastery of dervishes. (Dervishes were ascetic Moslems who used whirling dances and religious language so that they could induce a state of collective religious ecstasy. Some kabbalists identified dervishes with unclean spirits and idol worshippers.) Caro went for a walk in the garden of the *tekiye*. His friends used frankly erotic language, which led Caro to have what he would normally have considered sinful thoughts. Later the walkers witnessed an unrecorded but evidently unchaste activity, and again such thoughts emerged.

This experience excited Caro, who recorded that later that night he had a nocturnal emission. Such emissions were considered deeply immoral by kabbalists, who believed that they created more demons instead of human beings, and only humans, after all, could serve the Lord. Caro was greatly upset. He remained awake and troubled until an hour later, when he had relations with his wife.

Still later he got up to study, and a voice came to him, berating him for his behavior but telling him that the relations with his wife had allowed him to reenter a sphere of holiness. (The kabbalists saw marital relations as a kind of sacrament that could redevelop a communion between human beings and the Shekhinah [the Divine Presence, or the immanence of God in the world].) Caro became determined to avoid contact with places where his heart could be turned away from the Torah.

CHAGALL, MARC (1887–1985)
Artist.

It took a terrible accident for Marc Chagall to feel not just physical pain in himself, but emotional pain in other people as well.

A rabbi from Mohiliff deeply impressed Chagall as a child. The young

Chagall attempted to learn Judaism from the rabbi and had already stopped swimming on Saturday and started studying the Bible.

Chagall would go to the rabbi's house on Sabbath afternoons. It was the rabbi's habit to sleep while waiting for his young pupil. Chagall had to knock loudly on the door to wake the rabbi.

One day the loud knocks aroused the rabbi's dog rather than the rabbi. The reddish-brown dog was old, and he had a bad temper and sharp teeth. The dog made its way down the staircase with its ears pointed up. Chagall stared as it approached. Suddenly, the dog attacked, biting the boy.

Chagall was given some ice and taken to his home. The police searched for the dog and killed it only after firing twelve bullets. That night, Chagall went with his uncle to Petersburg to seek a doctor. The doctors who examined him concluded that the dog had been rabid: The boy would be dead within four days.

Chagall acted as though he were in a dream. He began to enjoy his situation. He liked the bed, the food, the chance to walk in the garden, and the nurses' smiles. He especially admired the beautiful toys the other children owned, for he had no toys at home. His uncle encouraged him to "take" a toy left unattended.

Chagall eventually recovered, but even after he left the hospital, he kept hearing the child who owned the toy weeping.

CHISSIN, CHAIM (1865–1932)
Early Zionist pioneer.

Seventeen-year-old Chaim Chissin was among the first of the Russian Jews to react to the pogroms that started in 1881 by deciding that only in their own ancient homeland would the Jews be safe. Chissin consequently set out for the land of Israel, full of enthusiasm, hope, and a deep sense of idealism. That idealism was sorely tested even before he reached his destination. On July 22, 1882, Chissin's ship landed in Constantinople. He was met by associates from the Central Bureau for the Rebuilding of the Land of Israel and taken to the hotel. He found three youthful representatives of the Central Bureau there. They arose, ordered tea, and, after discussing whether cake should be ordered, decided against it because of the cost.

After the tea arrived, the three provided a report on the Central Bureau's financial condition. Chissin heard the worst: They had no assets and several debts. They had pawned all they owned except for their clothes. They had no one from whom to borrow money.

The young would-be pioneers drank a lot of tea because the hotel provided it free for each room. They told Chissin what had happened the previous morning. They had drunk all the tea they could bear and yet had only a half-franc for breakfast. One of the three suggested that the half-franc be used to buy a loaf of bread. A second wanted to know what would happen after the bread was eaten. The third complained that he wished to smoke but that there was no tobacco.

It was either bread or tobacco. The three decided to vote. Two voted to buy the tobacco and one the bread.

Chissin was shocked. This, after all, was the Central Bureau. This was how they lived. These were the problems they discussed.

It was the first deflation of his idealism, but the reality of the desperate situation helped harden him for the difficulties he would endure.

Chissin kept a diary of his pioneer experiences from 1882 until 1887. In October of 1887, he returned to Russia, where he he worked as a pharmacist and as "government rabbi." In 1898 Chissin went to Switzerland, where he studied medicine. In 1905 he returned to Israel with his family and became a well-known physician. He remained active until his death in Tel Aviv.

COHEN, ELIE (1924–1965)
Israeli intelligence agent executed in Syria.

Elie Cohen was one of Israel's greatest spies.

Before his arrest in January 1965 by the Syrians, Cohen had infiltrated the highest offices in the Syrian defense establishment. There had even been talk of his being given a very high post in the Syrian Defense Ministry.

Many stories make up the Cohen legend. Here is one I was told:

One day Elie asked a Syrian military leader to provide him with a guided tour of the Golan Heights. The Syrians had two divisions on the Heights, from which they flew their aircraft into Israeli air space and bombarded the Israeli kibbutzim below. Elie knew that in the event of another war, the Golan would be invaluable.

Elie made several military observations during the tour and then reached his conclusion. He told the Syrians that the soldiers on the Golan Heights were too hot. They were using up valuable water, and the heat made their life difficult. They would be better fighters if they didn't have to endure the heat. Elie suggested that the Syrians plant clumps of trees near each large massing of troops. The trees would provide the needed shade. The Syrians thought this was a brilliant idea, and the trees were planted.

In June of 1967 the Israeli Air Force, while flying over the Heights, was able to pinpoint Syrian troop locations by the trees. The decisive action by the air force helped Israel capture the Golan and eliminate a crucial military threat.

COHEN, HENRY (1863–1952)
American rabbi.

Many famous non-Jews developed their sympathy toward Jews and Judaism because of the kindness shown them by individual Jews. Rabbi Cohen became famous in Texas for such kindness, which was especially evident in his concern about prison reform and the rights of prisoners of all faiths. He would note on his shirt cuff each morning the names of those who needed his immediate attention, and he would try to solve their problems before he went to sleep that night.

One day he learned of a man named Sidney Porter who was imprisoned on what seemed to be a false charge. Rabbi Cohen undertook his own investigation and determined that, in fact, Porter was innocent. The rabbi took his case to the governor, requesting that Porter be freed.

Several months later, Rabbi Cohen was sitting in his study. There was a knock at the door. The rabbi opened the door to find a man holding a suitcase.

"Are you Rabbi Cohen?" the stranger asked.

"I am."

The man looked up. "I am Sidney Porter, the man you got out of jail. I can't tell you how grateful I am. I can't pay you for your help now, but I'm a writer, and I'll do what I can to help your people."

Years later, Rabbi Cohen read a story about a rabbi who saved an innocent man from jail.

The story was written by O. Henry, the pen name chosen by Sidney Porter.

COHEN, HERMANN (1842–1918)
German philosopher.

Hermann Cohen was one of Judaism's greatest modern philosophers. His specialty was Judaism's philosophical and theological underpinnings.

One Friday evening, Cohen was sitting in synagogue when another worshipper asked him how he conceived of God. Cohen provided a lengthy and lucid explanation of his abstract idea of God. After he had completed his discourse, the man asked, simply, "But where is the creator of the world?"

Cohen then wept at the gulf that separated his philosopher's God from the God of the ordinary Jewish worshipper.

COWAN, PAUL (1940–1988)
American author and journalist.

Paul Cowan embraced his Jewish heritage only in adulthood. His return to a Jewish way of life was aided by his wife, Rachel, who, years after their marriage, converted to Judaism. One of Cowan's major influences on his spiritual journey was Rabbi Joseph Singer, whose traditional way of life was to provide a powerful model.

Cowan learned one crucial lesson from Rabbi Singer during the initial days of Hanukah in 1976. Cowan's parents had died in a tragic fire only a month before, on November 18. At the same time as he was pursuing a spiritual search for a more profound understanding of his life, Cowan was enduring continuing sadness at his parents' death.

Cowan came to see Rabbi Singer at the United Jewish Council on the lower East Side of Manhattan. Cowan approached the rabbi's small work area and observed Singer speaking to an elderly woman who was clearly reluctant to enter a hospital. The rabbi paced back and forth, juxtaposing Yiddish and English, yelling, begging, and kidding the woman. He reminded her of her religious obligation to maintain her health. He cited an appropriate talmudic passage. Finally he persuaded her to enter the hospital. After he arranged for someone to take her, he turned to Cowan.

He told Cowan that he, as a rabbi, had been called upon to deliver a eulogy for an elderly Jewish man who had remained outside synagogue life. The two of them walked together toward the funeral home. The rabbi linked arms with Cowan, telling him to be careful about the potholes, because "this is a very holy neighborhood." Then Rabbi Singer shifted to a discussion of how Moses had persuaded Pharaoh to allow Jewish slaves a day of rest on the Sabbath even before Moses received such a commandment at Sinai.

The two men approached Grand Street and waited at a red light. The rabbi told Cowan that the light was a mitzvah because it reminded pedestrians that they must protect themselves. He said a prayer to recall the wonderful gift of life that had been given. They arrived at the funeral home. The rabbi said, "It isn't right to speak of mournful things on a happy time like Hanukah." Cowan said that he didn't feel that he could attend another funeral. The rabbi said a blessing and asked him to call.

Cowan left. While riding uptown on the train, he realized that although he had heard a discussion with a woman about illness and had been on his way to a funeral home, the rabbi's religious insights had pushed away the thoughts of the death of his parents. It was a step toward belief.

CRESSON, WARDER (1798–1860)
American convert and Zionist.

Warder Cresson was put on trial and charged with insanity after he converted to Judaism. His family and others believed that his decision was an indication of mental imbalance.

Warder Cresson seems to have been a particularly zealous seeker of religious truth. Born a Quaker in an established family in Philadelphia, Cresson rejected his religion and went in search of a religion more compatible with his own needs. He became a Shaker, a Mormon, a Millerite, and a Cambellite.

Cresson's restless search eventually led to an acquaintance with Isaac Leeser, the Jewish editor of *The Occident*, then a leading defender of traditional Judaism in the United States. Cresson began to consider the Jewish situation. By 1844, he had become convinced that God was calling the Jews back to their ancient homeland. He therefore decided to visit the Holy Land for himself, but not simply as a tourist or pilgrim.

Through a congressional connection, Cresson received an appointment as the first American consul to Jerusalem. The appointment was soon cancelled, however, when the secretary of state received a complaint from Samuel Ingham, a former secretary of the treasury, that Cresson was "laboring under an aberration of the mind." Despite this setback, Cresson continued to Jerusalem. At the time, he still accepted the widespread Christian belief that converting Jews was a divinely mandated activity.

From 1844 until 1847 he worked with missionaries, but his humane conscience was troubled by what he thought of as "soul-snatching" – using economic incentives to persuade starving Jews to accept Christianity. His religious quest was also continuing. By 1848, publicly expressing his anger at the nature of missionary activity and identifying almost completely with the Jews in the land of Israel, Cresson decided to make one final spiritual journey: Despite fierce opposition by the chief rabbi of Jerusalem, he converted to Judaism. Cresson was circumcised and accepted the new name Michael C. Boaz Israel.

Cresson returned to Philadelphia in 1849, anxious to settle the affairs of his life in the United States before permanently moving to the Holy Land. Cresson hoped to persuade his family to sell their farm and move with him. Instead, his wife and children, shocked and bewildered by his religious conclusions, had him committed to a mental institution. A court ruled Cresson insane, but the verdict was appealed.

The trial, which was held in a higher court in May of 1851, lasted for six days and received extraordinary publicity. Well-known lawyers were hired by both sides. Almost a hundred witnesses were called. Finally, a decision was reached. The original verdict of insanity was overturned. Cresson was declared sane.

After the famous trial, Cresson divorced his wife. He returned to the land of Israel and attempted to establish an agricultural colony. Despite some financial help from such benefactors as Sir Moses Montefiore and Judah Touro, Cresson's efforts failed.

In 1851 Cresson published an autobiographical book, *The Key of David.*

From 1851 on, he lived according to Sephardic customs and married a Sephardic woman. He was widely regarded as a great man.

When Cresson died, he was buried on the Mount of Olives. To remember the man they called the American Ger Tsedek (righteous proselyte), all Jewish-owned businesses in Jerusalem were closed on the day of his funeral.

DAVID *(reigned 1010–970* B.C.E.*)*
Second king of Israel.

(1) King David's practical wisdom was legendary.

Once, one of king's infant children became critically ill. David prayed and fasted. He slept on the ground for the week of the illness. After that week, the baby died. The king's servants were afraid to tell him of the tragedy. Against such expectations, when David heard the sad news he changed his clothes, went to pray, and then ate a meal.

The servants, quite surprised at his reaction, asked him why when the child had been ill he had fasted and cried, yet when the child died, he had gotten up and eaten.

The king replied, "While the child was yet alive, I fasted and wept for I thought, who knows whether the Lord will not be gracious to me that the child may live. But now that he is dead, why should I fast? Can I bring him back?"

(2) King David went to the court jeweler. He told the jeweler to make him a ring and to inscribe on it some statement that would temper excessive delight in an hour of triumph, but also lift him from despair in an hour of loss. The jeweler thought long and hard about what kind of statement should be inscribed. But he was perplexed; he could not find suitable words.

Solomon finally offered a suggestion: "Inscribe on the ring the words *Gam Zeh Ya-avor*—This, too, shall pass."

(3) During Saul's reign as king, a rich, youthful widow was courted by a prince. The woman did not like the prince and so, to avoid marrying him, she decided to move away from the city. She had a lot of gold, which she did not want to carry with her, so she devised a plan. The woman secretly filled several jugs with

gold pieces, poured honey on the top to hide the gold, and, in the presence of witnesses, gave the jugs for safe keeping to one of her deceased husband's friends.

Some time later, after the prince had died, the woman wished to return home. In her absence, however, the man to whom she had entrusted the gold had used it to celebrate his son's wedding. He had at first intended only to use the honey, but then he had discovered the gold pieces. He'd emptied the jugs, removed the gold pieces, and refilled the jugs with honey.

After the woman returned, she asked that the man give back her property. The man asked that she bring the witnesses who had originally seen her give him the jugs. She did this, and the man returned the jugs. She quickly discovered that the man had stolen her gold. She went to the judges, but they ruled that no witnesses had seen her put any gold in the jugs. The judges advised her to go to King Saul. The king, in turn, gave the case to the Sanhedrin, but they, too, concluded that there was no proof that the man was guilty of stealing the gold pieces.

The woman began her journey home, saddened by the result. She met David, then still a shepherd boy, who was busy tending his flock. They talked, and she asked whether he could help her. David said that she should request of King Saul that he, David, be permitted to speak on her behalf. Saul agreed to this.

David, the woman, and the thief appeared before the king. David held up the jugs and asked, "Are you sure that these are the jugs that you gave to this man for safe keeping?" The woman said that they were, and the wily man agreed. David then broke one of the jugs. He found two gold pieces nearly covered with honey attached to the side of the jug. Then he turned to the man and said, "Return the gold that you have stolen from this woman."

The entire court was astonished by the shepherd boy's abilities.

DAVIS, SAMMY, JR. (1925–   )
American entertainer.

When Sammy Davis, Jr., converted to Judaism, the media created a sensation. The black entertainer's fame and faith gave courage to others who were considering their own religious situation. Davis's interest was first aroused by Eddie Cantor. While waiting to appear on Cantor's television program, Sammy admired a mezuzah-like ornament in his dressing room. Cantor gave it to him, and Davis wore the ornament every day until, one day in 1954, he misplaced it. That very day he had the automobile accident that cost him an eye.

While convalescing in the hospital, Davis discussed his feelings with the Jewish chaplain. The chaplain gave Davis several books to read.

Once he had recovered, Davis began to have extended talks with various rabbis. After several months of study, he decided to convert to Judaism.

His parents did not object to his decision, but several friends warned him that people might view the conversion as some sort of a publicity stunt. But Davis was adamant; he went through with the conversion.

His new faith was put to a test not long after he adopted Judaism. He was filming *Porgy and Bess*. Davis told the director that his religion forbade him to work on Yom Kippur. The director paled and called producer Samuel Goldwyn immediately. Goldwyn wasted no time in calling Davis.

"What's this I hear, Sammy? You won't be on the set tomorrow?" Goldwyn asked.

Sammy told the tough, no-nonsense producer that as a Jew, he could not work on the Day of Atonement.

There was silence on the other end of the line. Then, in an uncharacteristically quiet voice, Goldwyn said "Bless you" and hung up.

There was no production at all on Yom Kippur, a stoppage that cost Goldwyn $30,000.

DAYAN, MOSHE *(1915–1981)*
Israeli military and political leader.

(1) Moshe Dayan learned how to fight from a Bible-believing non-Jewish British army officer. It was a debt that Dayan—and Israel—would always remember.

In 1938 the British were facing an Arab campaign of terror. In particular, the British were concerned because marauders kept attacking the crucial oil pipeline that linked Iraq to Haifa. The British faced no similar terror campaign from the Jews. Jewish leaders had formed a secret armed force called the Hagana, but the Jews had developed a policy of self-restraint that involved never attacking unless directly attacked. Thus they never attacked the British or the Arabs unless they were themselves attacked.

The British sent in an Army captain named Orde Wingate to deal with the Arab terror. Wingate met Moshe Dayan for the first time in mid-1938, after Wingate sought secretly to help the Zionist cause.

Dayan watched as Wingate arrived, accompanied by a secret Hagana leader, in a broken-down old car, with a large revolver at his side and a Bible in his hand. It was just before sunset, and the fading light made this stranger even more mysterious to Dayan. Dayan asked the captain to speak. Wingate announced to the group that he wanted to teach them how to fight. For a while Wingate insisted on speaking Hebrew, which he had not mastered, but the men asked him to go back to speaking English. He told them of his experiences. He finished his talk and made a surprising proposal: that they go out immediately and set up an ambush.

Wingate got a map. Dayan expected him to set up the ambush near an approach to a Jewish village, as had been the traditional practice. But Wingate overturned the traditional strategy. He pointed to an ambush site at a crossroads near the Arab village of Mahlul. He was determined to end the notion of self-restraint and bring the fighting to the Arabs. This concept was new to Dayan.

Dayan stayed close to Wingate as they moved along. Originally, Wingate had sent out two scouts who knew the area. But Wingate did not think they moved quickly enough, so despite his own lack of familiarity with the terrain, he took the lead. Wingate, surprisingly for a military officer, was not a strong man. He bumped into bushes and other objects. He would frequently stop to listen to his left and right. Dayan, who had an intimate knowledge of the entire area, nevertheless let Wingate lead.

This notion of a military leader actually leading the unit became an important element in Dayan's (and Israel's) military thinking. Dayan continued to be impressed by Wingate's daring and courage.

The unit reached the crossroads. Wingate divided his men up into two groups and set them up 100 yards apart. His orders were to let any Arab terrorists go between them and then attack them in a crossfire.

There were no terrorists that night, but the evening's lessons were never to be lost on Dayan.

For his part, Wingate vowed to train soldiers for a Jewish army. Such efforts directly contradicted British policy. Wingate's method was simple. He persuaded his superiors to use Jewish Special Constables—essentially police officers—as part of the Special Night Squads that would attack the Arabs. The British agreed because these constables already had training in weapons use (the British had not wanted any Jews to have weapons training that could then be used to attack British forces) and because Jewish rather than British lives would be in danger during the night patrols. In fact, Wingate constantly rotated the squads, so that many young Jewish fighters were trained.

Wingate's Zionism eventually angered his superiors, and he was ordered out of the country. He died in a military plane crash in Burma.

(2) Dayan was once stopped for speeding by a military policeman. Dayan had his defense ready: "I have only one eye. Which do you want me to watch—the speedometer or the road?"

(3) Dayan's visit to the Western Wall after its liberation symbolized the Jewish recovery not only of a holy site but of a history and destiny as well.

On June 7, 1967, Israeli troops had broken into the Old City of Jerusalem, site of Judaism's most sacred site, the Western Wall.

Moshe Dayan entered the Old City through the Lion's Gate, turned left, and came to the Temple Mount. He spotted an Israeli flag over the Dome of the Rock, a mosque holy to Islam. Dayan ordered the flag removed. He then walked the entire length of the mount, turned right to pass through the Mograbi Gate, and came to the wall. The plaza in front of the wall was crowded with the soldiers who had liberated Jerusalem. Many of the soldiers were crying, and many were praying.

Dayan stood silently, looking at the wall. After a few minutes he withdrew a notebook from his pocket. He planned to follow the ancient Jewish tradition of writing a prayer on a piece of paper and stuffing the paper into one of the wall's crevices. Dayan wrote: "May peace descend upon the whole House of Israel."

DISRAELI, BENJAMIN (1804–1881)
British prime minister and novelist.

(1) Disraeli was justly famous for his wit. Never did he love wielding it more than against someone who attacked his Jewish background.

In 1835 in the House of Commons, the Irish leader of the Roman Catholics, Daniel O'Connell, launched one such attack on Disraeli's Jewish ancestors. Disraeli rose to face O'Connell.

"Yes, I am a Jew," Disraeli said. "And when the ancestors of the right honorable gentleman were brutal savages in an unknown island, mine were priests in the temple of Solomon."

(2) Otto von Bismarck, chancellor of Germany, also faced the Disraeli wit. The chancellor once said to Disraeli, "The Germans have just bought a new country in Africa where Jews and pigs will not be tolerated."

Disraeli immediately responded, "Fortunately, we are both here."

DOV BAER (died 1772)
Preacher and successor to the Baal Shem Tov as leader of the Hasidic movement.

Dov Baer was beloved for his teachings. He himself would not write, but he did let his disciples copy down his sermons and his actions. Here is one example of his wisdom.

A rich Hasid came to Dov Baer for a blessing. "What is your diet? What do you eat each day?" asked the great preacher.

"I eat only dry bread and salt," said the rich man.

Dov Baer looked at him angrily. "You should eat meat and drink wine as becomes a wealthy man." He spoke to the rich man for a long while until a promise was extracted that future meals would be much more sumptuous.

When the rich Hasid left, Dov Baer's disciples inquired what difference it made what the man ate.

The preacher said, "It matters a great deal. If he eats a good meal with fine meats, then he will understand that the poor must have at least dry bread with salt. But if, being wealthy, he renounces all enjoyments of life and lives so frugally, he will believe it sufficient for the poor to eat stones."

DREYFUS, ALFRED (1859–1935)
French army officer falsely tried and imprisoned for treason.

The Dreyfus case created an international sensation. It also contributed to the development of Zionism.

Two weeks after Captain Dreyfus was wrongly convicted of treason, he faced a military degradation. On the morning of Saturday, January 5, 1895, a crowd gathered at the *Champ de Mars*. The ceremony would be performed on the parade grounds of the *Ecole Militaire*, and angry citizens did not want to miss the chance to express their outrage. It was a cold day; the wind made matters worse.

The courtyard itself was restricted to several French officers and a few journalists. Among the journalists was Theodor Herzl, correspondent for the Viennese paper the *Neue Freie Presse*. A double line of guards was stationed outside the iron railing that served as a fence around the quadrangle. The crowd began to shout "Death to the traitor" and "Death to the Jew."

At a few minutes after 9:00 in the morning, a trumpet sounded. A soldier gave some orders, and a door quickly opened. A sergeant of the guard led four soldiers, each with a drawn sword. Captain Dreyfus walked in the middle of the four. The soldiers marched up to General Darras, who was sitting on a horse. The crowd was absolutely silent. Darras drew his sword and called out, "Alfred Dreyfus, you are not worthy to carry arms. We now degrade you in the name of the French people."

Dreyfus, at attention, lifted his head and raised his right hand. "I swear you are degrading an innocent man. Long live France!"

Just as Dreyfus finished speaking, a loud drum roll was sounded. The sergeant tore off Dreyfus's insignia. His sword was broken in half and thrown at his feet. Dreyfus did not move.

He was then led past soldiers lined up in columns. There were units from every regiment in Paris, a total of 5,000 men. Dreyfus professed his innocence several times. A group of soldiers shouted "Judas" at him. He yelled back, insisting he would not accept their insults.

Then he passed by the journalists. Herzl stood in his heavy coat staring at the degraded Dreyfus. Dreyfus spoke to the journalists. He said, "Tell all of France that I am innocent." Some of the journalists jeered at him.

The mob then changed its cry. No longer was the call just for Dreyfus's death. The new cry went up: "Death to the Jews!"

Dreyfus was led away.

Herzl, deeply agitated, walked back to his house to write a story for his paper. In Vienna, his editors censored his article. They deleted the phrase "Death to the Jews" and replaced it with "Death to the traitors." They claimed to be trying to avoid increasing the atmosphere of anti-Semitism in Vienna.

Herzl kept the memory of the degradation. It continued to torment him.

Four months later he wrote a letter to Baron de Hirsch, and on June 2 he interviewed the baron about a political plan for the Jews. Herzl had begun his Zionist career.

EBAN, ABBA (1915–   )
Israeli diplomat and political leader.

(1) Abba Eban was once introduced in a Bronx synagogue with the following words: "I'm honored to introduce Mr. Abba Eban, who is well known throughout the civilized world as well as here in the Bronx."

(2) Abba Eban became world famous in June of 1967 as he defended Israel at the United Nations. Eban's famed oratorical skills were never sharper, his words never surer, than during the General Assembly meeting at which the Six-Day War between Israel and the Arab countries was to be discussed.

Eban knew fully what was at stake. The Soviet Union wished to lead the condemnation of Israel by the entire United Nations and call for an unconditional withdrawal of forces. Such a withdrawal would have left Israel again vulnerable to attack.

Eban stayed up most of the night of June 18 preparing his speech. He wrote and dictated the speech and then reread it. He kept redrafting parts of it as he ate sandwiches and drank coffee. At 2:00 A.M. he began to read cables from Jerusalem. The cables reported on various commentaries that had appeared in the Israeli press. One scientist had published an article highly critical of Eban; the ambassador was so hurt by the attack that he fleetingly considered not appearing at the General Assembly session. Soon, though, he recovered enough to continue to work. He finished at 5:00, just as dawn was breaking, and went to sleep for a few hours.

At 10:00 A.M., US president Lyndon Johnson appeared on television and gave an address strongly supportive of the Israeli position. Buoyed by that support, Eban went to the United Nations building and struggled through a crowd of reporters to get to Israel's desk in the General Assembly hall.

Various Israeli delegates were at his side, including Golda Meir, then secretary-general of Israel's Labor party. Eban surveyed the scene. There were ten prime ministers and numerous foreign ministers. Beyond them, though, Eban was acutely aware of how many millions of people throughout the world would view the proceedings on television.

Aleksei N. Kosygin, the Soviet prime minister, spoke first. He condemned Israel and then blamed various western powers, including the United States, for "encouraging Israeli aggression."

Eban began to speak at exactly noon on June 19.

He spoke passionately for two minutes and then looked up. Somehow he felt that the vast audience was with him. In ringing language and in a voice that many believed embodied Israel itself, Eban spoke about his nation's history, the Holocaust, and the Six-Day War. At one point, he paused to look for Kosygin and Foreign Minister Gromyko. Eban pointed a finger directly at them and accused the Soviets of advancing the arms race. This gesture, symbolizing as it did the tiny country of Israel standing up to the mighty Soviet Union, electrified the hall.

Although very pleased as he finished the speech, Eban had no way of knowing that his talk would be considered not only one of the finest political speeches of the century, but also one instrumental in successfully defending Israel's actions.

EGER, AKIBA (1761–1837)
German rabbi.

Rabbi Eger was widely recognized as the most accomplished Talmudist of his age. The rabbi was praised as well as an *onov*, a meek person, modest about his talents and achievements.

Rabbi Eger once received a very complimentary letter from a rabbi. The writer went on at great length in the most flattering terms, praising both the scholarship and saintliness of Rabbi Eger.

Rabbi Eger's disciples were surprised as they watched him read the letter so carefully and with such obvious delight. He usually shunned such extravagant praise. Finally one of the disciples approached the rabbi and asked why he had read the complimentary letter so carefully.

"You don't understand," Rabbi Eger answered. "I don't believe that these words of praise apply to me. But I examined them carefully and thought, this is what I should strive to be—the sort of person who deserves such praise."

EINSTEIN, ALBERT (1879–1955)
German and American physicist, developer of the theory of
relativity, and Nobel Prize winner.

(1) Even extraordinarily intelligent people had difficulty grasping Einstein's theories. Chaim Weizmann was among the puzzled. Weizmann and Einstein once sailed together to the United States on a Zionist mission. When they arrived in New York, Weizmann was asked how he and Einstein had spent the voyage. Weizmann replied, "Throughout the voyage, the learned professor kept talking to me about his theory of relativity."

"And what is your opinion of it?" Weizmann was asked.

Weizmann responded, "It seems to me that Professor Einstein understands it very well."

(2) Chaim Weizmann died on November 9, 1952. Israel's first president, who had long been dissatisfied with the ceremonial job which had little if any power, had nonetheless been a world-famous man, and his loss left Israel in need of a president of comparable stature.

On the day following Weizmann's death, an Israeli newspaper had a suggestion: Offer the presidential job to Albert Einstein. Einstein's acceptance would provide enormous prestige for the Jewish nation.

Prime Minister David Ben-Gurion approached Einstein about the job. Ben-Gurion assured the scientist that his acceptance by the Knesset would almost be automatic and that he could continue his scientific endeavors.

Einstein, then 73, turned down the offer. First, he thought that he was too old. In addition, while he admitted having some knowledge of the natural world, he believed that he "lacked both the natural aptitude and the experience to deal properly with people."

(3) Einstein was giving a lecture. He startled his audience by saying, "I'm sorry I was born a Jew." He waited for the expected shock to set in before he continued: "Because it deprived me of the privilege of choosing to be a Jew."

(4) During a 1921 trip to Israel, Einstein visited a kibbutz. His guide was a 22-year-old woman who headed the young community of kibbutzniks. Among many questions, Einstein asked the woman, "What is the relationship here of men to women?" The woman was clearly embarrassed; she thought that the great professor subscribed to the common belief that the women of the kibbutz were common property to be shared by the men. Finally, she said, "Herr Professor, each man here has one woman."

Einstein started to smile. He took the woman's hand and said, "Don't be alarmed at my question. We physicists understand by the word *relationship* something rather simple—namely, how many of one thing to how many of another. So what I meant was, how many men are there and how many women?"

(5) While listening to the radio, Einstein heard the news of the dropping of the first nuclear bomb on Hiroshima. He felt some burden of responsibility because his theory of relativity had been the theoretical basis of the bomb, and his letter to President Franklin Roosevelt had launched American efforts to build a bomb. For a long while after the radio broadcast, all he could bring himself to say was "Oy vey."

(6) Einstein was the guest of honor at a banquet. He was describing conditions in Nazi Germany when the dean of Harvard University interrupted him with a question. The dean wanted to know how Germany could have accepted Nazism.

Einstein replied, "The German people were imbued with three qualities: honesty, intelligence, and Nazism. However, our Creator, in his wisdom, decreed that because we mortals are partly creatures of free will, a German could possess only two of the three qualities. That is why a German who is honest and also a Nazi cannot be intelligent. If he is intelligent and a Nazi, he cannot be honest. And if he is honest and intelligent, he cannot be a Nazi."

(7) Dr. Einstein was invited to give a speech at a dinner honoring the president of Swarthmore College. After a glowing introduction he stood and announced to the crowd, "Ladies and gentlemen, I am sorry, but I have nothing to say." He then sat down. A second later he was back up again. "If I ever do have something to say, I'll come back."

Six months later, Einstein sent a wire to the president: "Now I have something to say." Another dinner was scheduled. Einstein came and made his speech.

(8) The artist Sir William Rothenstein once prepared a portrait of Einstein. Einstein was accompanied to one of the sittings by a stranger. The artist thought this stranger very odd. Einstein talked and talked, explaining untested theories; he was clearly excited about the possibility of a new discovery. But every once in a while the stranger would shake his head, which would cause Einstein to pause, consider what he had said, and begin to speak along a new line of thought.

As the artist was leaving, Einstein finally explained. Pointing to the stranger, Einstein said, "He is my mathematician. He examines problems that I put before him and checks their validity. You see, I am not myself a good mathematician."

ELIEZER BEN HYRCANUS *(end of first–beginning of second century)*
Major rabbinic scholar.

One story about Eliezer illustrates the traditional Jewish love of learning.

Eliezer wanted above all to be a scholar, but his father refused to allow him to pursue his desires. Eliezer's father was a rich man who owned a lot of land. He insisted that his son work in the fields alongside the poor laborers.

One day, Eliezer had to plow a field. The field was covered with so many rocks that plowing was extremely difficult. Eliezer sat down and wept. His father saw this and said, "If this work is too hard for you, my son, then tomorrow morning you may begin work on another field, one that is already plowed."

So the next morning Eliezer went to work in the new field. But here, too, he no sooner began his labors than he started to cry.

"Why are you weeping now?" asked his exasperated father.

Eliezer said simply, "I want to study the Torah."

"But that is nonsense," his father said. "You're already 28 years old. It's too late for you to study the Torah. It would be better if you got married so your children could become scholars."

For three weeks Eliezer remained saddened by his father's harsh words. Then, one night, he dreamed that the prophet Elijah told him, "Go to Jerusalem and find Rabbi Yohanan ben Zakkai. He will teach you Torah."

Eliezer traveled to Jerusalem without telling anyone of his intentions. He found his way to Rabbi Yohanan's house and sat down by the door.

Rabbi Yohanan looked out the window and saw a man sitting by his door and weeping.

"Why are you crying?" the rabbi asked.

"I cry from my longing to study the Torah."

"Whose son are you?"

Eliezer remained silent.

"What learning have you had?"

"None."

Rabbi Yohanan then began to teach Eliezer, beginning with the Shema, grace at meals, and some prayers. They studied two sections of the Mishna every day.

Eliezer studied hard, but he had no food and would not beg for any. He soon became unpleasant to be around, and Rabbi Yohanan asked him to leave. But Eliezer remained seated outside the door and asked, "Why did you drive me away as though I were a leper?"

"Whose son are you?" Rabbi Yohanan again asked.

"I am the son of Hyrcanus," Eliezer said.

"What! Why haven't you told me that you come from such a great family? Come in to my house and eat."

But Eliezer was still proud. "I have already eaten."

Rabbi Yohanan found that Eliezer had not eaten for eight days, and he praised Eliezer for his pious suffering.

Meanwhile, Eliezer's brothers used his absence at home in their schemes to have him disinherited. His father agreed to the disinheritance, but he had to see Eliezer in order to make such an action legal.

Hyrcanus came to see Rabbi Yohanan. The two sat with other learned people around a table. Rabbi Yohanan asked Eliezer to join them and speak about the Torah.

"How can I, Rabbi? I am like a well. I can give no more water than has been put into me. All I know is what I have learned from you."

"No, you are like a spring. You send water up from your own source."

Three more times Rabbi Yohanan asked Eliezer to speak about the Torah. Eliezer demurred each time. Finally, Rabbi Yohanan observed that his pupil was awed by his presence in the room, so he left. Eliezer then gave a beautiful discourse about the Torah, for which he was praised by all.

Hyrcanus rose out of respect for his son, but Eliezer saw him in the crowd and said, "Oh, Father, how can I sit and discuss the Torah while you stand?" Eliezer asked his father to sit down next to him.

After the discourse, Hyrcanus said to his son, "I confess to you that I came here to disinherit you. Now I am prepared to make you my sole heir and instead disinherit your greedy brothers."

"No, father," Eliezer replied. "I want nothing that rightfully belongs to my brothers. I did not ask the Almighty for great wealth or land. I asked only to study the Torah. This much has already been granted. I am happy and want nothing more."

(2) Rabbi Eliezer used to tell his disciples, "Turn to God one day before your death."

This advice puzzled them, and they asked, "How can we know the date of our death?"

The rabbi responded, "Then you should turn to God today; perhaps you will die tomorrow; thus every day will be spent in returning."

ELIEZER BEN YAIR *(first century* C.E.*)*
Commander of the Masada fortress.

Masada has become a symbol in Jewish life of resistance to tyranny and also of
an iron determination that never again will the Jews be deprived of their nation.
Masada's story is one of the most dramatic in Jewish history.

The Roman conquest of Judea was almost complete. There remained a
single center for those who refused to accept Roman rule. The Zealots had
gathered at a fortress at Masada, a sheared-off rock that rose above the Dead
Sea. The Zealots who were there, all 960, had taken a vow to resist Roman
slavery by fighting to the death.

Flavius Silva, the Roman general, attacked Masada. The entire fortress
was surrounded by a wall of earth, called a siege wall, or circumvallation. Its
purpose was to prevent anyone on Masada from escaping. The wall was
strengthened by towers. Silva then set up eight camps around Masada. Ballistae
and battering rams were brought in. (The ballistae would be used to haul heavy
projectiles during battle, and the rams were to be used to break down the walls.)
An assault ramp of earth and stones was used to bring forth the Roman soldiers
and their weapons.

Eventually the rams did their job, and part of one of the fortress' walls was
broken through. But Eliezer was a good military strategist: Behind the first wall
he had built a second wall composed of crossbeams filled with earth so that a ram
would actually harden the earth. When the Romans finally realized this, they
prepared to set fire to the beams. Masada was finally about to fall.

It was the first day of Passover in the year 73 C.E. Eliezer called together the
Zealots. He spoke. "My loyal supporters, we all decided long ago to serve neither
the Romans nor anyone but the Lord. We cannot choose to be slaves now."
Eliezer went on to describe how human frailties had wronged God. "But for
those wrongs let us pay the penalty not to the Romans, but to God, and by our
own hands." He described the horrors of a slave's life, especially for women and
children. He asked that all be destroyed, except the food, to show that at
Masada the Zealots perished not for want of food, but because they had freely
chosen death over slavery.

Not all of Eliezer's listeners supported his call for self-destruction. Some
spoke of their wives and families. Again Eliezer tried to rouse them through
rededication to the Zealots' ideal to live honorably or die. He continued to
argue, finally winning all of his fighters over to his view.

All of the goods at Masada were then set on fire. After that, individual
men slew their families. Of the remaining fighters, ten were chosen to slay those
who were left. The fighters lay down next to their wives and children, put their
arms around their families, and then cut their throats. The ten then drew lots.

One was chosen to kill the other nine. This he did, and after checking to make sure that no one remained alive, he killed himself.

The Romans conquered Masada in an eerie silence.

As it turned out, an old woman, a younger woman related to Eliezer, and five small children had hidden in water conduits and remained alive. They were carried off.

ELIJAH (c. 875 B.C.E.)
Biblical prophet.

Many sought Elijah's wisdom. Most came away wiser.

A rabbi once approached the prophet. The man asked Elijah to point out those men in the marketplace who were going to be admitted to paradise.

Elijah agreed to do this. He looked over the crowd and pointed to two jesters. The rabbi was surprised because these two were not noted for their religious knowledge or fervor. The rabbi asked Elijah why they would be chosen to enter paradise. Elijah responded that it was the jesters' job to bring happiness to those who are in distress, and such a job merited a place in paradise.

ELIJAH BEN SOLOMON ZALMAN, GAON OF VILNA (1720–1797)
Great modern spiritual leader.

(1) Whenever Rabbi Elijah wished to do penance, he would dress in beggar's clothes and wander as would an ordinary poor man in search of a meal. Once during such a journey, on his way back to Vilna, he was stopped by a drunken peasant driving a wagon. The peasant ordered the great rabbi to drive the wagon. The rabbi agreed and began to drive. As the rabbi drove the wagon on into Vilna, the inebriated peasant fell asleep.

Rabbi Elijah was immediately recognized in his native city. But the townspeople, who had never seen him wearing his beggar's clothes, were amazed. One of those who saw him ran to the synagogue shouting, "The Messiah is coming!" When he was asked what he meant, the poor man said, "The Vilna Gaon, dressed as a beggar, is driving a wagon. Who else but the Messiah could be his passenger?"

(2) The Gaon, who was dying, lay weeping. His disciples asked him why he was weeping. After his exemplary life, they assured him, he was certain to go to heaven. The Gaon considered this and replied, "That may or may not be true, but there is something about which I am certain: Only in this life is there the joy

of carrying out the commandments. In heaven there may be a reward for keeping the mitzvot, but this cannot compare with the joy of actually carrying out the mitzvot."

(3) A young man, a scholar of the Talmud, came to Rabbi Elijah asking for a testimonial for a book that he had just written. Rabbi Elijah gazed upon the enthusiastic young man and said, "My son, you must accept the realities of your profession. If you want to write learned books, you must resign yourself to the fact that you will have to peddle those books from house to house as though you were a salesman selling pots and pans. You must accept hunger as a way of life until you reach the age of 40."

The young scholar saw a glimmer of hope in the final words. "And what happens after I'm 40?"

Rabbi Elijah smiled. "By the time you reach 40, you will have become quite used to it."

(4) The leaders of the Jewish community met to decide what to do about the large number of poor strangers who came into the city begging for funds. At the mass meeting, the leaders concluded that only closing the city to poor strangers would prevent their placing an economic burden on the city. The Vilna Gaon had been invited to the meeting without knowing its purpose. The great scholar had interrupted his studies for what he had been told was an important matter. When he heard the suggestion to close the city off to poor, wandering Jews, the Gaon sought out Reb Feitel, the head of the community.

"I'm sorry that I left the study of the Torah for this meeting," said the Gaon. "I told you that I did not wish to discuss community affairs except when a new custom is to be adopted for which there may not be a precedent."

"But that is exactly the case," said Reb Feitel. "We are adopting a new custom. No community prohibits strangers from entering its gate."

"That is not new," the Gaon said. "Indeed it is is one of the oldest customs in history. Do you not remember that it was the custom of Sodom and Gomorrah not to let strangers enter?"

Reb Feitel understood the Gaon and concluded that the city could not go forward with its plans.

The poor continued to be allowed to enter the city.

ELIMELECH OF LYZHANSK (1717–1787)
Rabbi and hasidic leader.

When they were young, unknown, and poor, Rabbi Elimelech of Lyzhansk and his brother, Rabbi Zusya of Hanipoli, came to the village of Lodmir. Because their clothes were shabby, none of the townspeople came out to welcome the strangers except for one man. This man was Reb Aaron, who was a poor tailor.

Many years later both rabbis became famous. They returned one day to Lodmir in a huge carriage drawn by many handsome horses.

All the townspeople came out to see them. The wealthiest citizen gave an address welcoming the distinguished visitors. He finished his speech by telling the two rabbis, "You will give me the greatest possible honor if you will allow me to have you as guests in my house."

Rabbi Elimelech suddenly recognized Reb Aaron in the crowd. He said, "My brother and I will be honored if Reb Aaron would invite us to his home."

The wealthy man was astonished. "Rabbi, it's unbecoming for men of your fame to stay in that poor man's hovel. He can't even feed you properly."

"We would far sooner eat that poor man's black bread and cabbage than all your fine roasts. When we were poor and unknown, but no different than we are now, you closed your door to us, but Reb Aaron showed us true Jewish hospitality. Now we come riding in an expensive carriage drawn by fine horses. You wish to welcome us. Clearly, it's the horses, and not us, you are welcoming. In that case, I'm delighted to accept your invitation. Please be good enough to care for our horses while we stay as Reb Aaron's guests."

EPHRAIM BEN SANCHO (c. 980–1060)
Community leader.

Jews were often forced to defend their faith, sometimes jeopardizing their safety. Ephraim faced such a trap.

King Don Pedro, ruler of Aragon, heard from his counselor, the troubador Nicholas of Valencia, that the Jews were inferior people. The king had heard of a wise Jew named Ephraim ben Sancho and asked that this man be brought before him. Ephraim came, and the king asked him directly which of their faiths was superior. Ephraim recognized the dangers inherent in either answer, and so he said, "Our faith is better suited for us Jews, for our God led us into freedom and out of our slavery in Egypt. Your faith is better for the Christians, for you have been able to rule over much of the world."

The king was not satisfied with the answer. "I don't want to know the benefits each of us gets from our religion. I want to know which religion is superior."

Ephraim said, "Let me consider this question for three days, for it is a difficult question requiring much thought. I will give you my answer at the end of the third day."

The king agreed.

Ephraim could not eat or sleep for the three days. He prayed constantly for guidance. Finally, it was time to go back to the palace. The king immediately noticed how sad Ephraim looked and asked the Jewish sage why.

"I look so sad because of what happened today. May I tell the story for your majesty to judge?"

"You may speak," said the king.

"A month ago my neighbor, who is a jeweler, went traveling to a distant land. He had two sons, who always fought. Before he left, he gave each of his sons an expensive gem. Today these brothers are still arguing, for they came to me to judge which of the gems is more valuable. I reminded them that their father was the jeweler and the best expert on the value of gems, and I suggested that they ask him because he could judge far better than I.

"When I told them this, they became angry at me, and then they beat me. Don't I have a right to be sad?"

"You have been mistreated," said the king. "They deserve to be punished for how they have behaved."

"My king. May your ears hear the words your mouth has spoken. You asked me which of two gems is superior. How can I give you the right answer? There is only one expert on these types of gems, and that is the Lord. He must tell you which is better."

The king was greatly impressed with Ephraim's wisdom.

ESHKOL, LEVI (1895–1969)
Third prime minister of Israel.

(1) Before becoming prime minister, Eshkol served as minister of finance. One day he entered a well-known and lavish restaurant in Tel Aviv. Many of the city's important business leaders were having lunch there. After a pleasant meal with a companion, Eshkol requested his check. When the check arrived, he took one look at it and said, "It's not my bill I wanted, but those of the people at the other tables."

The waiter looked surprised. "But you didn't invite them."

"No, perhaps not. But then, I'm the finance minister, and they're all eating at my expense."

(2) After Eshkol became prime minister, one of his main responsibilities was to make sure that enough food was available. Farmland was at a premium in Israel, so much of the country's food came from the United States.

One day, an aide came in and told Eshkol that a serious drought seemed all too probable.

Eshkol became agitated. "Where?" he asked.

"In the Negev."

Eshkol's face relaxed. "For a moment I thought you meant in *Kansas*."

EYBESCHUETZ, JONATHAN (c. 1690–1764)
Rabbi, talmudist, and kabbalist.

(1) Rabbi Eybeschuetz had been full of life as a youngster. Once, after his mother had roasted a chicken, he sneaked in and ripped off one of the legs, which he then promptly ate. His mother knew of his antics and so naturally accused him of eating the missing leg. He answered that the chicken had always had just one leg. His father, quite knowledgeable about a chicken's anatomy, punished his son.

The next day the two were walking to synagogue. The boy spotted a chicken standing on one leg. He pointed excitedly; the chicken was evidence that his father had punished him for no reason. His father raised his walking cane over the chicken, which then ran away on both legs. Jonathan was not impressed. "If you had raised your cane like that over our chicken, it, too, would have shown its other leg."

(2) An anti-Semitic army officer came to see Rabbi Eybeschuetz and presented a mocking question: "In the Bible it says that the patriarchs used asses to travel, and even the Messiah is supposed to arrive on an ass. How is it that you modern Jews have given up loyalty to this ancient tradition and instead ride horses?"

Rabbi Eybeschuetz said in reply, "Let me explain that to you. Since the passing of ancient times, asses have succeeded so that they now occupy prominent positions. It would be audacious for a Jew even to suggest riding on them."

FACKENHEIM, EMIL (1916–   )
Major Jewish philosopher and author.

The following anecdote, written by Emil Fackenheim, will be included in his memoirs.

Bringing their superior psychological wisdom to bear on the victims of the Holocaust, [men] such as Bruno Bettelheim, Elie Cohen and S. M. Elkins have not hesitated to compare these victims to victims of quite other sorts, such as slaves, or for that matter anyone else in "extreme situations." Other people have set themselves up as experts as to what constitutes extreme situations. Of these not a few have not hesitated to find Auschwitz almost anywhere, including Beirut earlier in this decade and, at this time of writing, in Algeria—this by Klaus Barbie's defense attorney at that criminal's trial in Lyon.

What I think of the above-named psychologists the interested reader can find in my book *To Mend The World* (New York: Schocken, 1982, pp. 226–230). Here I will only report a personal experience of mine in my three months in Sachsenhausen (November 1938–February 1939) which (unlike Bettelheim, who seems to have rushed into print with his conclusions about Buchenwald very shortly after his own release from that camp) I for the first time report here, nearly fifty years later. The above-named psychologists may know all there is to know about the victims, for after all they are experts in human relations. No expert but merely a philosopher sworn to be faithful to the victims, I claim no such knowledge.

My Sachsenhausen before the war, just as Bettelheim's Buchenwald, was, of course, nothing compared to Auschwitz or Treblinka
later. Still, it was bad enough; and psychologically the worst thing was
that, unlike regular prisoners sent to penitentiary, say, for armed
robbery, we had no way of knowing how long it would last. And here
our psychological experts come on the scene, saying that the inmates,
like children, sought refuge from reality in dreams and false hopes. I
can testify that we did nothing of the sort. We *knew* that we might
never be released, and each day (with its hard labor, inadequate food
and, worst of all, bitter cold that caused a dozen or so to drop dead
every day) was just barely bearable. So we practiced an act of resistance
that, so far as I know, has gone unnoticed all these years. We *quite
consciously* played a game with ourselves. We gave the Nazis a week:
One can stand almost anything for a week. When the week was up we
gave them another two weeks, and so on during my entire stay. The
game, as I say, was completely conscious. Moreover, far from "out of
contact with reality," it was completely *in* contact, for first hundreds,
then dozens, were in fact released every day. This game was played not
only by me, but by all the comrades I knew. And I defy anyone to call
it by any name other than resistance.

And now comes my personal experience. The original number of
Jews carted to Sachsenhausen following Krystallnacht was about
6,000. On February 7, 1939, only about 280 of these were left. During
that night two things happened. I heard someone vomit, and found
out in the morning that he had vomited on my jacket. This was
serious, for I had to wash it off, yet risked pneumonia in the wet jacket
in the bitter cold. More serious still, however, was something else.
When in the morning I discovered what had happened to my jacket I
for the first time allowed the idea to enter my mind that perhaps a core
remnant would *never* be released—and my morale collapsed. That
morning at roll call three names were called for release, and mine was
one of them.

I dedicate this brief memoir to my comrade Erich Kohlhagen. A
pal from my home town, he never was released, yet survived. No one
but his family knows about him. I for one shall never understand how
he mustered the morale necessary for survival when, following the
outbreak of war, the resistance-game I had played was no longer
possible. Erich, a dentist but otherwise a simple man, is one of the
countless unsung heroes and saints of the Jewish people.

FOX, WILLIAM (1879–1952)
American film producer.

Fox always remembered the poverty of his youth and those who had helped his family. He was finally able to repay the kindness shown to him by one particular man.

As a boy, Fox was once sent to the local butcher. The boy's father was out of work, and the family had almost no food left. Young William asked to "borrow" a pound of meat.

The butcher smiled at the boy and asked when he intended to return the borrowed meat.

"Some day I'm going to be wealthy. You'll be old and won't be able to work, and I'll take care of you."

The kind butcher provided the meat.

Fox remembered the incident. Later, after his success, the movie producer hired the butcher, who worked at Fox's movie studio for fifteen years.

FRANK, ANNE (1929–1945)
Author of a diary written while hiding from the Nazis.

On July 5, 1942, the Germans sent a summons for Margot, Anne Frank's 16-year-old sister, to report to be deported. On the morning of July 6, Anne Frank and her family left their home and went to their hiding place, called the Secret Annexe.

From the first, Anne hungered for news of her cat and her school friends. She especially wanted two of the Dutch Gentiles who had protected her to have dinner at the Annexe. The two, Henk and Miep, promised to do so, and soon an appropriate occasion for such a dinner was found. It was Henk and Miep's first anniversary, and so on Saturday, July 18, a dinner was held in their honor.

Miep remained behind at the office below the Annexe that night. Henk came to join her. They both had dressed up. They entered the hiding place and immediately smelled the food.

Anne had prepared a special menu and had even typed it. She had gone the previous morning to a private office just to use a typewriter. The dated menu read: "Dinner provided by Het Achterhuis on the occasion of the first anniversary of the marriage of Mr. and Mrs. Gies, Esquire." (It was Anne who first used the term *Het Achterhuis,* meaning "the Annexe," although, technically, the hiding place was not an annex.) Anne then listed all the courses to be served that evening, providing each of them with its own name. For example, she named the soup *Bouillon a la Hunestraat*, which was the name of the street on which Miep and Henk lived. The next course was *Roastbeef Scholte*, named, fittingly, after Miep's butcher. Her annotation to the gravy was that only tiny portions were available because the butter allowance had been lowered in the ration tickets. Rice was to be provided, as was "sugar, cinammon, raspberry juice," and, finally, "coffee with sugar, cream, and some surprises." The nine diners, in nine very mismatched chairs, sat around the table, eating. Mrs. Van Damm, one of those hiding, had been a gourmet cook. All enjoyed the meal. Miep promised Anne that she would save the menu.

Anne didn't record the dinner in her diary, which she had received for her 13th birthday and which she used to record many of the events in her life.

On August 4, 1944, the Secret Annexe was invaded by the police. All were taken away. Only Anne's father, Otto, survived the Holocaust. Anne died in March of 1945 in the Bergen-Belsen concentration camp, two months before Holland was liberated and three months before her 16th birthday.

Miep kept her promise. She saved the menu for the anniversary meal. The menu still exists.

FRANKFURTER, FELIX *(1882–1965)*
US Supreme Court justice.

Felix Frankfurter was very proud of being Jewish; he defended slurs against Jews regardless of who made them.

One of Frankfurter's college professors once made an anti-Semitic remark to Frankfurter about his name. Frankfurter wisely predicted, "Some day you will be proud to have known the owner of that name."

FRANKL, VIKTOR *(1905–   )*
Austrian psychiatrist and founder of logotherapy.

Even as a concentration camp inmate, Frankl could not forget his psychiatric training. He remained a close observer of the incredible human behaviors he witnessed in the camps. He was particularly surprised at the nature of the humor that he heard; indeed he was fascinated by the fact that humor existed in the camps at all. As a psychiatrist, he viewed humor as almost the only weapon the inmates had to preserve their sanity. He saw humor as allowing the inmates to escape their surroundings in their minds, even if only for a few seconds. At times Frankl even made an effort to teach other inmates to develop whatever sense of humor they could. He suggested to a doctor friend who worked next to him that, as they labored, they should invent one amusing story each day about what would happen after they were liberated from the camp.

The jokes that worked were those directly related to camp life; they were not "funny" jokes, but pertinent ones. For instance, Frankl once told the doctor about a future operating-room scene. At their building site, the foreman tried to get the men to work harder by yelling "Action! Action!" This often happened when a supervisor came to inspect. So Frankl suggested that in the future, the doctor would be in an operating room working hard on an important abdominal operation when an orderly would rush in to announce that a senior surgeon was coming by shouting "Action! Action!"

Sometimes the humor was painfully, even shockingly, realistic. One of the popular jokes envisioned a future dinner party. According to the joke, inmates would forget where they were when it was time for the soup and ask, as they did in the camp, that the soup be ladled from the bottom.

FREIER, RECHA *(1892–1984)*
Founder of Youth Aliya.

Henrietta Szold is usually the person most associated with Youth Aliya, the program that began bringing children to Israel in the early 1930s. But the idea for Youth Aliya came not from Henrietta Szold, indeed not from the Zionist movement, but from a woman in Berlin named Recha Freier. Recha Freier was the wife of a rabbi, an accomplished musician, and an ardent Zionist. She was also a very determined woman.

It was 1932. A group of teenage Jewish boys had just been fired from their jobs solely because of their religion. Despondent because of their loss, anti-Semitism in the society, and the general economic depression then rampant in Germany, they came seeking an answer from Recha Freier. Less than a year later, Adolf Hitler would be chancellor of Germany, but even then Freier knew that the future for young Jews in Germany was filled with potential danger.

Recha tried to do what she could. On the day after the boys called on her, she went to the Jewish Labor Exchange. The director told her that the boys would get jobs when the economy improved. He implied that nothing could be done for them, and therefore nothing should be attempted.

That answer did not satisfy Recha. It didn't take her long to come up with a simple and clear, but revolutionary, idea. Its very improbability had an appeal. She concluded that the boys should go to the land of Israel to work on an agricultural settlement.

Recha presented this idea to the German Zionist leadership, which was indifferent. Their rebuff, characteristically, did not deter her in the least. She spoke at a Zionist elementary school. Here, speaking mostly to Eastern European youth, she found a more receptive audience. Students rushed to be included.

Their excitement led the German Zionist leaders to reconsider. They told Recha that they would accept her plan if the Vaad Leumi, the National Assembly of the Jews in Israel, could establish some group to arrange for settling the children and assume financial obligations. She was told to contact the director of the Social Service Bureau in Jerusalem—Henrietta Szold.

Recha dutifully sent a letter outlining her audacious proposal. Henrietta Szold, a realist, was at first shocked at the idea. She knew the facts of pioneer life. Ten thousand children already living in the country had never attended a school. Suddenly, a German rebbitzin wanted German Jewish children to be sent to the Land. Henrietta Szold was also concerned because the German children would come without their parents; this seemed particularly cruel to the childless but maternal Szold, who unhesitatingly rejected the idea.

Back in Berlin, the indomitable Recha Freier had found a new way to get children to the Promised Land. In June 1932 she discovered that at least a few German Jews could be sent to the Ben Shemen Children's Village. One of Recha's friends pawned jewelry to guarantee the children's support. A few boys finally departed from a crowded Berlin railway station on October 12, 1932.

From this small beginning came the effort to save Jewish children from the Holocaust, and eventually from oppression everywhere in the world.

FREUD, SIGMUND (1856–1939)
Austrian psychiatrist and father of psychoanalysis.

(1) Freud was always the psychiatrist, even during seemingly casual conversations.

In the summer of 1933, Freud was visited in Vienna by the prominent American rabbi Stephen Wise. The two drank wine, smoked cigars, and talked about the Jewish situation. At one point in the conversation they decided that it would be fun if they could agree on a list of the five most important Jews in the world. Wise started off the list by saying, "Of course you belong, Dr. Freud. Also, I'd select Albert Einstein, Chaim Weizmann, Justice Brandeis, and probably Henri Bergson." Freud considered the list and said, "And why not also include Stephen Wise on the list?"

"Oh, no, no, no, no," was Wise's response.

Freud removed his cigar, smiled, and said, "My dear Dr. Wise, if you had answered 'no' only once, I would believe you mean it, but when four 'no's' come out, I cannot believe you really meant it."

(2) When Freud was 12 years old, he had a conversation with his father about anti-Semitism. His father told the boy about how a Gentile had knocked his new fur cap down into the mud of the road and shouted at him, "Jew, get off the street." Young Sigmund was fascinated by this but indignant at the hatred shown. He asked his father how he had reacted, expecting his father to reply that he had fought the man. Instead, his father merely said, "I went into the street and got my cap." Sigmund was shocked at this lack of action; he never forgot the incident.

GAMALIEL (c. 80 C.E.)
Rabbi and tamudic sage.

(1) Rabbi Gamaliel once told his servants, "Bring me something good." The servants returned with a tongue. The rabbi then said, "Go to the market and bring me something bad." Again, the servants brought a tongue, saying, "A tongue, my master, may be the source of either good or evil. If it is good, there is nothing better. If it is bad, there is nothing worse."

(2) An emperor spoke to the rabbi, saying, "Your God is a thief."
"Why?" asked the rabbi.
"Because he made Adam fall asleep, and without his consent removed a rib from his body. Is that honesty or is it thievery?"
The rabbi's daughter was listening and asked to respond. "Your majesty," she began, "the other night robbers broke into our house. They took a silver jug, but they left a gold jug in its place. What do you think of such robbers?"
"Robbers! I wish such robbers visited my house every night."
"But that is just what God did," she continued. "He took from Adam merely a rib and gave him a woman for it. Don't you think Adam was satisfied with that?"

(3) A pagan philosopher once approached Rabbi Gamaliel with a question about God. "Rabbi," the pagan began, "I do not understand your God. He gets angry at idolators when He should be angry at the idols. If there were no idols, after all, people could worship only Him."
Rabbi Gamaliel said that he thought the question intelligent, but then said, "You are wrong, however. I agree that idols are without the power ascribed to them. Even so, it would not be better to do away with them. Think of all the

idols that would have to be destroyed, all the ones that are worshipped. The sun and moon and stars are worshipped, so they would disappear. So, too, would animals and trees, for these are seen as gods by some.

"To destroy all the objects that people make idols of would be to destroy the world. Instead, God blesses people with the free will to worship or not worship as they see fit."

(4) A man came to the rabbi asking where God was to be found. The rabbi answered simply that he did not know. Such uncertainty bothered the questioner. "How can you pray to Him each day if you do not even know where He is?" the man asked.

Rabbi Gamaliel said, "You are asking about the Holy One, Who is very far away from us. Let me ask you about something that is with you each day and each night. Tell me, where is your soul?"

The man thought and finally said, "I do not know."

"Ah," said Rabbi Gamaliel, "You cannot even say where the soul is, something you always carry with you. Yet you ask me about the Lord, Who is so far away. He sees the work of His hands, but it cannot see Him."

(5) A heretic once mocked Judaism in front of the visiting Gamaliel. The heretic spoke: "You rabbis claim that whenever ten people assemble in prayer, the Shekhinah is among them. Just how many Shekhinahs are there that they can be among so many people?"

The rabbi saw a shaft of sunlight coming in through the windows. He then called the heretic's servant over and struck him with a ladle. "Why did you hit my servant?" asked the heretic.

"Because there is sunlight here," replied the rabbi, "and sunlight has no place in the house of an infidel."

The heretic was astonished. "But the sun shines all over the earth. I cannot stop it from being everywhere."

"It does shine all over," said Rabbi Gamaliel. "But if the sun, which is but a single part of God's creation, can be in all parts of the world, how much more so can the Shekhinah shine throughout all the universe?"

GEBIHAH BEN PESISA (fourth century B.C.E.)
Scholar.

(1) Gebihah was often called upon to defend his people. His only means of defense was his knowledge of the Torah.

Once Egyptians appeared before Alexander the Great to bring a lawsuit against the Jews. The Egyptians claimed that when the Jews departed Egypt during the exodus, they took an enormous amount of gold and silver, jewels and clothing. The Egyptians pointed to Exodus 12:35–36 to justify their claim that the Jews had "stripped" such items.

When confronted by this evidence from the Torah itself, Gebihah referred to the same chapter but used the fortieth verse to show that the Jews had stayed in Egypt for 430 years. He then issued a counterclaim, asking the Egyptians to pay the wages owed the 600,000 Jews who left for the 430 years of enforced labor. Alexander told the Egyptians that they would have three days within which to make a reply. Instead, they left and never returned to the court.

The Arabs, too, quoted the Bible to Alexander. They used Genesis 25:12 to claim that because Ishmael is called Abraham's son just as Isaac is, the holy land belonged to Arabs as well as to Jews.

Gebihah again used the same chapter as his opponents had to prove his point. "In Chapter 25, verses 5 and 6, it clearly says that Abraham gave all he had to Isaac; but to the children he had by concubines, including, of course, Ishmael, he gave gifts, and he sent them away from Isaac to a land to the East. Therefore the land of Israel belongs to the children of Israel. Your claim was settled by none other than Abraham himself."

(2) Gebihah was widely admired for his great debating skills.

A man once came to him and asked, "How is it possible for you to believe in resurrection? If those who are now living continue to grow old and die, how can those who are already dead come back to life?"

Gebihah said to him, "The answer is quite the opposite of what you suggest. For if those who never lived at all can be made to live, think of how much easier it will be for those who have already lived to live again."

GINZBERG, LOUIS (1873–1953)
Talmudic scholar and author of The Legends of the Jews.

While working on his *Legends*, Ginzberg developed an exceptionally close friendship with Henrietta Szold. Although she was thirteen years older than Ginzberg, Szold nevertheless fell deeply in love with him. This was awkward to say the least, because Ginzberg was not sure that he wished to marry her.

Ginzberg was on a trip to Berlin in 1908. He attended synagogue services there one day. While at the services, he looked up to the women's gallery and saw a very attractive young woman. He met Adele Katzenstein that day, saw her the next, and then went away for two weeks. During his absence he wrote to her regularly. (She could not read his penmanship, so her uncle had to decipher the letters for her.) After the two weeks had passed, Ginzberg sent a marriage proposal in one of his letters. She accepted.

The only unhappy person left in the wake of this romance was Henrietta Szold.

GLUECKEL OF HAMELN (1645–1724)
Yiddish-language memoirist.

Glueckel, who was born in Hamburg, married Hayyim Hameln, a merchant. She helped her husband in his various economic enterprises and also managed to bring up twelve children.

His death left her devastated. She wrote an autobiography mainly to console her children. One of the many moving events she retells involves the few days during which her husband was injured and died. She recounts these events with great sadness.

On the 19th of Tevet in 1689, Hayyim journeyed into town for a business meeting at a merchant's house. He stumbled and tripped over a stone near the house. He then came back home and told Glueckel that he had fallen. She emptied his pockets and tried to make him comfortable. They didn't realize that a persistent rupture from which he had suffered had been worsened by the fall.

Hayyim was brought upstairs. Glueckel stayed with him through a bitterly cold night. Some time after midnight, Glueckel realized that he was not going to get any better on his own. She asked if she should call a doctor. Evidently embarrassed at having tripped over a stone, he told her, "I would rather die than let the world know of it."

She shouted at him, "What kind of talk is that? Why shouldn't people know? You haven't been hurt because of some sin." He persisted, saying that it would hurt the children if people thought there was some kind of weakness in his blood.

By dawn he was in so much pain that he was forced to agree to see a physician. The physician, Abraham Lopez, reassured the family. Lopez treated the wound early in the morning. By noon it was clear that the patient's condition was worsening. The next day more physicians were brought in.

By the following Sabbath, all signs indicated that Hayyim would die. Each member of the family in turn came to see him. None could do anything to ease the pain. At the end, in the company of a man named Feibisch Levi, who stayed and read to him, Hayyim simply said the Shema and died. He was buried on the 24th of Tevet (January 16, 1689).

Glueckel was left to raise her twelve fatherless children.

GOODE, ALEXANDER DAVID (1911–1941)
American rabbi and army chaplain.

Rabbi Alexander Goode was an Army chaplain. In January 1941, he was assigned to be the Jewish chaplain in Greenland. Although Rabbi Goode would have preferred to go to Europe or to someplace closer to the war, he agreed to the new assignment.

He embarked for his new job during the last week of January on the freighter *Dorchester*. The *Dorchester* was very old and quite rusty. Worse still, it was slow, a fact that bothered Rabbi Goode because he knew of the large number of Nazi submarines in the North Atlantic.

Goode was joined on the voyage by three other chaplains—George L. Fox and Clark V. Poling, who were Protestants, and John P. Washington, who was a Roman Catholic.

By February 2, the convoy of ships that included the *Dorchester* reached St. Johns, Newfoundland. The stopover was used to get new supplies and to mail letters.

At 8:00 that night, the convoy again set sail. At 1:00 A.M., as usual, a single bell sounded, announcing the time. Almost immediately thereafter, a torpedo struck the *Dorchester* below its water line.

An order was issued to abandon ship. One man, John Mahoney, rushed to leave, only to realize that he had forgotten his gloves, which he would desperately need to survive in the icy waters. Mahoney started to race back to his cabin. He met Rabbi Goode on the way, and the rabbi gave Mahoney his own gloves. The rabbi assured Mahoney that he had a second pair. Mahoney was later to learn that there was no other pair, and that Rabbi Goode had earlier given his life preserver to an enlisted seaman who had no preserver of his own. The other chaplains had done the same.

John Mahoney was one of only two men in his forty-man lifeboat to survive the cold, thanks in part to the rabbi's gloves.

Some who had been in the lifeboats believe that they saw the four chaplains linked arm in arm, standing together waiting to die, having given their lives so that others could live.

GORDIS, ROBERT (1908–   )
A leading American Conservative rabbi, founder and editor of Judaism.

The following anecdote was supplied by Dr. Gordis.

At an anniversary celebration of an important New York Jewish institution, a symposium was held on what the state of American Judaism would be a century hence. The meeting was crowded with young people who, at the time, were strongly attracted to left-wing causes.

There were three speakers. One was a famous historian. The second was a distinguished professor of philosophy. Rabbi Gordis was the third speaker.

The historian offered some enlightening comments from the perspective of the past. The philosopher made it clear that he maintained no useful relationship with traditional Jewish life. He explained that he did not believe that Judaism had a future as a religion because he didn't believe in any religion. Nor, he said, did Judaism have a future as a nationalism, because he was opposed to all nationalisms. As for Jewish culture, the philosopher rhetorically wondered what there was to that culture. He answered his own question by suggesting, disparagingly, that Jewish culture amounted merely to a few short stories by Sholom Aleichem, some special dietary preferences, and some humor. This, he claimed, was not enough to sustain Jewish life in the future.

Rabbi Gordis then spoke. He said that in view of what had just been argued, he didn't see how the philosopher, or perhaps his children, could remain Jewish if he didn't believe in Judaism as a religion, as a culture, or as a nationalism.

The philosopher shot back: "I object to the rabbi's excommunicating me. I want him to know that I was circumcised on the eighth day of my life."

Rabbi Gordis returned to the microphone to say, "I appreciate the autobiographical reminiscence, and regret that I was not present for the occasion. But I am certain that the guest of honor must have yelled like hell!"

GRATZ, REBECCA (1781–1869)
Humanitarian and literary figure.

Rebecca Gratz's tortured love story became the basis of a famous novel.

Rebecca was the daughter of one of the most important merchants in the United States. The family's home in Philadelphia was an important gathering place for well-known intellectuals of the day, including such writers as Washington Irving.

Rebecca fell in love with Samuel Ewing, a minister's son, but she finally decided that she could not marry him. This romantic tale of anguish deeply affected Irving, who eventually told the story to Sir Walter Scott. Scott created a "Rebecca" character, modeled on Rebecca Gratz, in his novel *Ivanhoe*. In the book, the hero, as had been the case in real life, does not marry the Jewish heroine.

GREENBERG, IRVING (1933–   )
A leading American Orthodox rabbi.

There was a famous dreydel-spinning contest held annually at the City College in New York. The president of the college, Robert E. Marshak, had won twice. The president was a theoretical physicist who had made a private study of how the dreydel spins. He provided the following answer to the question on every Jewish child's lips at Hanukah: "What you need is the biggest angular momentum you can produce over the shortest period of time to give you the greatest torque. This will maximize angular acceleration, which is the change of angular velocity with respect to time." President Marshak even developed equations, using the Greek letter alpha to represent angular acceleration.

Unfortunately, many of the president's competitors could not understand either particle physics or the explanation. Marshak was so confident that he would win, however, that after his first year's victory he had offered the presidency of the college to anyone who could better him at dreydel-spinning— but no one could.

Then came the third year. This time President Marshak faced a stiff competitor, Professor Irving Greenberg of the Jewish Studies department at the college.

Marshak had a green dreydel; Greenberg, an orange one. Greenberg wanted to know whether he would lose his tenure if he emerged victorious. Marshak didn't say, but neither did he repeat his offer of the presidency.

The first spin was exactly even. On the second spin, Rabbi Greenberg's dreydel spun for a tiny bit longer than the president's. The final spin had the president in a tizzy. His dreydel rolled off the table; this unfortunate spin was ruled a false start. Nevertheless, Rabbi Greenberg emerged victorious.

When Rabbi Greenberg was asked about his victory for the Jewish Studies department, his comment was, "The wisdom of the ages has triumphed over physics."

GRODNER, NACHMAN (1811–1879)
Rabbi of Grodno.

(1) Rabbi Grodner devoted his life to helping the poor. He became well known throughout Lithuania for the extent to which he'd go to get money for the poor. The masses of poor Jewry loved him for his folk preaching and his many acts of charity. The people called him Reb Nochemke, or sometimes, the Father of the Poor.

Reb Nochemke, a learned student of the Talmud, was also extremely modest. His modesty caused him to shun becoming the rabbi of a congregation, because he believed that such a position would distance him too much from the people. Instead he worked in a synagogue cleaning up, lighting the stove, running errands for the rabbis, and performing other tasks. He spent all his free time collecting alms for the poor, although this was not required as part of his work as a shammes for the synagogue. He gave to widows, orphans, the ill, the hungry, and those who had been abandoned. He took care to give the money without undue attention.

Because his work at the synagogue occupied so much of his time, it was only late at night that he could begin to seek funds. He often went to the taverns and inns of the area, where people were up and were often in a mood to be generous. He would sit among a group of card players and talk with them, making jokes, and then ask for a percentage of their winnings for the poor.

It was late one night when he sat in among some card players who didn't know him. As they played, he interjected, "What will you give me for the poor?"

The men just laughed at him. One of them then said, "I'll give something to you, but not a thing for your poor." The man then hit Reb Nochemke on the mouth, and the rabbi began to bleed.

But Reb Nochemke laughed and said to the man who had hit him, "Okay, you've given me something, now give something for the poor."

The astonished man gave Reb Nochemke ten rubles.

(2) On another occasion, Reb Nochemke heard that a wealthy Jew was staying overnight at a particular inn. As usual, it was only late at night that he was free to approach the man. But when he got to the inn, he found that the door to the gate was bolted. Reb Nochemke became concerned that the wealthy Jew would leave early the next morning, before he had had a chance to speak with him. Reb Nochemke decided that he was small enough to lie flat on the ground and crawl through one spot under the fence to get into the inn's courtyard. As he did this, an angry dog began to bark. A servant came running out, saw Reb Nochemke, and began to shout, "Thief, thief!"

The "thief" was taken inside, where he was immediately recognized. The innkeeper asked why Reb Nochemke had crawled onto the grounds.

"I had to ask your wealthy guest for a contribution," was the answer.

The innkeeper felt obliged to wake the wealthy man, who listened to the story. He was very much impressed by Reb Nochemke's devotion and made a large donation.

(3) Reb Nochemke was particularly concerned about not hurting the feelings of the poor he helped or making them feel humiliated.

One day a man asked Reb Nochemke to be the godfather at a circumcision for his newborn son. Reb Nochemke learned that the man was very poor and lacked even sufficient money to celebrate the boy's entry into the covenant. Reb Nochemke went to visit the man and asked, "Tell me, are you going to visit Kovno?"

"Kovno? Why do you ask me this?"

"I thought that perhaps you would be visiting Kovno," said Reb Nochemke.

"What if I were going to visit Kovno?" asked the man, by now quite curious about what Reb Nochemke was talking about.

"If you were going to visit Kovno, I intended to ask a favor of you. You see, I owe twenty-five rubles to a man who lives there. I wanted you to return that money to him for me."

"I haven't been to Kovno for two years. I have no idea when I'll be going there."

"Really, there's no hurry. The man from whom I borrowed the money can wait." Reb Nochemke then gave the man twenty-five rubles. "The next time you are in Kovno, I would appreciate it if you could return the money. Of course, should you need the money for some reason between now and when you go, you can certainly use it and then replace it later."

The man, secretly pleased, took the money. He spent it on a joyous party for his new son.

As Reb Nochemke arrived for the bris, the man said to him, "You did not give me the name and address of the man in Kovno to whom you owe this money."

Reb Nochemke acted as though he was trying to remember the name. "I'm sorry. I don't seem to be able to recall the name and address. I must have them at home. I'll tell you some other time. Come, let us enjoy this festive party."

Reb Nochemke later told the man that the name and address had been lost. In time, the man proudly saved twenty-five rubles and returned them to Reb Nochemke.

(4) Reb Nochemke continued to help the poor despite his failing health.

Once, late at night, he was walking on a deserted road when he had a heart attack. Losing consciousness, he fell to the ground. Eventually he awoke and began to call out. A man driving a wagon heard the cries and came to help him. The wagoner took the good shammes into the wagon and began to drive him home. As they drove, Reb Nochemke began to feel better. He asked the driver to stop and let him off.

"What are you doing, shammes? You're not in any condition to go walking around in the dark."

"But there are many people I must look after," Reb Nochemke answered.

"You are too sick."

Reb Nochemke thought for a minute. "Suppose I offered to pay you to drive me through the forest even at this late hour of the night. Would you do that?"

"Of course. I make my living by driving this wagon. I've got a wife and five children who I must support."

"I have many more to support than you do," said Reb Nochemke as he climbed out of the wagon.

H

HARIF, IZEL *(died 1873)*
Rabbi of Slonim.

The Jews have always considered charity an important virtue, not only for the good it does, but also for what it reveals about a person.

Rabbi Harif and a companion once came to the home of a wealthy man to seek funds for the building of a new Talmud Torah. The wealthy man refused to give a donation to build the school. Rabbi Harif's companion was surprised by the refusal, and as the two men walked away from the house, he expressed his views to Rabbi Harif, adding, "He usually gives whenever he is asked."

Rabbi Harif said, "This time he may be right in his refusal."

"How is that possible?" asked the companion.

"You see, those who give to charity usually do so out of fear that the misfortune that they are helping to alleviate might one day afflict them. For instance, one person might help the crippled because he thinks one day he himself might be crippled; another might give to the blind out of fear of becoming blind; and so on. But why should this man have given to education? He is never likely to be afflicted by the thirst for learning."

HART, KITTY *(born 1927)*
Holocaust survivor and author.

No concentration camp survivor ever forgets the first day spent in that camp. Kitty Hart was imprisoned in Birkenau, a part of the Auschwitz concentration camp. In her autobiography, *Return to Auschwitz*, Kitty described the day she and her mother arrived in the camp.

Female German criminal prisoners were in charge of newcomers. After a roll call early in the morning, the newcomers were told to strip. While their clothes were taken away to be "decontaminated," the women showered in cold water. They were then submerged in a blue-green, malodorous liquid. The *fryzerki*—"hairdressers"—arrived. Arms and legs were stretched while body hair was removed. Oversized new clothing was issued. When Kitty and her mother saw each other, they could not refrain from laughing at their ridiculous appearances.

The women were then put in a long line, where they made their way to a series of desks. Each woman gave full information to the woman at the desk. After providing her information, Kitty had a number tattooed on her arm. Her number was 39934. The needle kept digging into her arm, becoming more painful with each insertion. Finally, she was finished. She looked at the tattoo. She didn't like it, but she figured that she would just wash it off. The possibility that the mark was permanent was not considered. She left the room as a band played a march.

The awful horror of that day never left Kitty; it echoed throughout her life.

HARTMAN, MAY WEISSER (born 1900)
American philanthropist and author.

May Hartman's parents were among those who founded the Hebrew National Orphan Home at 37 East 7th Street in New York City. The home cared for Jewish male orphans between the ages of 6 and 14. It was run according to Orthodox Jewish tradition.

The home was owned by the Bessarabian Verband Association, a group of lodges and societies whose members, like the Weissers, were emigrants from Bessarabia, a Rumanian-speaking province in Russia. The house was purchased from Rabbi Philip Klein.

At age 14, May began to perform various services on behalf of the home.

One day, when May was 15, the chairman of the Finance Committee came to see her. He told her that he wanted her to go to see Rabbi Klein and tell him that the association didn't have enough money to pay the interest on the mortgage. He told May to ask for more time.

The girl went to see the well-known rabbi. Rabbi Klein listened to her and then asked, "Why did they send a child to ask me this?"

She looked at him and answered as honestly as she could: "I suppose they were too embarrassed to come themselves."

The rabbi smiled. "You can go back and tell them that you accomplished your mission. I'll wait until they have the funds."

HECHT, BEN (1893–1964)
American author and Zionist.

(1) In the early 1940s, Ben Hecht went to see David O. Selznick, then especially famous as the producer of *Gone With the Wind*. Hecht had the idea of lining up twenty Jewish leaders to support the idea of a Jewish fighting division under British command in the land of Israel. Of course, Hecht knew very well that such a group could form the nucleus of a Jewish army in a Jewish nation.

Hecht approached several people with the idea, but they all turned him down.

Selznick was no different. He told Hecht, "I am an American, not a Jew, and I am not interested in Jewish political problems."

Hecht immediately challenged Selznick to a bet. Selznick was to come up with the names of three people who could be called right at that moment. Each of the three would be asked whether he considered Selznick an American or a Jew. If even only one of the three answered "an American," Selznick would win the bet, and Hecht would not bother him again. But if Selznick lost the bet, he would have to help Hecht.

Selznick lost the bet. Later in his life Selznick would head the United Jewish Appeal's Motion Picture Division.

HEIFETZ, JASCHA (1901–1987)
American violinist.

Heifetz often played his violin accompanied by Arthur Rubinstein on the piano and Gregor Piatigorsky on the cello. Although Heifetz appreciated the music the trio produced, he was upset because Rubinstein got the top billing. Heifetz once remarked; "If the Almighty Himself played the violin, the credits would still read 'Rubinstein, God, and Piatigorsky,' in that order."

HEINE, HEINRICH (1797–1856)
German author.

(1) Early in his life, before his apostasy, Heine was offered a job as head librarian in the library at Weimar if he would become a Christian. He replied with a poem:

If I believed, as you believe,
In Jesus and the Trinity,

I'd earn my bread, I do believe,
And thrive in your vicinity,
But how can any Jew believe
Another Jew's divinity?

(2) Heine often made fun of atheists with this line: "In Frankfort, I met a watch that did not believe in the existence of watchmakers."

HERTZ, MARCUS *(1747–1803)*
German physician.

Hertz drove a carriage to the houses of his ill patients. On the door of the carriage were his initials, M. H.

One day Heinrich Heine asked him why he drove around in a carriage inscribed with those letters. "Don't you know that in Hebrew, M. H. stands for *malech hamoves* [the angel of death]?"

But Hertz was not impressed. "Heine, you're just a pessimist. Don't you know that M. H. in Hebrew also stands for *mechayai hameissim* [to give life to the dead]?"

HERZL, THEODOR *(1860–1904)*
Founder of modern Zionism.

(1) Many of Herzl's early efforts on the road to establishing the Zionist movement were fraught with difficulty. (See *Dreyfus, Alfred.*)

In 1893, Herzl was casting about for a solution to the widespread hatred of the Jews. He thought through a variety of proposals to end this hatred. He first considered challenging all those who hated Jews to a duel, but he quickly realized the impracticality of attempting to duel to the death every anti-Semite in Europe.

He also very briefly considered solving the "Jewish question," particularly in Austria, by converting Jews to Christianity. He thought of getting Austrian Catholic help in encouraging the pope to meet with him about his plan. According to that plan, mass conversions would take place in broad daylight at noon on Sundays in St. Stephen's Cathedral. Herzl could almost hear the pealing of the bells. But he envisioned a small group of Jewish leaders, including himself, remaining Jewish.

Herzl was finally dissuaded from the plan by Moritz Benedikt, one of the publishers of the paper for which Herzl wrote. (Ironically, Benedikt was later a vehement opponent of Herzl's Zionist enterprise.) Benedikt argued that Jews had retained their religion for a hundred generations, and Herzl had no right to terminate that line.

Satisfied that no real solution lay in the area of conversion, Herzl began to think about other solutions. Eventually and fatefully, he came to conclude that Jewish nationalism was the best response to anti-Semitism.

(2) Herzl dedicated the last seven years of his life to rebuilding a Jewish nation in Israel. His efforts included the publication of his Zionist pamphlet *Der Judenstaat* ("The Jewish State") in 1896. The incredibly enthusiastic response that greeted the pamphlet prompted Herzl to convene the First Zionist Congress.

The congress was scheduled to convene in Basel, Switzerland, on August 29, 1897, and Herzl was extremely agitated about it. He knew that the movement to create a Jewish nation was weak, with almost no financial resources and too few supporters. The congress itself was a calculated gamble; he was trying, despite the fact of the movement's weakness, to impress the world. Herzl's plan to make a financial deal with Turkey (which controlled the land of Israel) depended in part on Turkish and international perception of Jewish nationalists as financially well off, as intellectually impressive, and as representing the dynamic leadership of world Jewry. The congress was conceived to further that perception. Herzl had invited the press, many diplomats, some contacts that he had established, and representatives of the sultan who ruled Turkey. Herzl feared that the press and the diplomats would take one look at Zionism's poor followers—and Herzl wasn't even sure how many of them would actually show up—and cease to think of Jewish nationalism as anything more than a small, powerless, quixotic movement.

Herzl arrived in Basel by train four days before the opening session of the congress was due to convene. After making his way in the heat to the Hotel Trois Rois, Herzl checked the location that the city had provided for offices. The offices turned out to be a converted tailor's shop. The shocked Herzl could predict the humorous jibes that would be evoked by the fact that the new movement's offices were located in a shop associated with such a traditionally Jewish trade. He ordered the tailor sign covered. He then walked to the assembly hall where the congress would meet. His associate in Switzerland had rented a huge beer cellar with a stage and backdrop used mostly for gymnastic shows. Herzl cancelled the lease and instead rented the Basel Municipal Casino. The municipal hall seemed less frivolous; it provided a more serious, even somber, atmosphere. One of Herzl's assistants, David Wolffsohn, was assigned the task of putting a banner over the entrance to the hall. Wolffsohn used the blue and white of the traditional Jewish prayer shawl and included a star of David—thus giving birth to the national flag.

Herzl, trained as a dramatist, carefully considered how he could produce his Zionist drama for his audience. He ordered that black formal attire and white neckties be worn by all at the opening session. He wanted those who attended to feel, in their bones, that they were a national assembly, and he wanted to make them appear so to the world.

Herzl knew that of all the factions that might attend, he would probably have the most trouble with the religiously observant delegates, so on the Sabbath before the congress was to begin, Herzl attended services in a synagogue. He was called up to the Torah and, having memorized the blessings, said the appropriate words without a single error.

On Sunday morning, August 29, some 208 delegates and 26 correspondents arrived at the hall, along with many curious Swiss Gentiles.

The platform, draped in green, looked out upon tables crowded with reporters and stenographers.

The senior delegate, Dr. Karl Lippe, spoke for half an hour and then turned the gavel over to Herzl. Herzl rose and walked erectly. Some reached out to kiss his hand; others wept. He reached the rostrum, but successive waves of applause prevented him from commencing his speech. The cheering continued for fifteen minutes.

Finally, Herzl was able to talk. When he concluded, Max Nordau spoke about the desperate situation of the Jews. The assembled group then divided into commissions. Herzl chaired a debate.

Over the next three days, going virtually without sleep, cajoling factions and a wide variety of idiosyncratic followers, Herzl weaved the strands of mayhem into a fabric of order. The congress passed the Basel program. The World Zionist Organization had been formed.

Herzl closed the congress, and exultation filled the hall. There was wild hugging, singing, crying, and cheering. Cries of "Next year in Jerusalem!" resounded. The Jewish soul had found a voice.

(3) At one point during the congress, seven agitated rabbis came to see Herzl at his hotel. They left smiling and pleased. One of Herzl's aides saw them and asked whether Herzl had promised that he would eat only kosher food and maintain the Sabbath. One of the rabbis said that that was not the case at all. In fact, he added, had Herzl kept kosher and kept the Sabbath, the rabbis would have been deeply perturbed. The aide looked puzzled, so the rabbi continued, "We would not then have been able to join the movement, because if he were also observant, we would have had to accept him as the Messiah."

(4) In 1898, Herzl was on a visit to Motza on the western approach to Jerusalem. The Zionist leader planted a cedar tree there with his own hands, beginning the tradition, later carried on by the Jewish National Fund, of planting trees to make Jerusalem green. (Jerusalem's afforested area now covers more than 7,500 acres.)

The cedar Herzl planted was eventually destroyed. Another tree was planted in its place by Herbert Samuel, the first British high commissioner. Since that time, Motza has been used as the traditional tree-planting site for the various presidents of the state of Israel.

(5) Herzl was discussing the establishment of a Jewish state in East Africa with Joseph Chamberlain, British secretary of state for the colonies. Herzl was not intrigued and said so. Chamberlain then pointed on his map to an area of Egypt that, he said, Britain would be willing to provide for the Jews.

Herzl looked at him. "Egypt? My people would surely not hear of it. We have already been there."

HESIL, JOSHUA (died 1664)
Hasidic rabbi.

Rabbi Hesil took the rights of all beings, including animals, very seriously.

He often traveled to visit his disciples. On one of those journeys he was a passenger in a wagon drawn by an old, slow-moving horse. The wagon came to a stop at the foot of a steep hill. Rabbi Hesil descended and climbed the hill on foot. His attendant was astonished at this behavior and asked why the rabbi had climbed the hill.

Rabbi Hesil said, "I was afraid that the horse would bring me to court claiming that I did not have sufficient pity if I made it climb this hill."

The attendant was not satisfied by this response. "But surely, Rabbi, you would have won the case. After all, horses were meant to serve people."

"Yes," agreed the rabbi. "There is no doubt that I would have won, but I'd rather climb this hill a dozen times over than find myself being brought to court by a horse."

HILLEL (first century B.C.E.–first century C.E.)
Famous scholar of the Second Temple period.

(1) This is the most famous of the many stories about Hillel.

A stranger came to the house of Shammai. Shammai greeted the stranger and asked what he wanted. The stranger said that he wanted to learn the whole of the Torah while he stood on one foot. Shammai immediately saw that the stranger wished to make fun of him. He became angry and told the stranger to go away.

The stranger then went to the house of Hillel. Hillel greeted him and asked what he wanted. The stranger repeated his jeering request to be taught the whole of the Torah while standing on one foot. Hillel also saw that the stranger was mocking him, but Hillel did not become angry. Instead, Hillel said that he would teach the stranger as was wished.

Hillel began the lesson. "What is hateful to you do not do to your neighbor."

The stranger waited for more. Finally he asked, "Is that all the Torah?"

"Yes," said Hillel. "That is the foundation. All the rest is commentary. Go and study."

The stranger said, "Thank you Hillel. If that is the foundation, I will study all the Torah."

(2) Hillel had a reputation for never losing his temper. Knowing of this reputation, and believing that not even a sage could live up to it, a man made a wager of 400 zuzim that he could make Hillel angry.

One late Friday afternoon just before the Sabbath—the worst time to receive visitors—this man went to Hillel's house and loudly knocked on the door. Hillel answered.

"Are you Hillel?" the man asked.

"I am," Hillel responded softly. "What is it that you wish of me?"

"I have an important question to ask you. Why do the Babylonians have round heads?"

"You have asked a very intriguing question," said Hillel. "The reason is that Babylonia lacks expert midwives."

Just a few minutes later, the man again knocked loudly on the door. Hillel opened the door and again asked what he could do to help the man.

"I have a difficult question for you. Why are the Trudians red-eyed?"

"Sir," Hillel said, "you've asked a very sensible question. It is because they live in the desert, and the sand gets in their eyes."

Hillel tried to get back to work, but the man would not quit. Again, he pounded loudly. Again, Hillel answered and was ready to help.

"I have another question for you. Why do some men have large feet?"

"That is a most interesting question. Some men live in swamps—a condition which tends to flatten their feet."

"Are you Hillel the prince?" asked the rude man.

"I am."

"I certainly hope that not many like you will be born in Israel."

"Why is that?" the puzzled Hillel asked.

"Because of you I lost a lot of money. I made a wager of 400 zuzim that I could make you angry."

"Sir," said Hillel, "even if you were to lose twice 400 zuzim, I would not get angry."

(3) When Hillel was still young, he had a deep thirst for knowledge. Unfortu-nately, he was too poor to go to school. Finally, however, he resolved to attend. He worked as hard as he could, living on half of his wages and taking the other half to the doorkeeper of a famous school. He offered the doorkeeper the money in return for being allowed to enter and sit in the assembly to hear the lectures. He did this for several days, but eventually his money had completely run out, so that he could no longer even afford to eat. The doorkeeper then refused to allow him to enter.

Hillel maintained his desire to learn.

One Sabbath eve, he climbed on to one of the windows and sat on the sill, from which he could see and hear the wisdom inside. The next morning as the rabbis entered the academy, the room seemed peculiarly dark. They searched for the reason and discovered the frozen Hillel on the sill covered with snow, blocking the light. He had stayed there all night. Despite the fact that it was the Sabbath, the rabbis decided that it would not be a sin to kindle a flame. They gave food and drink to the young stranger.

(4) A heathen had gone to Shammai and asked, "How many Torahs do the Jews have?"

Shammai answered, "Two, the written and the oral."

The heathen said, "I believe in the written Torah, but not the oral one. Will you accept me as a convert if I believe in only the one?" Shammai threw the man out.

The heathen then came to Hillel and asked the same question, got the same answer, and made the same request to be accepted as a convert despite his belief in only the written Torah. Hillel accepted the man for study.

On the first day, Hillel taught the would-be convert the Hebrew alphabet in the correct order. On the next day, however, Hillel reversed the order. The man was upset. "Yesterday, you taught me the opposite," he complained. "Which way is correct?"

Hillel looked at his pupil. "You see, you must depend on me to teach you something as simple as the letters of the alphabet. So, too, must you depend on me to explain something infinitely more complex—how to understand the Torah."

HIRSCH, EMIL (1851–1923)
American rabbi and scholar.

Rabbi Hirsch was an advocate of Reform Judaism, but a man unusually tolerant of those Orthodox practices that he didn't accept.

One day he was being berated by a minister who was critical of Orthodox funeral practices. The minister claimed that there was much more order and discipline at a Christian service. There was no screaming, no open display of emotion. The minister contrasted this especially to Orthodox Jewish funerals, with their sometimes wailing participants. Hirsch looked at him in anger. "You are quite right," he said. "I would rather see ten Christian funerals than one Jewish funeral."

HOBSON, LAURA Z. (1900–1986)
American author.

Although her name would have allowed Laura Hobson to pass for a Gentile, the author consistently maintained a fierce pride in her Jewish heritage.

Just before the Second World War, Hobson—whose maiden name had been Zametkin—was at a dinner party in New York. The conversation naturally turned to the subject of the emerging Nazi menace. Some at the table talked of "those awful Germans." Others did not consider the Nazis to be a genuine menace. One guest was of the opinion that "the chosen people ask for it, wherever they are." Another uttered the cliché, "Some of my best friends are Jews." Laura Hobson then spoke up. "Some of mine are, too. Including my father and mother."

IMBER, NAPHTALI HERZ (1856–1909)
Poet and author of Hatikvah, *the Israeli national anthem.*

As a young man, Imber rebelled against some religious traditions. By his old age he had come to understand those traditions in his own way and to recognize their insight.

Imber was 15 years old and a student in Hebrew school. It was customary at the time for students to spend Monday and Thursday nights in the *Bet Hamidrash,* the house of learning. The *Bet Hamidrash* was like a synagogue, though not quite as sacred. Eating was allowed, as was discussion of subjects not strictly religious. The *Bet Hamidrash* remained open all night so that students could sleep on the wooden benches or study or read a book from the large library. At about 3:00 in the afternoon, pious Jews gathered there to talk of the destruction of Jerusalem, to drink tea (and sometimes liquor), and then to talk of other matters. Life after death was a favorite subject.

One horrible winter evening, Imber sat alone in the *Bet Hamidrash,* studying the Talmud. As he looked out the window, he was overcome by a common superstition of the day. He saw white sheets that had been hung out to dry. His poetic mind transformed the sheets into wandering souls of the risen dead. The local belief was that the dead arose at midnight and wandered into the synagogue to read the Torah. The belief was so powerful that Jews stayed away from the synagogue near midnight.

Several pious Jews then came in to join Imber. They sang some lamentations and then lit their pipes and began to talk.

Mendele, an ox trader, spoke to Moshe, a teacher. "Do you know that Shlome the shoemaker, whom we buried several days ago, is now a wanderer at large in the *Olam Hatohu* [world of confusion]?"

"Yes," answered Moshe. "Even the Gentiles say they have seen him wandering."

Imber listened, fascinated by the conversation. According to the beliefs of the day, the *Olam Hatohu* was a state of being that was without pleasure or sadness. Such a state was, it was thought, reserved for the simple person who had done others no harm but who had not engaged in any philanthropic work. Upon death, such a person would be neither punished nor rewarded, but would wander in the world of confusion.

The shoemaker under discussion had been famous for his beer drinking, an activity that had made him enormously fat.

Imber felt obliged to enter the conversation. "That such things as the *Olam Hatohu* exist I know from my reading of Jewish lore, but I cannot conceive it possible for a man of his bulk to have gotten out of the grave unaided. Think of it. Here was a man who weighed more than 350 pounds. Six men were needed to bury him. If he could get out of the grave by himself, why couldn't he have gotten into the grave by himself and spared those six men the trouble?"

Moshe, the teacher, jumped up, stuck a fist in Imber's face, and yelled, "Herzel, you are a heretic!" Word spread that young Imber was a nonbeliever. He was forced to leave town, having acquired a firm determination to use only his common sense as his guide in life.

It was thirty-five years later, after having seen the world and met many people, that Imber, while writing an autobiographical fragment, professed a belief in his own version of the *Olam Hatohu*, for the older Imber observed that "we all wander aimless in this world of confusion."

ISRAEL MEIR HA-KOHEN (1838–1933)
Known as the Hafetz Hayyim, rabbi and talmudist, a leader of the Musar movement.

(1) The following anecdote was supplied by Bernard Medintz.

In 1913, Israel Medintz was a young boy attending the Yeshiva of Raden, which had been established by the Hafetz Hayyim. One day young Israel and two friends went for a walk in the woods near the Yeshiva. They carried sticks in their hands. They had found the sticks during their walk. Then the Hafetz Hayyim himself passed the boys. He greeted them in a friendly manner and stopped to talk to them. "*Kinder*," he said, "never walk with a stick in your hand. You might be provoked by someone and, before thinking, use the stick to hit or beat someone. A Jew should never carry a stick. Without a stick in the hand, physical violence will not be so easy."

The young Israel remembered this incident all his life and passed it on to his son.

(2) The Hafetz Hayyim came to Navaradok. He had just written a book on the evils of malicious gossip, and he sought approval for the book from the town's rabbi, Y. M. Epstein. Rabbi Epstein heard about his plans and sent two of his most brilliant pupils to where the rabbi was staying. They spoke to him for two hours, seeking to get him to say an unkind word about a rabbi or community leader. But the Hafetz Hayyim refused to utter a disparaging word about anyone. The two students recounted the meeting to Rabbi Epstein, who then agreed to write his recommendation for the book. In the recommendation, Rabbi Epstein wrote: "This author practices what he preaches."

ISSERLES, MOSES (c. 1525-1572)
Polish rabbi and Halakhic authority.

There seemed to be a desire among many Jews, even the learned and traditional, to engage in secular studies. Such a desire seemed at variance with tradition. Isserles sought a way out of this dilemma.

In addition to the sacred literature, Isserles was particularly interested in studying philosophy. He approached various authorities and ultimately concluded that the Bible, the Talmud, the Codes, and the commentaries on all sacred writing formed the sole source of study. He accepted the view that other fields of study were not appropriate.

Nevertheless, he did find a way from within the tradition to read philosophy. He concluded, "It is permitted to study other sciences occasionally, provided this does not involve reading historical works. This is called by the sages 'strolling in paradise.' A man must not 'stroll in paradise' until he has filled his stomach with meat and wine, namely the knowledge of that which is forbidden and that which is permitted, and the laws of the precepts." Isserles urged that philosophy be studied only on holidays or on Sabbath, when other people spend their time simply walking.

J

JABOTINSKY, VLADIMIR (1880–1940)
Zionist leader and founder of the Revisionist movement.

It took a jail term to turn Vladimir Jabotinsky into a Zionist.

Jabotinsky was spending time as a guest in the house of a friend. His friend's two sisters were being watched by the Russian police because of their connection to the Socialist movement.

The police also suspected Jabotinsky because of this connection, and so, in the spring of 1902, the police searched Jabotinsky's home and confiscated what they claimed were suspicious publications. One of the publications was an illegal copy of a memorandum to the czar from the Russian minister of finance. There were also four copies of *Avanti*, an Italian Socialist paper published in Milan. The paper carried articles that Jabotinsky had written. One of the police officers said that because the newspapers were in an "unintelligible language" they would be taken and turned over to one of the czar's official translators to determine whether they contained any offensive passages.

Jabotinsky was arrested and sent to the prison in Odessa to wait for the results of the translation.

The prison term was eventful for Jabotinsky. He met revolutionaries who wanted to overthrow the czarist government. He had never before met social revolutionaries, and their sincerity deeply impressed him.

At least three-quarters of the prisoners were Jewish, and each had a nickname, many of which were taken from Jewish life. One of the inmates, for example, was nicknamed Zeide (grandfather). Jabotinsky's nickname was Lavrov (heart of a rabbi).

The prison rules called for solitary confinement, but the inmates organized lectures and musical programs.

Zeide's lectures particularly impressed Jabotinsky. Zeide gave three lectures on the history of the Jewish Socialist Bund. Jabotinsky later wrote that it was after these three lectures that he became a Zionist. This claim was somewhat exaggerated, but it is clear that prison life prepared Jabotinsky to receive ideas that he might otherwise have ignored. He had previously filtered out Jewish concerns from his life; the prison term filtered them back in.

Jabotinsky was released after seven weeks. He remained under police observation.

Before long he would begin his remarkable Zionist career as founder of the Jewish Legion and Revisionist wing of Zionism. Jabotinsky was to serve as a political mentor to many Zionist leaders, including Menachem Begin.

JACOB DAVID (*late nineteenth–early twentieth century*)
Teacher and Slutsker rebbe.

It was just after the horrible massacre of Jews at Kishinev in 1903. Rabbi Jacob passed a hall on the East Side of New York. In front of the hall was a sign announcing a dance to raise funds for the victims of the massacre.

The rabbi was horrified at the idea that people would dance as the way to remember such a terrible event. He walked into the dance and mounted the stage. The dancers and the musicians stopped to listen to him.

"Your dance reminds me of a story. A farmer hired an old Hebrew teacher to instruct his children. One night the farmer was awakened and saw the old teacher sitting on the ground in front of a candle, sobbing over a moth-eaten prayer book.

" 'What's the matter?' the farmer asked.

" 'Don't you know?' responded the teacher. 'Once we had our land, our own government, our own temple. Then the Romans came and sent us into exile. Shouldn't we weep over our tragedy?'

"The farmer agreed, and for two hours they sat on the ground, crying and praying.

"Finally the farmer stopped crying. He suggested that the two have a drink of whiskey to gain strength for further prayer.

"They had one drink, but it was clear that it did not revive their energy. So they kept on drinking until they began to sing and dance. Soon the farmer's wife came down and demanded an explanation for their behavior.

" 'Don't you know that our temple was destroyed, our people killed? Now we are in exile. Come, have a drink.' "

Then the rabbi stared at the crowd. "You are also dancing and singing because your brethren were butchered."

JACOB JOSEPH OF POLONNOYE (died c. 1782)
Rabbi and hasidic preacher.

Rabbi Jacob Joseph came one morning to his synagogue in Sharogrod. There were no worshippers. The rabbi asked the shammes where all those who regularly prayed had gone. The shammes told him that the faithful were all at the market. The rabbi was surprised that they would be there at the hour of prayer. Then the shammes explained why they were there: There was a stranger telling fascinating stories, and the people wished to listen to him. The rabbi became furious and ordered the shammes to bring the stranger to the synagogue immediately.

The shammes quickly made his way to the market, worked his way through the crowd to the stranger, and transmitted the order. The stranger calmly agreed to go to the synagogue.

The rabbi, still angry, did not rise respectfully as the stranger entered. Instead, the rabbi accused the man of turning the congregation from the ways of the Lord.

"Don't be angry," said the stranger. "Instead of getting angry, you should listen to a story."

At first, this suggestion made the rabbi even angrier, but eventually something about the stranger drew the rabbi's attention. He agreed to listen.

The stranger was the Baal Shem Tov, the founder of Hasidism. This is the story that the Baal Shem Tov told the rabbi:

"I was riding along a road in a coach drawn by three horses. Each of the horses was of a different color, but, strangely, not one of them was making a noise that horses make. This did not make sense to me. Finally we came upon a peasant on the road. He shouted to me that I had to loosen the reins. Suddenly all three horses started to neigh."

In a single instant, Rabbi Jacob Joseph understood how the parable applied to him. A religious soul, too, needs to cry out and is prevented from doing so by too many restrictions. The rabbi began to cry.

Rabbi Jacob Joseph became a leader in the new Hasidic movement.

JACOBSON, EDDIE (1891–1955)
Former business partner of President Harry Truman.

This is the story of how Eddie Jacobson, a shopkeeper, got the president of the United States to help the Zionist movement.

Three months had passed since the November 29, 1947, United Nations vote for partition of the Holy Land. But early in 1948 there were setbacks on the road to Jewish statehood. Arabs were dividing the land of Israel with highway outposts. The settlements in the Negev were cut off from the rest of the country, except for the Haganah, the Jewish army, which could fly in planes to the settlements.

It was a common perception that the Jews simply would not survive after the British withdrew in May. Rumors quickly spread that the United States believed that partition would not work, and that it was planning to suggest a trusteeship to take the place of the British mandate. The idea, of course, would forestall or even end the dream of an independent Jewish nation.

The Zionist leaders concluded that with so many bureaucrats in the state department pushing for trusteeship, the only way to persuade the United States not to back off the partition plan was to make a face-to-face appeal to President Harry Truman. At the time, Truman was not particularly sympathetic to hearing any more about the Middle East. He was irritated about the entire partition battle, especially after the Zionists had unleashed efforts to get the United States to persuade other nations to support partition. Through the winter following the partition vote, Truman would not see any Zionists at all. In addition, Truman found many American Zionist leaders politically or personally unpalatable. The only Zionist leader for whom he had any respect was Chaim Weizmann, but Truman resisted seeing even him.

The Zionists were desperate. It was then that they turned to Eddie Jacobson.

On March 13, Jacobson walked into the White House. He did not have an appointment. Truman's secretary for appointments, Matthew Connelly, begged Jacobson not to discuss the Middle East. But Jacobson simply answered, "That's what I came to Washington for."

Connelly allowed Jacobson in to see the president only because Jacobson and Truman were such old friends.

Once in the Oval Office, the two discussed their families and various business questions. Jacobson finally brought up the subject of the Jewish nation. Truman became tense. In a way he never had before, Truman spoke bitterly to his old partner. Jacobson argued back, reminding the president of his admiration for Weizmann. Jacobson said that he simply couldn't understand why Truman wouldn't see him.

But Truman would not be moved. He told Jacobson that too many Jewish leaders had been disrespectful and mean to him. Jacobson was shocked. His dear friend sounded like an anti-Semite, and Jacobson wondered what some of the Jewish leaders must have done.

The two men were at an impasse. Suddenly Jacobson saw a model for a statue of Andrew Jackson. Jacobson summoned his courage and spoke. "Harry, all your life you have had a hero. You are probably the best-read man in the United States on the life of Andrew Jackson. Well, Harry, I too have a hero — a man I have never met but who is, I think, the greatest Jew who ever lived. I too have studied his past, and I agree with you, as you have often told me, that he is a gentleman and a great statesman as well. I am talking about Chaim Weizmann. Now you refuse to see him because you were insulted by some of our American Jewish leaders. It doesn't sound like you, Harry."

Truman listened as he drummed his fingers on his desk. Jacobson paused, and Truman swung in his swivel chair to face the Rose Garden. Several seconds passed. Suddenly the president swung back. He stared Jacobson straight in the eye and said, "You win, you bald-headed son of a bitch. I will see him."

Jacobson left, went back to his hotel, and then went to a bar. For the first time in his life he drank a double bourbon.

The Weizmann–Truman meeting that emerged was directly responsible for Truman's determination during the next several months that an independent Jewish nation would be born.

JAVITS, JACOB (1904–1986)
US senator and statesman.

Javits made his first of many visits to Israel even before that nation was officially declared. He arrived in December of 1946, worried about the fate of Hitler's victims and increasingly concerned about how the British were administering their mandate. Javits had just been elected to Congress for the first time but had not yet begun his service. Most of his constituents seemed to favor a United Nations trusteeship for the area rather than a partition into two states, one Jewish, the other Arab. Javits determined to see for himself.

One incident crystallized Jewish life under British control. One evening, Javits was walking along a narrow street in Tel Aviv. Suddenly a British tank came rolling down the street. The tank's searchlight swept back and forth across the street, from the wall on one side to the wall on the other. Javits saw that other pedestrians were flattening themselves against the walls. He did the same. The tank passed so close to him that Javits could have stretched out his arm and touched it. It was at that moment that he fully understood how Tel Aviv's residents felt under British rule.

Javits determined to support partition and the creation of a Jewish nation. On January 20, 1947, Javits gave his first speech as a member of Congress. The speech was about the need for more Jewish immigration into their Holy Land.

JEREMIAH (c. 627–585 B.C.E.)
Second of the major prophets.

Jeremiah was a witness to the fall of Judea in 587 B.C.E. He had begun to preach as early as 627, arguing wherever he spoke that Judea was being judged. He warned people of the consequences of what he considered the anti-Jewish apostasy that was prevalent. Jeremiah prophesied that Judea would be captured.

When Nebuchadnezzar in fact came and conquered the land and put shackles on the Jews to lead them away to captivity, Jeremiah asked that he, too, be shackled. Nebuchadnezzar saw this and ordered the chains removed. Jeremiah observed that the older Jewish captives wore halters around their necks. He put a halter around his own neck and went among them. Nebuchadnezzar again learned of his behavior and came to Jeremiah.

"Either you are a false prophet, or you cannot feel pain, or you wish me to die. Didn't you foretell this disaster for your people? Yet you grieve over it as though you are surprised. I have tried to spare you pain, but you look for it. You know I must keep you safe so as not to anger your God. Yet you seem determined to destroy yourself, thus bringing forth your God's wrath on me."

Jeremiah continued to accompany the captives. As the group reached the Euphrates River, Nebuchadnezzar said to Jeremiah, "You may come with us to Babylon, or, if you wish, you are free to return to Jerusalem."

Jeremiah prayed and concluded that it was more important that God go with the captives while he remained behind to comfort those who were not forced to leave. He told Nebuchadnezzar of this decision, but the captives cried when they heard that Jeremiah would not join them. Jeremiah called out, "Had you but listened to my warnings in Jerusalem, you would have been spared all these trials!" Two tears rolled down his cheeks. The captives began to cry openly.

The Babylonian commanders saw these tears and ordered the captives to stop crying. They beat the captives and told them that they would be killed if they continued their weeping.

The captives again asked Jeremiah to accompany them, to lament and pray openly on their behalf. Jeremiah blessed them and reminded them, "God will not abandon you, even in exile. Have hope and put your trust in Him!"

Jeremiah put them in God's hands.

JOB (c. 500 B.C.E.)
Biblical figure noted for his righteousness.

Job was concerned about the welfare of the poor. He built his house with four separate entrances, one on each side of the house, so that the poor could find their way inside the house from whichever side they approached. Job fed all the hungry who came to his home.

Job grew to be a very wealthy man. Knowledge of his wealth spread throughout the land.

One day, Job heard that a very poor man had died, leaving a widow and many children. Job decided to do what he could to help the family.

Job went to see the woman. First he offered words of consolation. Then he went to her neighbors to inquire whether her husband had left her any money or fields. He was told that nothing had been left, though the dead man had owned a small field which had not been productive for many years. Job then concluded that he would help the widow.

After the *shiva* period ended, Job went to the woman and offered to provide servants and animals to help cultivate the field.

"I cannot accept aid from a strange man. God will not abandon us in our need," she responded.

"Let me then at least provide a vegetable garden for you," Job persisted. But she would not accept this offer either.

When it came time to sow the field, the woman sold all her household goods. She rented an ass and cultivated the field, but the ground was tough and the results were meager. She and the children grew hungry.

Job again heard of their dilemma and sent enough grain to last the family one year.

Again the woman refused the gift. She informed Job that she would become a servant so that her family could live by her own labor.

The woman did find work as a servant, but the pay was poor and the family remained hungry.

Job then decided to tell everyone he knew that the widow was one of his blood relatives. People who heard this immediately thought, "Imagine the man lucky enough to marry this woman. He will inherit money from Job."

Eventually a good man married the woman, and Job, discovering that he was good, helped him. The couple lived in peace and great happiness.

JOSE DUMBROVER (*eighteenth century*)
Rabbi in Dumbrova.

Rabbi Jose was especially beloved because of his efforts on behalf of the poor, the widowed, and the orphaned. People were always very generous with their gifts when Rabbi Jose made his requests. Reb Favish, one of the wealthiest Jews in Dumbrova, was particularly helpful.

One day, however, as Rabbi Josele, as he was affectionately known, came to Reb Favish to seek another donation, Reb Favish uncharacteristically refused the request.

"Why have you refused?" asked Rabbi Josele, adding, "I hope it isn't that you yourself are now poor."

"No, that isn't it," Reb Favish answered. "It is just that the other day, Mordecai the beggar died. They found thousands of ranishes on him. This made me think that the poor are impostors, and that I shouldn't waste my money on them."

Rabbi Josele said, "Surely you have seen a poor person who desired to appear rich by wearing expensive clothing and living well. The rich are not blamed for such people. Similarly, if one rich man wishes to appear poor, why should all the poor be blamed?"

Reb Favish considered this and then gave a considerable amount to help the needy.

JOSHUA BEN HANANIAH (first and second centuries C.E.)
Rabbi and scholar of Jewish law.

(1) The emperor came to Rabbi Joshua and said, "I wish to see your God."

The rabbi responded, "You cannot see him."

The emperor was insistent. "I will see him."

Rabbi Joshua didn't know what to do. Finally, he took the emperor outside and had him face the sun during the summer solstice. The rabbi said, "Look up at it."

The emperor, blinded by the blazing sun, averted his eyes and said, "I cannot."

Rabbi Joshua said, "If you cannot look at the sun, which is but one of the ministers that attend the Holy One, how, then, can you presume to look upon the Divine Presence?"

(2) The emperor came to Rabbi Joshua and asked, "How is it that when I eat with you on the Sabbath, the food smells so pleasant?"

Rabbi Joshua said, "We Jews possess a special spice that we include to make the food fragrant."

The emperor asked if he could have some of the spice. Rabbi Joshua said, "No, because this spice is available only to those who observe the day of rest, for the spice is the Sabbath itself."

JUDAH HALEVI (c. 1075–1141)
Hebrew poet and philosopher, author of such works as The Kuzari.

(1) Halevi's daughter had reached a marriageable age but remained unmarried. Halevi's wife became angry at the poet for not making sufficient efforts to find a good husband for his daughter.

Angry at the reproach, Halevi took an oath that the next man to walk through the door would marry his daughter.

Just after the oath had been uttered, a poor wanderer, dirty, seemingly unlettered and ignorant, entered. Halevi's wife was shocked, but Halevi would not violate his promise. He gave the wanderer food and shelter and began to teach him the rudiments of Hebrew.

At the time, Halevi was struggling unsuccessfully to complete a poem about Purim. Frustrated, he went for a walk. While he was gone, the stranger went into Halevi's study and wrote a beautiful final stanza.

When Halevi returned home, he was very much surprised and asked who the author of the stanza was. "Only an angel could have written it, or perhaps Abraham Ibn Ezra," he said, referring to the great poet and philosopher.

"Ibn Ezra did write it," said the stranger. And so Ibn Ezra married Judah Halevi's daughter.

(2) Judah Halevi wished for a long time to immigrate to the Holy Land. This decision was in part an intellectual one. Halevi had made a profound political analysis of Jewry's future in the Diaspora and found it wanting. Of course, these political elements were buttressed by his theology, which emphasized the unity of the Jewish religious experience—tying God, the Jews, the land, and holy language together. His personality was such that he spoke out against those he perceived as engaging in self-deception—those who spoke and prayed for a return to Zion but never acted on it.

On September 8, 1140, Halevi, accompanied by the son of Abraham Ibn Ezra, arrived in Alexandria, Egypt, where he stayed for several months. After a journey to Cairo and back, Halevi boarded a ship at Alexandria. He was ready to make *aliyah*, to ascend to the land of Israel, in what he saw as an act of personal redemption. But the ship's passage was delayed by bad weather. Halevi evidently returned to Egyptian soil, where he died early in 1141, without returning to the Holy Land.

JUDAH HA-NASI (end of second–beginning of third century C.E.)
Rabbi and editor of the Mishnah.

(1) Rabbi Judah was lecturing to his students when he smelled some garlic that one of his students had evidently been eating. The rabbi asked that the guilty

student leave the room. No one moved. Finally, Rabbi Hiya, though not guilty, left the room so that the offender could do so. Then another student left, and a third. In a few moments not a single student remained in the room.

(2) As a wealthy man, Rabbi Judah was willing to provide for others. However, he was concerned that those whom he aided be learned. During a famine, Judah announced he would feed anyone who was hungry, provided only that the person prove his knowledge of the holy books.

A man, poorly dressed, showed up one day at Judah's house and asked for food.

"Do you know the Scriptures?" asked Judah.

"No."

"Do you know Mishnah?"

"No."

"Do you know Aggadah?"

"No."

"Then I'm sorry, but I cannot give you any food."

The stranger asked only for the food that Judah would give to a hungry animal.

So Judah fed him, though he later expressed regret that he had fed such an unlettered beggar.

Judah's son Simon said to his father, "Perhaps he was a scholar who did not wish to use the Torah as a means of obtaining support."

Judah undertook to discover the beggar's identity. Indeed, as his son had said, the beggar had been Rabbi Jonathan ben Amram, a well-known scholar.

After that, Rabbi Judah fed all those who came asking for food.

(3) The Emperor Antoninus sent a messenger to Rabbi Judah Ha-Nasi. The messenger carried a vital question. "The Imperial Treasury is rapidly being depleted. Can you advise me on how I might increase it?"

Rabbi Judah did not respond. Instead, he took the messenger into his garden and began to work. He uprooted large turnips and planted much smaller turnips in their place. Then he did the same with beets and radishes.

The messenger, seeing that the rabbi would not answer, requested that he write a letter, but the rabbi said that no letter was needed.

The messenger returned to the emperor.

"Did Rabbi Judah give you a letter for me?" the emperor asked.

"No."

"Did he say anything to you?"

"No, he didn't do that either."

"Did he do anything?"

"Yes, he led me into his garden, dug up large vegetables, and planted smaller ones in their place."

"Then I understand his advice," said the emperor.

The emperor then dismissed his governors and tax collectors. They were replaced with less well-known but more honest officials. Before very long, the Imperial Treasury was replenished.

(4) King Artaban of Parthea one day sent a gift to Rabbi Judah. The gift was an exquisite and quite expensive pearl. The king's only request was that the rabbi send a gift in return that was of equal value. Rabbi Judah sent the king a mezuzah.

Artaban was displeased with the gift and came to confront the rabbi. "What is this? I sent you a priceless gift and you return this trifle?"

The rabbi said, "Both objects are valuable, but they are very different. You sent me something that I have to guard, while I sent you something that will guard you."

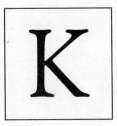

KAFKA, FRANZ *(1883–1924)*
German author.

Kafka felt intense, unrelenting loneliness in his life until he reached the age of 19 and found a friend.

One day Kafka decided to enter the Reading and Lecture Hall for German Students at his university. The place was really a clubhouse set aside for Zionists—those Jews who called their nationality "Zionist" before they called it "German" or "Czech." Kafka was not certain whether they would even let him in. He didn't even feel extraordinarily Jewish. (In his diaries is an entry, "What have I in common with Jews? I have hardly anything in common with myself.")

Summoning his courage, he went in. Nobody challenged his Zionist credentials. This was his first effort at seeking out the friendship of others. He sat around the table intently following the debate, at first venturing only a single, small observation during the course of the entire meeting. He made some jokes and almost apologetically added his comment.

It took several weeks, but Kafka began to notice that others actually listened to him. More than once he saw other conversations stop so that its participants could hear what he had to say. This was extraordinary to a young man whose family—especially his father—had told him that he had no worthwhile opinions. Once he even heard a student remarking to another, "That Herr Kafka, he's hit the nail on the head again."

One of the members of this club who most admired Kafka was a student named Max Brod. The two soon began to talk. It was an intense relief for Kafka finally to find someone who was willing to listen to him. All his ideas and thoughts came rushing out. Kafka realized more than once how intense his conversational barrage had been. He sometimes paused in the middle of a street to offer an apology, and Brod would always laugh in response.

In 1917, after he was diagnosed as having tuberculosis, Kafka gave all his unpublished manuscripts to Brod with instructions that they were all to be burned. Brod could not bring himself to do so because of the quality of the work.

After Kafka's death, Brod began to publish such literary masterpieces as *The Trial* and *The Castle*.

KAHANE, MEIR (1932–   )
Rabbi, American-born Israeli Knesset member. Founder of the Jewish Defense League.

Rabbi Meir Kahane is one of the most controversial figures in Israel's history. His plan to, if necessary, force the emigration of Arabs from Israel and the administered territories has aroused some passionate support and engendered much equally passionate hostility. These conflicting views met head-on in the city of Afula in 1985.

In July of that year, two teachers, Yossi Eliyahu, age 35, and Leah Almakais, age 19, were murdered in Gilboa. Three Arab shepherds were arrested and confessed to the crime.

Rabbi Kahane appeared in Afula in an atmosphere of anger and confusion. Many of Afula's 20,000 citizens were Sephardic Jews; many Arabs worked in the city. Afula was to become a symbol of how Kahane's views were acted out in real life.

Kahane himself never got out of his car in Afula. His young followers chanted that Kahane was their leader. They began to throw stones at Arab-owned automobiles. Arabs were attacked in the market area. The felafel stands that were run by Arabs were overturned. Cars with license plates from the administered territories were stopped and damaged.

Arabs stayed away from the town for the next several days while the still-angry Jews continued to loot some of the Arab-owned stores.

Rabbi Kahane was barred from entering the city, but his initial presence and the actions precipitated by the murder of the teachers and the rabbi's fiery arguments became important news stories in Israel. Kahane's proposal to throw out the Arabs had been heard by all of Israel.

KALIR, NATHAN (1824–1886)
Banker and community leader.

To remind him to pray regularly, Nathan Kalir's wife had to resort to trickery.

Prior to becoming the first Jewish deputy in the Austrian parliament, Kalir had been a banker from Brody. Kalir was an observant Jew, but his arduous political duties in Vienna sometimes made him neglect putting on his prayer shawl and tefillin to pray.

His wife heard about this behavior, and so when he came home on a vacation, she asked him whether there was truth to the rumor. He assured her that he remained an observant Jew. Before he returned, his wife packed all the clothes he would need for the upcoming cold winter.

When winter arrived, however, Kalir could not find his much-needed heavy underwear. He wrote to his wife, inquiring about its location. She wrote back: "Pray to God, and your wish shall be granted." Kalir immediately understood. He opened the bag which held his prayer shawl and tefillin and found the missing clothing.

KAPLAN, MORDECAI M. (1881–1983)
Rabbi and founder of Reconstructionism.

Some of Rabbi Kaplan's theological ideas—especially his denial of the existence of a supernatural Being and his attack on the idea of chosenness—often provoked controversy, but never more than in 1945. In that year Kaplan and various colleagues from the Reconstructionist movement had finished editing the movement's Sabbath prayer book. The book's publication was greeted with an uproar of criticism, especially from the Orthodox movement. The Union of Orthodox Rabbis (Agudat Harabbanim) organized a protest meeting. At the meeting the rabbis issued a herem, excommunicating Kaplan. Afterward, there was a public burning of the prayer book, although Agudat Harabbanim later denied responsibility for that.

The Reconstructionists defended themselves. They issued a pamphlet denouncing the herem. The Conservative movement, which Kaplan had served with great distinction for many years, seemed at first to be on his side. The Rabbinical Assembly of America condemned the Agudat's actions.

Both sides continued the struggle through the summer of 1945. Then an extraordinary split in Conservative ranks became public. In October, three professors from the Jewish Theological Seminary—Louis Ginzberg, Alexander Marx, and Saul Lieberman—broke ranks with their seminary colleagues. This was the first time in the seminary's history that internal differences were aired in a public arena. The three professors wrote a letter in *Hadoar*, the Hebrew-language weekly. They opposed the imposition of the herem, essentially because it could not be enforced, but attacked Kaplan as "not learned in the Law" and advised the rabbi to turn to homiletics instead.

Public debate eventually died down, but Dr. Kaplan's relations with a significant segment of traditional Judaism were never fully repaired.

KAUFMAN, GEORGE S. (1889–1961)
American playwright and wit.

(1) Kaufman often entered into witty conversations with various writers and artists at the Algonquin Hotel. Among those who ate lunch at the famous Round Table were the half-Jewish Dorothy Parker, who had conflicting feelings about her Jewish heritage, Alexander Woolcott, who pretended to be anti-Semitic, and Kaufman, who was proud of being Jewish.

One day at lunch, Woolcott loudly called Kaufman "you Christ-killer." Kaufman rose and told the assembled group. "I will not stay here and listen to any more slurs on my race. I am now leaving this table and the Algonquin." He turned to leave, paused for a second, turned back around, stared at Dorothy Parker, who had remained silent, and said, "And I hope Mrs. Parker will follow me – halfway."

(2) Moss Hart, a playwright who often cowrote with Kaufman, was thinking about transforming the Laura Z. Hobson novel *Gentlemen's Agreement* into a film. The book, about a Gentile who pretends to be a Jew in order to examine anti-Semitism, had gotten considerable publicity. Hart asked Kaufman about the book. Kaufman said, "I don't have to pay $3.50 to find out what it feels like to be a Jew."

KOCH, EDWARD I. (1924–   )
American politician, mayor of New York.

President Jimmy Carter's re-election campaign in 1980 against Ronald Reagan proved politically troublesome for Mayor Koch. He was, of course, a loyal Democrat, but he was also an avid opponent of American policies toward Israel that he thought were not in the best interests of either country. In particular, he wanted assurances that all anti-Israel United Nations votes would be vetoed, and he wanted the US Embassy to be moved from Tel Aviv to West Jerusalem.

One day in October of 1980, as the campaign drew to a heated close, Koch received a telephone call from William Safire, the well-known Washington columnist for the *New York Times*. Safire reminded the mayor about a lunch with former secretary of state Cyrus Vance. Koch had sought a political reconciliation with Vance after the two had fought over American Middle East policy. Koch said that he recalled the lunch. Safire continued. He wanted a confirmation of a rumor. Supposedly during that lunch, someone had asked Vance whether Carter would "sell out" Israel after he was re-elected, and Vance had responded affirmatively. Safire wanted the mayor to either confirm or deny the rumor. The mayor said that he couldn't do that because otherwise people would stop having lunch with him.

Safire, ever the undaunted journalist, then asked Koch whether he knew the Washington game called "wave off." Koch had not heard of it. Safire then explained the rules of the game: A trusted reporter would come to someone and discuss a story, but one he doesn't want to pursue without confirmation; the reporter discusses the story and if it is not true, the listener is supposed to say "wave off." Koch said that he couldn't wave Safire off the story. Safire appreciated the candor and hung up the telephone to continue working on the politically sensitive story.

That afternoon Koch refused to appear with President Carter before Jewish audiences. Koch knew that refusal followed by the Safire column would be devastating. Perhaps because of that, Koch felt an obligation to Vance to alert him about the story that was about to appear in Safire's column. With some difficulty, he got through to Vance and told him the story.

Vance was adamant. He wanted the mayor to call Safire and tell the columnist that Vance had not said that Carter would sell out Israel. Koch knew that the lunch had taken place three months earlier and that Vance was honest. Koch agreed to make the call, feeling sorry he had ever learned the rules of "wave off."

Safire was understandably upset. He told the mayor that the story had already been written and that it would be difficult to rewrite it before the deadline for the column. Nevertheless, Safire did rewrite the column. It appeared in the October 15 issue of the *Times* without reference to Vance's supposed assertion. Even without it, the column was devastating in its attack on the soon-to-be ex-president.

KOHEN, SABBATAI (*seventeenth century*)
Rabbi.

A search was being conducted in Vilna for a cantor. Rabbi Moses Rivkes was one of the candidates for the post. Unfortunately, Rabbi Rivkes's voice was considered by many to be inferior to those of previous town cantors. The leaders of the community came to Sabbatai Kohen with the problem. Rabbi Kohen announced that he was in favor of Rabbi Rivkes, saying, "There are five qualities necessary in a good cantor: He must be married, be learned in Jewish law, be filled with the love of God, have a good reputation, and have a good voice. Rabbi Rivkes has the first four qualities. It's true that he does not have a wonderful singing voice, but, tell me, where is it that you can find a perfect individual?"

KOHUT, ALEXANDER (1842–1894)
Rabbi and scholar.

Rabbi Kohut was widely known as an extraordinarily hard-working student. He studied at Breslau with Rabbi Zecharias Frankel, one of the intellectual founders of Conservative Judaism. The usual length of time required to complete the studies was between seven and ten years. Kohut, however, completed his studies and received his rabbinical diploma in approximately five years. Another student went to complain to Rabbi Frankel. The student said, "I have been in this institution for ten years and I have no diploma, while Kohut gets his in five."

"You are mistaken," Rabbi Frankel answered. "Kohut has actually been here for over seven years."

"How is that possible?" the student asked. "I was here when he began his studies in the seminary. That was exactly five years and four months ago."

Frankel answered, "Ah, but Kohut turned his nights into days for the purpose of study. If you had been as serious a student as he has been, I would gladly credit you with twenty years of study."

KOHUT, REBEKAH (1864–1951)
American educator and community leader.

Rebekah Kohut, daughter of a Hungarian rabbi, married the well-known rabbi Alexander Kohut in 1887. The rabbi, twenty-two years older than his wife, was then a widower who had eight children. After his death seven years later, Rebekah was left to support the family. She relied on the advice and help of friends of the family.

Rebekah had spent hour after hour by her husband's bed as he lay ill. To pass the grueling and difficult days, she would write lecture notes about literature.

After her husband's death, it struck Rebekah one day that she could support the family if she delivered the lectures based on the notes. It was then very popular to have what were known as parlor lectures given in the home of a wealthy and powerful host before an invited audience of friends and acquaintances.

Excited by the prospect of supporting her family, Rebekah read over the notes. She realized that they needed additional work, so she went to the Columbia University library, where she did additional reading and revising.

Right after Rabbi Kohut's death, Jacob H. Schiff, a well-known Jewish financier and philanthropist, had cabled Rebekah from overseas telling her to wait for his return before making any decisions. Schiff visited the family on the afternoon of Rosh Hashanah. Rebekah told him of her financial straits and her plan to deliver the lectures. She wanted permission to deliver them in Schiff's home under his wife's patronage. But Schiff did not encourage her plans.

Several days later, however, Rebekah got a note from Mrs. Schiff, who agreed to have the lectures given in the drawing room of the Schiff home.

The lectures proved to be an enormous success, drawing as many as 200 to 300 women. The lectures also provided many valuable introductions for Rebekah Kohut and led to her preeminence in Jewish life and education.

KOLLEK, TEDDY *(1911–   )*
Israeli politician, mayor of Jerusalem.

Before he became mayor of Jerusalem, Teddy Kollek was involved in a series of important activities on behalf of his nation. One of the most important was raising money to pay for weapons that Zionist leaders couldn't purchase on the open market. The leaders of the Czech government were willing to provide desperately needed weapons, but they required a large, immediate payment.

Kollek was put in charge of raising the money. He met in New York at the Hotel Fourteen with a few friends. They were racing against time, searching desperately for someone wealthy enough who could help. One of those present, textile merchant Joseph Shulman, knew William Levitt. At the time, Levitt was mass-producing houses in Levittown, on Long Island. Shulman arranged a meeting between Kollek and Levitt at the Levitt offices on Northern Boulevard in Manhasset.

Kollek, then as later, did not have time for small talk. "We need money," he told the builder. "I can't tell you what it's for. But if you'll lend us the money, the provisional government of the state of Israel will give you a note and pay you back in a year."

Kollek was asking for $1 million. He offered no collateral, no interest, no certainty that the money would ever be returned.

Levitt gave him the money on the spot.

KOOK, ABRAHAM ISAAC *(1865–1935)*
First Ashkenazic chief rabbi of the modern land of Israel.

(1) Rabbi Kook was widely noted for his tolerance toward the non-Orthodox Jewish pioneers who built the Holy Land.

He was once asked by a reporter why he didn't protest the opening of motion picture houses and theaters in the land of Israel, since it clearly stated in the Talmud that "he who frequents circuses and theaters has no share in the world to come."

Rabbi Kook smiled and told the reporter, "There is another passage in the Talmud that says that in the Messianic era, all the theaters will be converted into synagogues. Well, then, the more theaters now, the more synagogues when Messiah comes."

(2) During his final visit to the Holy Land, a philanthropist called on Rabbi Kook to discuss with him the deplorable economic conditions of the Jews in Jerusalem. The philanthropist, Nathan Straus, noted the high unemployment and gave 100 pounds to relieve the hardship. Rabbi Kook thanked the wealthy American but asked to be permitted to tell Straus a little story. Straus agreed to hear the tale.

"There is an old story about a prince," began Rabbi Kook. "The prince had been hunting in a dense forest and lost his way. He wandered around aimlessly for several hours until he chanced upon a dirty hut in which there lived a poor woodchopper and his family. The prince announced his identity and said that he was quite hungry. The woodchopper fed the prince some bread and hard-boiled eggs. After eating, the now-satisfied prince asked what the cost of the meal would be. The woodchopper said, "The meal costs 1,000 pieces of silver."

The astonished prince asked, "Why do you charge so much? After all, you only served me ordinary eggs."

"Yes, that is true," admitted the woodchopper. "But you are so special that the price should be special."

Straus listened to the story and understood its point. He gave the rabbi a much larger gift for the poor Jews.

KORCZAK, JANOSZ (1878–1942)
Teacher and head of a Jewish orphanage.

Janosz Korczak trained as a physician, but he became especially interested in helping poor children. He wrote several books decrying the conditions under which the poor lived. In 1911 he became the head of a Jewish orphanage in Warsaw. He developed a system at the orphanage under which the children were self-governing. They produced a newspaper which appeared as a weekly supplement in *Nasz Przeglad,* a daily Zionist paper.

Korczak visited the land of Israel several times and was impressed by kibbutz educational methods. He considered settling in the Holy Land, but he would not abandon the orphans.

The orphanage was resettled within the Warsaw Ghetto in 1940, after the Nazi invasion of Poland. The Nazis gave a deportation order in 1942.

Korczak, who had refused numerous offers of escape, was with his children on Wednesday morning, August 5, 1942. Ukrainian police surrounded the house in which the orphans lived. Jewish policemen then came into the courtyard.

The police shouted, "Jews get out! Quickly, quickly!" Korczak had not told the 200 children about the deportation order. They had been told that they would be going on a picnic in the country that day, so they were well dressed, but they were surprised to have their breakfast interrupted. The children walked out in an orderly fashion and lined up in fives. Korczak came out carrying a green flag—the orphanage's emblem.

Korczak walked to the head of the group. Although he was weak with a heart ailment, he was determined, even at the end, to lead his children with dignity. The children were pulled, hit with rifles, and berated as they marched toward the cattle trucks. A 5-year-old girl had trouble walking, so Korczak picked her up. Some of the children sang.

When the group reached the assembly area, Korczak was called off to the side. He was offered a final chance to be released if he would abandon the orphans. Korczak flatly refused.

Korczak and his children were taken to Treblinka, where they were killed.

KOVLER, YANKELE (nineteenth century)
Russian rabbi.

Rabbi Kovler was widely known for his wisdom and his deep sense of justice. He was often called upon to settle legal disputes. His fairness was so admired that Gentiles frequently asked him to settle their disputes instead of using the Russian civil courts.

One day, a non-Jewish Russian merchant asked Rabbi Yankele to settle a complaint. The Russian charged that a Jew named Berka Aaronovitch Schmue-levitch had borrowed ten rubles from him, but now that the debt was due, he was simply denying that he had borrowed the money.

Rabbi Kovler called in Berka, who again denied that he owed the Russian any money. The rabbi turned to the merchant. "Are there any witnesses?"

"No," said the Russian.

"So," said the rabbi. "It seems that I will have to determine the truth for myself." After asking each of the men several questions, the rabbi concluded in his own mind that the Russian was telling the truth, and that Berka only dared to deny the debt because there were no witnesses to the transaction.

Rabbi Yankele then spoke to Berka in Yiddish so the Russian wouldn't understand. "You're lucky there are no witnesses. If you continue to deny the debt, there's no way he can prosecute you. You'll be able to keep the ten rubles."

"You're very wise, Rabbi," said Berka. "And I'm pretty wise, too. I know what I'm doing. I've thought the same thing from the moment I got the money."

The rabbi then grew stern. "Berka Schmuelevitch, you have admitted this debt to me. You must now pay this man immediately."

Berka was shocked, but he paid.

The Russian merchant was entirely satisfied with Jewish justice.

KOVNER, ABBA (1918–1987)
Lithuanian resistance fighter, Israeli poet.

After Abba Kovner arrived in Israel, he found himself feeling alienated from all he encountered. He joined a kibbutz and journeyed to the Western Wall, but in his mind he still felt himself a partisan fighting near the extermination camps in which his parents, friends, and other fighters had died.

One day a man came over and tugged at Kovner's sleeve. He asked Kovner to join nine other people to make a minyan. Kovner immediately put on something to cover his head and joined them. At the moment he prayed with them, he finally felt that he belonged, that he counted, that other Jews needed him.

Many years later, Kovner developed an idea for the Diaspora Museum, now in Tel Aviv. For the museum, he designed one special corner, which he termed "the minyan." In this corner there are waxed figures which represent a variety of Jewish communities praying together. Through their prayer, through a spiritual need for one another, they form one community. But there is something odd, too, about this minyan. There are only nine wax figures. Kovner was asked why, when every Jew knows that ten people are needed for a minyan, there were only nine wax figures. Kovner answered that the absence of the tenth figure was a call to the viewer, a call to join them, to be counted, to let the viewer know that the minyan cannot go on without the viewer's help.

KRANTZ, JACOB (1741–1804)
Rabbi, Preacher of Dubnow, and teller of parables.

Rabbi Elijah, the Gaon of Vilna, was deeply impressed by the ability of his friend, Rabbi Jacob Krantz, to have a parable ready for every problem he encountered. One day, Rabbi Elijah decided to ask how such a feat was possible.

Rabbi Jacob answered him by saying, "I will respond to your question about parables by using a parable. Once a nobleman decided that his son should be the very best musketeer. He therefore entered his son into a military academy to learn the martial skills. For five years the young man studied and learned and practiced until he was the most accomplished of musketeers.

"He graduated from the academy with a gold medal. While on his way home, he entered a village in order to rest. While standing on a street, he happened to notice a stable wall. There were the chalk marks of a target on the wall. Each target had a bullet hole at its exact center. Astonished at the skill of the marksman, the young man determined to meet the accomplished shooter. He asked throughout the village and finally discovered who had done the shooting—a small Jewish boy dressed as a beggar.

"The nobleman faced the child. 'Who taught you to shoot so well?' he asked.

"The boy answered, 'Let me explain. First I shoot the bullets at the wall. Only then do I take a piece of chalk and draw circles around the holes.'

"This is what I do," said the Preacher of Dubnow. "I don't search for the parable to fit the subject under discussion. Rather, I learn as many parables as I can. Eventually the right subject will come along for every parable."

KURZWEIL, ARTHUR (1951-   )
American author, editor, and genealogist.

(1) Arthur Kurzweil's first trip to the Jewish division of the New York Public Library took place in the spring of 1970. Kurzweil was there on a search that he himself doubted would be successful. Since childhood, he had been told a few stories about Dobromil, the shtetl in Galicia from which his family had emigrated. The town had evoked images of home in Kurzweil's imagination.

So there he was in the library, determined to search for information about the town. He stood in the doorway, surveying the wide variety of Jews in the room. Kurzweil crossed over to the card catalog and opened a drawer. He ran his fingers through the cards until he came across one with the heading "Dobromil." A book was described on the card. The reality of the book's existence was nearly overwhelming. Kurzweil filled out the necessary forms and sat down at a library table to wait for the book. It finally arrived. It was a Memorial Book, a work prepared by former residents of a particular place. Hundreds were produced after the Holocaust to preserve memories of each place and, when possible, to list the victims of the Holocaust so that their names would not be lost to history. Kurzweil flipped through the book, returned to the first page, with its photograph of Dobromil's main street, and simply stared, trying somehow to grasp the town.

Finally, Kurzweil went through the book a page at a time, examining the photographs. Again, he did not expect to find much. His father had left the town as a boy, and his grandfather, he knew, had been a tinsmith. Other relatives had similarly ordinary occupations.

Suddenly, there, in a group photo, was his great-grandfather, Avrahum Abusch, after whom Kurzweil was named. The young man began to shake and then ran to the librarian to show her the picture. He recalled that she wasn't quite as excited as he was.

After that day, Kurzweil often returned to the library to look at the book.

One day he decided to call the authors of the book. They were listed as members of the Book Committee of the Dobromiler Society. The society was in New York, so Kurzweil assumed that the authors also lived there. He searched through various telephone books and finally found the number of one of the authors, Philip Frucht.

Kurzweil called him, identified himself, and asked whether Frucht had known the Kurzweil family. Frucht thought carefully, but there was no sign of recognition. Kurzweil persisted, however, because of the picture of his great-grandfather. Finally, an idea hit him. His great-grandfather's Yiddish name was Yudl, and so he asked if Frucht had known Yudl the tinsmith. Frucht became excited. He asked Kurzweil to repeat the family name. Kurzweil repeated it, pronouncing it as he always did—"kerzwhile." Frucht, however, provided the original pronunciation—"koortzvile"—and suggested that that was why he had not recognized the name.

Kurzweil's experiences at the library were the beginning of the recovery of his past, and, in a way, the recovery of the past for all Jews.

(2) Arthur Kurzweil was an almost daily traveler on the F train. He rode it back and forth from his home in the Flatbush section of Brooklyn to his Manhattan office. It was a friendly enough subway ride; at certain hours, he recalls, there could have been a minyan in the passenger car.

One evening while going home on the F train, Kurzweil was reading *The Thirteen Petalled Rose*, by Adin Steinsaltz. (Steinsaltz is most famous for his on-going new translation, with commentary, of the Babylonian Talmud. *The Thirteen Petalled Rose* is an introduction to Judaism which Kurzweil found so insightful that he reads a chapter a day of the book.)

An elderly Hasid was seated next to Kurzweil on the train. As Kurzweil read, he thought of what one teacher had said in the Talmud: Given the opportunity, a Jew shouldn't travel two cubits without talking about Torah with another Jew. A cubit is equal to the length of the forearm from the elbow to the tip of the middle finger, so Arthur knew that two cubits was not very far, and with the Hasid sitting right next to him, he certainly had the opportunity. The problem, of course, was the rarely broken social rule of not speaking to a stranger on the subway. Nevertheless, buoyed by the talmudic teaching, Kurzweil did speak. He started by holding up the Steinsaltz book and saying, "Excuse me, have you ever seen this book?"

The Hasid said that he hadn't. Then he took the book, looked at it, and said that he never looked at any book that didn't have at least two *haskamahs*. (A *haskamah* is an introduction that approves or recommends a particular book. Seeking such approval for a book began in about the fifteenth century.) Kurzweil noted to himself that the man was reading the *New York Post*, a publication presumably without the required number of *haskamahs*, but he didn't say anything. The Hasid then said that the *haskamah* wasn't so important. He wanted to know what the book was about. Kurzweil then told the man the names of the chapters. He had a specific question in mind and decided to ask it.

In one of the chapters, one on man's soul, Steinsaltz discusses the belief that each letter of the Torah has a corresponding soul, and each soul has a part to play in the world. The soul that has fulfilled its task can wait after the body's death for the perfection of the world. But some souls don't complete their tasks. After death, these souls return to the body of another person to complete their tasks. Kurzweil had been surprised at this passage. He knew that reincarnation was important in some Eastern religions, but as far as he knew, that idea was foreign to Judaism. He decided to ask the Hasid whether Jews actually do believe in reincarnation. The Hasid said that they did, and wondered aloud about the extent of Kurzweil's Jewish education. Kurzweil then spoke of his background and the limited exposure he had had to Jewish learning.

Before Kurzweil got off the train, the Hasid said to him, "You're luckier than I am." Then he continued with his thought. "Every Jew is connected to God by a rope. When the rope breaks, as in your case, after you tie the rope back together you're closer to God than you were before. I'll never be that close."

Kurzweil got off the train at his stop, fully convinced then that it paid to talk about the Torah with other Jews.

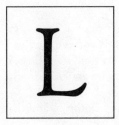

L

LAMM, NORMAN (1927–   )
Orthodox rabbi and president of Yeshiva University.

The following anecdote was provided by Dr. Lamm.

I was invited to speak at services one morning at the Knesset Eliahoo Synagogue in the Fort section of Bombay. Services began at the ungodly hour of 7:00 A.M.

Immediately after I was introduced by the president of the congregation and had ascended the pulpit, I heard sirens and, because they sounded identical to those of fire engines in New York City, I imagined there was a fire nearby. I complimented the congregation and then began to speak—whereupon I heard the sirens again, and imagined that more fire engines were being called out to extinguish the blaze. When I reached my peroration, the sirens grew in intensity, and I feared that the conflagration was serious and must be nearby. When I concluded my address, the sirens came on again, even louder, and I was truly frightened. As I descended the pulpit, I asked the president immediately, "Where is the fire?"

He looked at me rather quizzically and explained that he had no idea what I was talking about. "But if there is no fire," I said to him, "why all those sirens?"

He smiled and, pointing to the ladies sitting cross-legged on the floor of the balcony above, said that that was the traditional sound that Indian ladies make to signify their approval of a speaker.

LANDAU, EZEKIEL (1713–1793)
Authority on Jewish law; rabbi of Prague and author of Noda
B'Yehudah.

(1) Rabbi Landau made semi-annual trips to communities outside Prague to
settle religious disputes and render guidance. His driver liked to have fun, and
one day he told the rabbi, "My driving takes more skill than your work does. I
could settle the religious arguments as well as you can, but you couldn't do my
job."

The rabbi agreed to exchange jobs. The two switched clothing, and the
rabbi began driving.

In the first village to which they came, the "rabbi" was met by a committee
of prominent citizens. They took him to a house where he dined. After the meal,
they confronted him with a difficult problem that could not be solved even by
the brightest of the villagers. The "rabbi" considered the question and shrugged
his shoulders. "You have asked me a very silly question. Even my driver can
answer that. Here he is—ask him."

(2) A Jew from Prague traveled to a distant town in order to teach. As Passover
approached, he wanted to send one hundred gold crowns to his wife. Unfortunately, there were no postal connections in his small town, so he asked a
merchant going to Prague if he would bring the money to the teacher's wife. The
merchant said that he did not wish to take the money because there was a
chance he might lose it. The teacher promised to pay five crowns as a fee. The
merchant said, "Five crowns is not enough. Since, however, your wife is in need,
in this case I will deliver it provided you write to your wife that I may take as
much money as I wish to for my efforts."

The teacher agreed to this arrangement. When the merchant arrived in
Prague, however, he told the teacher's wife that he intended to give her only one
crown out of the hundred. The woman was enraged. The two were to settle their
dispute before Rabbi Landau.

The rabbi listened carefully to both sides and said, "I have decided that
you, the merchant, may keep only one crown and must give ninety-nine to this
woman. Her husband's note reads 'I am sending one hundred crowns with the
understanding that the bearer is to give to my wife as much as he wishes.' Since
you wish ninety-nine crowns, that is the exact amount you must give to this
woman."

(3) A new mayor was elected in Prague with the strong support of Jewish voters.
The Jews were not aware that the man secretly held anti-Semitic feelings.
Believing the mayor-elect to be a noble man, the Jewish community organized a

dance and banquet for him. Rabbi Landau was one of the important guests invited to the event.

The mayor-elect decided to ridicule the Jews while at the dance. He said to the rabbi, "Aren't the Jews really fond of dancing? It must be a tradition because when their ancestors built the golden calf in the desert, they not only bowed down to it in worship, but danced around it."

The rabbi immediately saw the true nature of the man who would soon lead the town, and he answered: "Why, yes, your honor, it is a tradition. Whenever the Jews select an ox or a calf for a leader, they begin to dance."

(4) Two men came to see Rabbi Landau to seek a charitable contribution. The rabbi asked them how much they needed. The men said, "We need 1,000 gulden immediately to help the people." The rabbi left the room and returned with a leather case. He showed the men that the case was filled with gold coins. "Here," said the rabbi. "I've got 990 gold pieces. You must get the other 10 pieces you need from people in your city."

The men looked at Rabbi Landau in astonishment. "Rabbi," one began, evidently unsure of how to proceed. "It is a mitzvah to give, and you are performing a great mitzvah. But why do you start such a mitzvah and stop almost at the end?"

"You are both learned," answered the rabbi. "You should know why. It is wrong to give and by so doing deprive others of the joy of giving. I want to help, but I also want to allow other Jews a chance to be charitable."

(5) Rabbi Landau was a rationalist, widely known for his protestations of certain practices. One of the practices he found most objectionable was the use of amulets. Some Jews believed that amulets possessed magic powers that aided in healing.

Even his deeply held dislike of such folk beliefs did not prevent Rabbi Landau from acting with wisdom when circumstances required it.

A group of Jewish leaders from Prague had come to the rabbi with a problem. "There is a woman in our city who is a good woman. She has helped many people, but she has now acquired a strange belief. She told us that she is extremely ill and that only an amulet you give to her will cure that illness. She says that she will die without the amulet. We believe that that is true because she refuses to see any physician. We know of your distaste for amulets, but we have come to ask for your help."

Rabbi Landau went to his study and found a plain piece of leather, then popular for use in making amulets. The rabbi took a blank piece of paper and sealed the amulet in it. "Here," he said to the men. "Give this amulet to the woman. Tell her that she must wear it around her neck for a month. After thirty days, she is to take it off. If the letters on the leather have disappeared, it will be a sign that she is cured."

The men did as they were told. The woman also followed the rabbi's orders. At the end of thirty days, she unwrapped the leather. The letters, which in fact had never been there, seemed now to be gone. She was convinced of her health, and she eventually recovered.

LAZARUS, EMMA *(1849–1887)*
American poet.

Emma Lazarus is most famous for the poem she wrote that appears on the Statue of Liberty. Ironically, that was one poem she had been very reluctant to write.

A friend of Emma's named Constance Harrison had begun to raise money to purchase a pedestal for the statue. Harrison had especially been interested in attracting original literary manuscripts that could then be sold at auction to raise the much-needed funds. She approached such well-known writers as Walt Whitman, Bret Harte, and John Greenleaf Whittier.

In the fall of 1883, Harrison went to Emma and asked for a new poem. Emma sarcastically responded that she could not simply write a poem on demand. But Harrison did not give up. She asked Emma to think of the statue's torch held out for the Russian Jewish refugees, about whom Emma felt so deeply.

A few days later, Emma gave Constance Harrison the sonnet "The New Colossus," which was eventually engraved as a memorial plaque and placed on the pedestal of the Statue of Liberty in 1903. The poem, in response to Harrison's call to remember the refugees, includes these memorably stirring lines:

> Give me your tired, your poor
> Your huddled masses yearning to breathe free,
> The wretched refuse of your teeming shore.
> Send these, the homeless, tempest-tost to me,
> I lift my lamp beside the golden door!

LEBENSOHN, MICAH JOSEPH *(1828–1852)*
Major Hebrew poet of the Enlightenment era.

Lebensohn's spirit of rebellion against traditional Jewish beliefs became evident at an early age.

Once, as a boy in Vilna, he was visiting with his father at the home of

Matthew Strashun, then famous for his talmudic erudition and his philan-
thropy. He asked the young boy a variety of questions and was amazed at his
clever responses. Finally, Strashun kidded the boy, "Micah Joseph, you are so
bright, I'd like to have you around me constantly. Indeed, I believe I shall create
a special job for you. I want you to remain standing on the promenade on the
roof and keep an eye out for the arrival of the Messiah. Just as soon as you
discover that he has arrived, you are to tell me immediately. I will pay you fifteen
rubles a month for this job."

The boy considered the proposal and then said, "The salary you offer isn't
very generous, but on the other hand, the position is permanent."

LEVENSON, SAM (1914–1980)
American humorist.

Sam Levenson enjoyed recalling the humor that came with growing up in a
poor, immigrant family. He was especially fond of his mother, who prided herself
on being able to feed any unexpected company. To do this, she kept a pot full of
chicken legs always going on the stove. The family was unable to afford whole
chickens, but the legs were readily available.

Then came Mama Levenson's greatest challenge. One day, Uncle Louis
and Aunt Lena and their eleven children dropped in unannounced.

Mama was in a panic. She simply didn't have enough legs ready. Her
honor was at stake. Hastily, she called her own children into the bedroom and
told them, "Children, do me a favor. Say you don't like chicken."

The children were understanding and sympathetic. They went back in
and dutifully refused all the chicken when the relatives offered to share.

Finally it was time for dessert. The same problem arose, but this time
Mama Levenson didn't have to call the children into the bedroom. Instead, at
the table, she said to one and all: "Now, all the children who wouldn't eat the
chicken don't get any dessert."

LEVI YITZHAK OF BERDITCHEV (c. 1740–1810)
Rabbi and Hasidic leader.

(1) The rabbi saw a man eating on Tisha B'av. Famous for his concern for people,
the rabbi decided to speak to the man.

"You have probably forgotten that today is Tisha B'av."

"No, I know what day it is."

The rabbi paused. "Then I guess you don't know that it is forbidden to eat on Tisha B'av."

"I know," said the man, obviously enjoying himself at the rabbi's expense.

But the rabbi would not be put off. "I imagine you are sick, and your doctor has told you not to fast."

"I'm healthy as can be."

The rabbi looked at the man. "You see how wonderful our people are? A Jew would rather admit he's a sinner than to tell a lie."

(2) The rabbi was visiting a hotel. The Jewish merchants who were staying in the hotel had come to the town for a fair. One morning the rabbi heard them racing through their prayers before they rushed to the fair. That evening he invited the merchants to his room. When they arrived, he spoke unintelligibly for several moments. The merchants were mystified. Finally, one said, "Rabbi, we appreciate being invited by you, but we can't understand your words."

The rabbi responded in words that were all too clear: "Now you can imagine how the Almighty feels when you mumble your prayers in the morning."

One shocked merchant spoke up. "Master, a little baby mumbles also. Nobody understands when he coos and cries, but his mother understands. We are the children of God, and the Lord understands us no matter how we speak."

"You are absolutely right," said the rabbi. "Please forgive me."

LEVIN, MEYER (1905-1981)
American author.

Levin knew from an early age that he wanted to become a writer. One day, having arrived home from his Hebrew class, the 9-year-old Levin sat down at the kitchen table, put his notebook on the oilcloth covering, and began to write a story. After dinner, Levin was standing with his back to the stove, which his mother had polished that afternoon. A kettle was steaming on the stove. Levin decided that this was the most appropriate moment to announce to his family that he wanted to be a writer. He opened the notebook and almost acted out the story he had written.

The story was about an innocent man wrongly jailed. The man escaped from the prison and hid in a car, intending to get to the city to prove he was innocent. The car was driven by a blonde, American young woman. (In later years Levin provided this analysis of his youthful story: The prison was his Jewishness, and the woman was a fantasy figure of the United States, a land which would free him; he wished to be reborn as an unhyphenated American.)

After the story was told, both parents expressed concern about their son's vocational choice. They told him that they would not stand in his way, but his mother especially was concerned about whether he could earn a living as a writer. Levin turned to his father and suggested that some writers made huge amounts of money, especially if they sold their stories to the movies.

The parents were afraid to tell the boy not to do what he wished. They considered themselves "greenhorns" and inferior even to a child brought up in the United States.

Levin became a writer.

LEVIN, SHAMARYAHU *(1867-1935)*
Zionist leader, orator, and author.

(1) Shamaryahu Levin tried to learn to blow the shofar when he was a child. It was just before the High Holy Days, and the boy was anxious. The shammes had taught as well as he could, and the boy had spent countless hours practicing, but he still could not do it. One day a Polish, non-Jewish peasant came to the Levin house, listened to the boy's feeble attempts, and blew a mighty sound.

The boy ran to the shammes. "How come I as a Jew practice and struggle and can barely produce a whimper, and this Gentile peasant, without any preparation, produces so mighty a sound?"

The shammes put his arm around the boy and said, "My son, the trick is not to blow the shofar; the trick is to listen to it."

(2) Levin met Julius Rosenwald, who tried to impress Levin. The philanthropist told the great Zionist of the new Rosenwald house in Chicago, which was named Tel Aviv.

"It would have been a lot better," Levin said, "if you had built a house in Tel Aviv and named it Chicago."

LEVIN, ZEVI HIRSCH *(1721-1800)*
Rabbi in England and Germany.

While serving in the city of Mannheim, Rabbi Levin grew close to the duke of the city. The duke was an intellectually curious man and studied Jewish customs carefully. One day, the duke asked Rabbi Levin this question: "I have for you a most puzzling religious question. At your beautiful ceremony, the Passover seder, one of your young children asks why that night is so different from all other nights. But why do you ask it on this night? The family is all around the table eating. It is not so different. Why not instead have the child ask such a probing question at your Succot holiday? There, at least, you leave your house, you live in some kind of hut. Is this not really the different night, eating and sleeping apart from what you normally do?"

Rabbi Levin answered him. "You ask a good question, but you do not know the soul of the Jew. It is Succot that is normal and Passover that is different. You see, Jews live in exile from their holy land. They suffer poverty and deprivation. They fear for their lives. They are persecuted to the four corners of the earth. At Succot, therefore, when they live outdoors in huts, this exile from their homes is what is sadly normal for the Jews. On Passover, though, the house is beautiful. All the best food is available. People eat and drink as kings and queens do. On Passover, the Jews are free from the worries of the world. That is why the night is so different."

LINDHEIM, IRMA L. *(1886–1978)*
American Zionist and author.

Irma Lindheim had been brought up in a highly assimilated American-Jewish family that was opposed to Zionism.

It was only as a young adult that she encountered Judaism. She was already married, had four children, and had served in the Motor Corps of the United States during World War I.

To enhance her appreciation of culture, Lindheim attended a series of lectures given by one of the leaders of the Ethical Culture movement. The lectures were on the Bible as literature, and the audience was made up mostly of Jewish women.

The lecturer spoke passionately one day about the Book of Job and its literary greatness, ranking it alongside Shakespeare and Goethe. Suddenly, as Lindheim looked on, the speaker turned from a calm teacher into an indignant one. He glared at the class and said, "Should I, a non-Jew, have to reveal to you who are Jews the greatness of your own literature?"

Lindheim felt humiliated and disgraced. She had systematically studied philosophy, history, and other subjects for several years. In that moment of humiliation she suddenly realized that she had neglected (and feared she had unconsciously avoided) Jewish subjects. She was shocked to realize that she had read the Upanishads but not the Bible. It was this disgrace about her own ignorance that propelled Lindheim to learn about her heritage.

That learning eventually led to a deep devotion to and leadership in the Zionist movement.

LURIA, ISAAC (1534–1572)
Rabbi and Kabbalist, known as Ha-Ari, *the lion.*

A pious man lived in Safed. He was so good that some spoke of him as one of the *Lamed-Vav Tzaddikim,* one of the thirty-six righteous people upon whom, according to Rabbi Abaye in the Talmud, God's goodness rests.

The pious man was extremely poor, yet he continued to share whatever food he had with those who were even less fortunate than he was. He endeavored, however, to avoid letting anyone know of his goodness, because he did not wish any praise, fearing that it would make him feel self-righteous.

This pious man was overtaken by illness at Passover. He could no longer continue with his work. His family suffered greatly from hunger. They despaired of purchasing matzoh and wine for the seder. The good man urged his family to remain steadfast in their faith in God; they refused to tell anyone of their situation.

Rabbi Luria was the only resident of Safed to know about this holy Jew. The rabbi determined to help.

Rabbi Luria removed his fine white garments and in their place donned the old clothes of a wandering beggar. He then put on a knapsack and found a walking stick. Wearing this disguise of a traveler, Rabbi Luria made his way to the good man's house.

Rabbi Luria greeted the man in the traditional fashion, "Sholom Aleichem."

The good man's response was also traditional, "Aleichem Sholom." Then the pious, poor Jew said, "May I help you? Is there someone you seek?"

"No, I do not seek anyone. It is only that I do not have a place where I can celebrate the Passover."

"I've got nothing for you, but you are most welcome to stay here."

The "traveler" thanked the man and said, "Here are a hundred dinar for you to prepare the Passover meal."

The good man stood amazed. "What is your name?"

"I am called Rabbi Nissim," said the traveler, who went off to pray while the meal was prepared.

The money was used to purchase all the needed food. The meal was ready, but the good man did not want to begin the seder until the traveler returned from the synagogue.

The traveler never returned.

The pious Jew then remembered that the word *nissim* meant "miracles."

MAIMONIDES, MOSES *(1135–1204)*
Rabbinic authority and philosopher.

(1) While Maimonides was busy working on the *Mishneh Torah*, he learned of the plight of the Yemenite Jews. The Yemenites were like the Marranos of Spain: In public they worshipped the God of their host country, but in private they remained Jews.

There arose in Yemen a Jew who was an apostate. He argued that Mohammed's arrival on earth had been foretold in the Torah, that Islam had replaced Judaism as the true religion, and that only by embracing Islam could the Jews usher in the arrival of the Messiah. The Jews would not listen to the apostate, but this rejection only strengthened the apostate's conviction. Finally, he told the authorities about the Jews' secret synagogues. He warned the Jews that he would destroy them if they did not follow him. Some Jews began to accept the apostate's teachings. This acceptance led Jacob al-Fayumi, a leader of Yemenite Jewry, to write to Maimonides to seek his advice.

Maimonides wrote an *Epistle to the Yemenite Jews* in reply. In it, Maimonides reminded the Yemenites that Jews had often been persecuted in order to get them to break their covenant. He appealed to the Yemenites to stay faithful. After writing the letter, Maimonides showed it to friends and students.

The rabbi from Cairo asked him the most important question: Would Maimonides send the letter under his own name? As his disciples pointed out, in the eyes of the Muslims, the Jews of Yemen were really Muslim. Maimonides's letter could therefore be interpreted as an appeal to a Muslim population to convert to Judaism. Such proselytizing carried the death penalty. When Maimonides said that he intended to send the letter under his own name, the rabbi from Cairo suggested instead that two men should be selected to memorize the letter and then go to Yemen to recite it in the secret synagogue, proclaiming that it indeed came from Maimonides.

Maimonides could not be convinced. "I do not wish to appear immodest, but Jacob al-Fayumi wrote to me . . . because he thought my name might have some influence with the Jews of Yemen. If that is so, I must answer in person."

Maimonides was reminded of the possibility of death by torture. The philospher pondered this and responded, "In Yemen there is a penalty of death by torture merely for being a Jew. Our brothers live with the threat of this penalty every morning when they say their prayer, at their noon meal, and every evening in their synagogues. Should I be so afraid for my life, living in the peace of this city, that I refuse to put on paper how grateful I am for their sacrifice?"

Maimonides sent his letter, which was read in every secret synagogue. The Jews there listened. The apostate was rejected.

(2) Maimonides wished to be buried in the land of Israel.

After his death, a delegation of Egyptians accompanied his coffin. The Jews in the Holy Land met the Egyptians and asked where the Rambam had asked to be buried. The Egyptians replied that no specific instructions had been given. Jews from the various communities then began to engage in a bitter dispute to determine the holy site at which the Rambam would be buried. The people of Jerusalem argued that their city was the spiritual capital of the Jewish people. The people from Hebron argued that the Rambam should be buried near the patriarchs. Finally, all the disputants realized that their wrangling was an insult to the great scholar. They arrived at an unusual compromise. It was decided that they would let the camel carrying the coffin wander freely wherever it chose. Wherever the camel stopped to kneel, that would be the scholar's final resting place.

The camel wandered for several days before finally coming to rest in Tiberias. It was there that the Rambam was interred.

MALBIM, MEIR *(1809–1879)*
Rabbi.

(1) Rabbi Malbim had come to a small town in Rumania to talk before the Jews of the area. The rabbi attended Sabbath morning services. Two things seemed unusual to him. First, he saw that in the synagogue he attended, the worshippers didn't directly kiss the Torah, but rather touched it with their fingers and then brought their fingers to their lips. The second unusual thing he noticed was that all those who were called to the Torah made very generous promises of funds to maintain the synagogue. Rabbi Malbim, surprised at the size of the pledges, asked whether the donors were wealthy. He was told that their pledges were never paid.

It was finally time for the rabbi's sermon. He got up on the bimah and said, "My friends, I see that in this town you kiss with your hands and make donations with your lips. For the sake of Judaism, I beg of you to reverse the order: Kiss with your lips and donate with your hands."

(2) A man decided to have fun with Rabbi Malbim. The man went up to the sage and said, "Rabbi, I have a question for you. Everyone knows that when you see a dangerous dog you should sit down. Jewish tradition says that you must stand up when you see a rabbi. Here's my question: What are you supposed to do if you see a rabbi and a dog at the same time?"

Rabbi Malbim pretended to contemplate the question. "That's a very difficult question to answer, since the response should be decided by the local custom rather than Jewish law. We can learn the local custom, though. Suppose you and I take a walk together, and we shall see just what the people will do."

MANASSEH BEN ISRAEL (1604–1657)
Rabbi and scholar from Amsterdam.

Although Manasseh was a rabbi, he enjoyed very little talmudic authority. His attention centered not on Jewish law, but on the speculative elements of religious thought. Most especially, Manasseh concerned himself with the question of how the arrival of the Messiah could be speeded. His conclusion from reading the Bible was that before the Messiah could arrive, Jews would have to return to their homeland; but before they could do that, they would have to be scattered throughout the world. At that time, England was considered to be the northernmost point on earth, so Manasseh concluded that Jews would have to be readmitted to England from where they had been banished in order that they might be fully scattered throughout the earth.

In 1650, Manasseh published and sent to the British parliament his work "Hope of Israel." Manasseh was aware of the political currents in England. The Puritan party had gained power in 1648. Manasseh carried on a regular correspondence with several Puritan theologians interested in the restoration of Jews to their ancient homeland in Israel. Manasseh was asked to appear before Parliament to speak about his request that Jews be readmitted to England. Unfortunately, a commercial war broke out between England and Holland, delaying any visit. In 1652, the British leader Oliver Cromwell sent Manasseh a passport and an invitation. In 1654, Manasseh asked his son and his brother-in-law to present his petition. (He didn't go himself because he feared that there would be considerable Orthodox pressure and opposition to any human interference with God's unfolding of history.) But Cromwell was not satisfied with the substitutes.

Manasseh finally arrived in London in 1655. He gave his petition and simultaneously promulgated a declaration throughout the country in which he stated his case for Jewish readmittance. In one famous passage in his address to the lord protector, Manasseh wrote: "Men are very prone to hate and despise him that hath ill fortune."

Although Cromwell spoke forcefully for readmittance, there was powerful opposition as well. The opponents made arguments based on centuries-old charges of ritual murders, to which they added such incredible views as the suggestion that Cromwell was a Jew, and that the Jews planned to purchase St. Paul's Cathedral.

Cromwell, unperturbed by the opposition, ordered a committee to consider the petition. Lawyers declared there were no legal barriers to readmission, but there was no agreement as to the extent and nature of readmission. The committee finished its work, but they did not reach a consensus. Manasseh, broken by this failure at the very moment of seeming success, journeyed back to Holland, where he died a year later.

Yet Manasseh's mission was not really a failure. Indeed, as early as 1656, Sephardic Jews, surreptitiously existing among the English, were granted recognition of their legal status as British subjects. This was tantamount to readmission.

MANSOOR, MENACHEM (1911–   )
Scholar.

Monsoor, who taught at the University of Wisconsin, was visiting Morocco to study that country's Jewish population. He constantly confronted angry Arabs. His hosts told him not to worry, that they would stay close to him; they reassured him that there was safety in numbers.

"Ah, yes," he said. "But being a biblical scholar, I would prefer safety in Exodus."

MARCUS, DAVID "MICKEY" (1902–1948)
American soldier, commander of the Jerusalem front in Israel's War of Independence.

(1) June 9, 1948, was the day before a cease-fire between the Arabs and the Israelis was to take effect. Everyone waited for 10:00 A.M. the next morning for the armistice to begin.

Mickey Marcus was staying at the central front headquarters of the

Palmach, the striking arm of the Israeli army. The headquarters was in the Arab village of Abu Ghosh, located several miles west of Jerusalem. Marcus spoke at length that night to Yigal Allon, who was then in charge of the Palmach.

Marcus was clearly excited. His dream of a nation of Israel was about to be realized. The war that he had played so prominent a part in winning was soon to pause. Marcus awoke in the night and went for a long walk. He started his return at 3:50 in the morning.

A sentry saw him approach. There was confusion involving language, then a common event in the army. Although most soldiers in the Palmach spoke English, the sentry on guard that night did not. Marcus spoke no Hebrew. In English, Marcus explained his rank. The confused sentry, hearing English, believed Marcus to be a British officer attached to the Arab Legion of Jordan. The sentry fired a shot. Mickey Marcus fell dead hours before the cease fire was to begin.

Marcus was laid to rest at West Point. David Ben-Gurion, Israel's leader, cabled Marcus's wife Emma: "His name will live forever in the annals of the Jewish people."

(2) Before his tragic death, Mickey Marcus had helped establish the Israeli Army.

Marcus had been recruited on December 9, 1947, by Major Shamir of the Haganah, who, on David Ben-Gurion's orders, had come to New York. Marcus was needed to serve as the chief instructor of the new Jewish army.

Shamir went to Marcus's new law office and made the suggestion. Marcus immediately agreed. The stunned Shamir thanked him and asked him why his answer had been so immediate. Shamir asked, "Why are you so willing to leave your office and your profession and your wife and your home to help a new, little country to which you owe no allegiance?"

Mickey looked at his Haganah visitor and then spoke, "Have you been to Dachau, Major? Have you ever seen and heard a group of Jewish skeletons singing *Hatikvah*? Have you ever stood and cried as I was crying then and as I am crying now, shedding tears which were and are at one and the same time tears of anger, tears of pride, and tears of joy?"

When Marcus came to fight for a Jewish state, he entered the country under the assumed name of Michael Stone. He worked quickly to establish the army by having American military publications translated into Hebrew, establishing schools to train officers, and planning military strategy and tactics. It took Marcus only three months to forge the Haganah into an army.

All the while, one of the Haganah's greatest worries was that the real identity of Michael Stone would be discovered, and the British would force him to leave the country before his enormous task was completed.

One day Marcus and David Ben-Gurion were driving together to a meeting. Their vehicle was stopped by a British patrol. Ben-Gurion was visibly upset. A British officer asked Marcus his name. Marcus coolly replied, "Michael Stone." The officer was not satisfied, however. "And what is your occupation?"

"I'm a foundry worker," Marcus replied. As always, his quick mind worked to Marcus's advantage. Not only had he been unhesitant in his reply, but his nose, misshapen during his boxing career, made him *look* like a tough foundry worker. Marcus even pulled out carefully worn identification papers. The forgery was excellent, and even though Marcus had in fact been in the country for only a short time, the soiled papers made him appear to have lived there for an extended time.

The officer let them pass.

It was only after their safe passage that Marcus remembered the gold ring he wore on the third finger of his left hand. To Ben-Gurion he explained, "It's my West Point ring with my real name engraved inside."

Mickey took off the ring and never wore it again.

MARX, HARPO (1893–1964)
American comedian.

The silent Marx brother was walking down Fifth Avenue when he was called upon to fight his own battle against anti-Semitism.

Harpo was elegantly dressed in his own odd way. He wore a yellow raincoat, a blue hat topped with a feather, and a sash around his middle.

He paused in front of a well-known jewelry store. As he looked at the diamonds, he overheard an argument between a cab driver, who clearly appeared to be Jewish, and the doorman, who just as clearly did not. The doorman let out a steady barrage of anti-Jewish insults. "Get away from in front here, you dirty Jew! Go on, before I break your dirty Jew head! There'll be a law soon keeping you and all Jews off this street. Go on, get back to the ghetto where you belong!"

Harpo walked away. He was back, however, in about fifteen minutes. He had used the intervening moments to buy a few dollars worth of paste emeralds, rubies, and diamonds. Using all his acting skills to appear as imperious as possible, Harpo stopped in front of the doorman and gave him a haughty stare. The doorman bowed deeply and opened the door for this distinguished-looking customer.

Harpo remained in the store for twenty minutes. As he left, he took a false step out into the street. The doorman watched in horror as the elegant shopper tripped and fell over. All kinds of precious stones rolled onto the sidewalk and into the street.

The doorman rushed about trying to gather all of the wandering "jewels," which he presumed had just been purchased. He stayed on his hands and knees for ten minutes, shooing away pedestrians and patiently gathering all the stones.

Finally, the doorman walked up to the elegant Harpo.

"Please, look quick. See if they are all there."

Harpo made a grand production of examining the jewels, finally saying, "Yes, they are all here."

"Thank God," said the doorman.

Harpo stood up and started toward the cab driven by the same Jewish man whom the doorman had earlier insulted. Now the doorman opened the cab door for Harpo.

Harpo paused before he entered the cab. He looked at all the paste jewels he still held in his hand. He picked the very largest of the diamonds, handed it to the doorman, and said, "Here, for your troubles."

Before the stunned doorman could utter a word, Harpo continued, "And give this one to your best girl, and to your dear mama, this ruby."

Harpo then said to the cab driver, "Drive me to the synagogue. I am late for my afternoon prayer."

The doorman was fired that afternoon. For some reason he had screamed at the assistant manager.

MARX, KARL (1818–1883)
Social philosopher and Communist theorist.

Despite his own antipathy toward Judaism, Karl Marx once unwittingly provided great political assistance to Jews.

Marx was born into a family that included rabbis on both sides. A year or two before Marx's birth, however, his father converted to Christianity. Marx grew up without any attachment to Judaism.

In 1843, Marx was just completing his work as editor of the *Rheinische Zeitung*. As editor, Marx was approached by leaders of the Jewish community in Cologne. The Cologne Jews sought political equality and wanted Marx to deliver a petition advocating such equality to the Landtag, the parliament.

Marx wrote a letter to a friend at the time the request came. In the letter, Marx revealed that he found the Jewish religion *Widerlich*, —that is, revolting or repulsive—but that he nevertheless planned to present the petition. Marx was convinced that the petition would never be granted. He certainly had no particular desire to help Jews obtain equality, but he believed that all petitions should be considered. The more failed petitions there were, he reasoned, the more bitterness toward the government would increase. Marx's real aim was to undermine the political structure.

Marx was in for a surprise. A number of Christian liberals supported the petition, and it was approved.

For the first time, a German parliament had granted political equality to the Jews.

MATLIN, MARLEE (1966–   )
American actress and Academy Award winner.

Marlee contracted roseola when she was 18 months old. The disease caused her to lose all hearing in her right ear; she retained 20 percent of her hearing in her left ear.

When she was 7 years old, Marlee met Rabbi Douglas Goldhammer. The rabbi intended to open a synagogue specifically for deaf Jews. Marlee and her parents were among the first congregants in the new synagogue.

Rabbi Goldhammer prepared Marlee for her Bat Mitzvah. They met weekly, and the rabbi taught the girl to read and translate Hebrew. At one point, the rabbi now recalls, he told her that she had to learn to project to the audience. At the Bat Mitzvah, Marlee read from the Torah and then used sign language to translate the text into English.

When Marlee won her Academy Award, seven different parties were hosted in her honor by families who were members of the Congregation for the Deaf.

MATTATHIAS (second century B.C.E.)
Leader of an uprising in 167 B.C.E. against
Antiochus IV.

The story of Hanukah started with a Jewish struggle for freedom.

In 168 B.C.E., the Syrians controlled the Holy Land. On the 15th of Kislev, the Syrians sacrificed a pig in the holiest sanctuary of the temple. Ten days later they held a pagan feast there. Jews, in despair, began to turn away from their ancient religion.

Mattathias lived then in Jerusalem. He had five sons, including Judah Maccabee. At first, Mattathias believed in simply following the religious dictates of his faith and passively ignoring the political and military oppression around him. Eventually, though, as he witnessed the incursion of foreign culture into his people's hearts, his mind changed. He took his family and left Jerusalem to settle in the small village of Modin.

The Syrian influence soon spread even into this village. Mattathias's five sons pleaded with him to call for open, armed rebellion. Judah was particularly forceful, arguing, "Even if we die, we die as fighting men in the name of the Lord. If we do not fight, we die anyway, but like pigs."

Mattathias was reluctant to issue such a call. He waited instead for a miraculous deliverance.

One day an order was issued that all Jews were to assemble in Modin's marketplace.

The Syrians used a cavalry and a war elephant to frighten the villagers. The effort was effective. The Jewish villagers came forward.

The Syrians already had a statue of Jupiter in the village. The Syrian governor of the area, Apelles, was about to test Syrian control.

After the crowd had assembled, the Syrian troops picked out ten strong males. Swords were held to their throats, and they were asked whether they would volunteer. They agreed, and were then forced to lay a stone pedestal in the marketplace. The statue of Jupiter was then placed on the pedestal. An order was given that the Jews were to reassemble in the marketplace the next morning.

When they were reassembled, Apelles read out a royal edict from King Antiochus. The edict proclaimed that from then on, the Jews had to worship Jupiter and forsake their God.

No one moved. Apelles asked, "Who is the leader here?"

Mattathias stepped forward. "I am the priest of Modin."

Apelles gestured for Mattathias to step forward to the idol, but Mattathias would not move. Apelles was about to order soldiers to drag the old man up when Mattathias spoke. "We will not worship the idol. If all the people obey this edict, I and my sons will remain faithful to the covenant."

Apelles seemed unsure of what to do. Finally, he decided not to challenge Mattathias's authority, but instead to ask for any elder to conduct the first sacrifice to Jupiter.

Apelles asked for someone to step forward, alternately threatening and promising rewards. No one moved, but Apelles glimpsed a merchant who seemed afraid.

He called the merchant forward and handed him a leather thong holding a young pig. Apelles also gave the merchant a sacrificial knife. The merchant looked at the soldiers and prepared to make the sacrifice. Mattathias saw that if the sacrifice were made, all the Jews would accept this foreign idol. Mattathias stepped forward and appealed to the merchant to keep the faith of his people. Suddenly, he turned and spoke to his sons, "Yes, we must have faith in the Lord and His goodness. But such faith does not relieve us from responsibility for making decisions."

Mattathias went to the merchant and took the sacrificial knife. Mattathias chanted, confessing his sin, and shouted, "Here is your sacrifice, Apelles!" as he stuck the knife into the merchant who had been about to offer the sacrifice.

Mattathias's sons withdrew their swords. Mattathias called for the villagers to join them. A battle ensued. Every Syrian soldier was killed.

That night Mattathias and his sons let it be known that they were at war with Antiochus, and that they would welcome the faithful to join them. Judah Maccabee trained the fighting troops.

Eventually Mattathias died, but Judah led the Jews to victory. The Syrian armies were destroyed, and the temple was cleansed. It was during the cleansing that the miracle of Hanukah occurred.

MEIR *(second century* C.E.*)*
Rabbi and major scholar who helped develop the Mishnah.

(1) Rabbi Meir was widely admired not only for his scholarly erudition, but for his warm humanity as well. He maintained in his own life the values of modesty and tolerance for the views of others with whom he disagreed, but others did not always understand this tolerance.

Rabbi Meir was once reproached for maintaining contact with a former teacher of his, Elisha ben Abuyah (Asher the Other). Elisha had become an apostate, renouncing his Judaism. Those who questioned Rabbi Meir believed that it was disgraceful to maintain contact with such a man. The rabbi responded to his critics by saying "Even when they err, the father does not deny his children." Asked how he could continue to converse with unbelievers, Rabbi Meir responded, "I take the kernel, but cast away the husk."

(2) Rabbi Meir lived in the land of Israel. He suffered from persecution and so was forced to flee.

He was on the road in Armenia when he came to an inn. The rabbi went inside to dine. Several of the guests, enjoying a pork dinner, thought that they recognized the fugitive rabbi. They weren't sure, though, so they decided to put the stranger to a test. They would invite him to taste their dinner. If he agreed, then he could not be Rabbi Meir.

They invited him over and asked him to taste their food. The trapped rabbi considered his situation. He dipped a finger into one dish and seemed to eat the food. The men returned to their conversation, sure that the stranger was not Rabbi Meir.

They had not noticed that the stranger had dipped one finger into the dish and put yet another finger into his mouth.

(3) Rabbi Meir gained a reputation as a peacemaker who would go to any lengths to restore calm, especially between wives and husbands.

One Sabbath eve, the rabbi's weekly lecture at the synagogue was especially lengthy. When one of the women, who had stayed to listen to him, returned home, she saw that the lamp that lit her house had gone out. Her husband was angry with her and demanded to know where she had been. When she told him of Rabbi Meir's lecture, the husband grew even angrier and told his wife that she could not return to the house until she had spat in the rabbi's face.

Rabbi Meir heard of her difficulties and vowed to do something to help her. At the next synagogue service, he pretended that his eye was sore and asked someone to help him. The woman's neighbor prodded her to step forward, which she did. The rabbi said to her, "Spit seven times into my eye and it will be better." She did as the rabbi asked. When she finished, the rabbi said, "Now go tell your husband that while he wanted you to spit only once, you have done so seven times."

After she left, the rabbi's disciples said, "Did you not read the Torah incorrectly? If she had but told us, we would have brought the man here and chastised him until he allowed his wife to return."

Rabbi Meir said, "Scripture allows the Divine name, written in holiness, to be blotted out by water so that peace can be established between husband and wife. If this is good enough for the Torah, how much more so is it for Meir."

MEIR, GOLDA *(1898–1978)*
Israeli prime minister, leader of Labor party.

(1) After the United Nations vote in favor of partition, the need for weapons became greater than ever before. Weapons were available for the Jews seeking to establish Israel, especially on the black market, and from some Communist-controlled countries such as Czechoslovakia. (These countries were anxious to oust Britain from the Middle East.)

The need for enormous sums of immediately available money was so vital that the first decision made was that only American Jewry had the resources to provide it. David Ben-Gurion believed that the need was so overwhelming that he wished to go himself to the United States to plead for funds. Golda Meir thought that Ben-Gurion was needed where he was. She reluctantly volunteered to go on the mission. Ben-Gurion refused her offer. He wanted Eliezer Kaplan, the Jewish agency treasurer, to go. Kaplan had come back from the United States at the end of 1947 with a sad report on the improbability of raising the funding needed.

Golda argued with her boss. "No one can take your place here, while I may be able to do what you can do in the United States." But Ben-Gurion refused to budge.

He didn't seem to realize with whom he was dealing. Golda asked that the question of her going be put to a vote. Ben-Gurion stared at her for a second and nodded. The vote was in favor of Golda's going to the United States.

She left that day, without luggage, wearing the dress she had worn to the meeting.

Her first appearance was in Chicago on January 21, 1948, at the general assembly of the Council of Jewish Federations and Welfare Funds, a non-Zionist group. Golda knew that these were professional fund raisers. She knew that if she were to succeed, she would have to get through to them. Kaplan had told her that she would, at best, be able to get $5 million, although all the Zionist leaders knew that this figure, however difficult it might be to obtain, was hopelessly low.

Tired, without a chance to rehearse her speech, talking to a group that she knew did not have Jewish nationalism on its agenda much less at the front of its concerns, speaking without being scheduled and without being announced prior to the meeting, Golda Meir approached the microphone. She had a single thought in mind: Whatever she had been told of the limits of fund raising, she was still going to ask for all that was needed.

She began by telling the crowd that the Jews intended to fight to the end, with stones if necessary. She told them that within the next few weeks Zionist leaders needed between $25 and $30 million dollars. She told them again that the decision had been made to fight, but that they would be making a decision as well. Their dollars would determine whether the Jews or the Arabs won the fight.

The audience wept openly. Then they pledged their efforts.

Golda stayed in the United States for six weeks, speaking all over the country. People came and listened. They provided their money and they took out loans.

In March, Golda returned with $50 million for the Jewish army. When a Haganah agent in Paris notified Ben-Gurion that he could buy tanks if he had $10 million, Golda's money was used. In Czechoslovakia, the money was used to buy planes and heavy guns.

When Golda finally returned home, it was Ben-Gurion, as usual, who summed it up best: "Some day, when history will be written, it will be said that there was a Jewish woman who got the money which made the state possible."

(2) Golda was touring a local hospital. The director of the hospital was introducing the prime minister to the patients. Suddenly the director spotted a familiar face in one of the beds. It was the janitor, who should have been sweeping the floors. The director said, "Yonah, what are you doing here? Are you ill?"

"No, sir," said the janitor. "I just borrowed pajamas and jumped into bed. Otherwise I never would have had a chance to talk to Golda."

After they spoke, the janitor jumped out of the bed and resumed sweeping.

(3) Golda never allowed her son to play with toy weapons when he was a child. He later told her, during a conversation about the Six-Day War, "You did not want to give me a toy gun. Now I have been given a real gun."

(4) Golda was introduced to Senator Stuart Symington, a Democrat from Missouri. The senator asked her to tell him the basic difference between the Israelis and the Arabs. Golda replied, "It's simply this. They want to kill us—and we don't want to die."

(5) On her seventy-fifth birthday, Golda was given an ancient Israeli jar. She looked at it and said, "Most appropriate—antiques for the antique."

(6) A man took his 4-year-old nephew to a Bar Mitzvah and pointed to Golda Meir, who was also a guest. The boy couldn't believe that the prime minister was actually standing there. He walked over and stared at her. Finally, he said, "How did you get out of the television?"

She laughed and told him, "I jumped."

(7) President Nixon once reportedly kidded Prime Minister Meir by making known his wish to swap generals with the prime minister. He purportedly said to her, "We'll take General Dayan, General Rabin, and General Bar-Lev."

She is supposed to have responded, "Fine, and we'll take General Motors, General Dynamics, and General Electric."

(8) On one of Golda's visits to the United States, President Nixon and Secretary of State Kissinger gave her an official reception at the White House. Nixon admired the prime minister, and they had a pleasant conversation. At one point, the president said, "Madame Prime Minister, it must be a source of great satisfaction for you to observe that in the United States Jews are so well-regarded and are given so much political equality that in my administration, a Jew serves as my secretary of state, or, to use the nomenclature employed in your country, my foreign minister."

Golda smiled and commented, "This certainly is one of the many indications that the United States is truly a genuine democracy." A twinkle crept into her eyes. "I am sure that you will be delighted to know, Mr. President, that our foreign minister is also a Jew who differs in one respect from your foreign minister. Our foreign minister [Abba Eban] speaks English without an accent."

(9) When she was interviewed for a book by Julie Nixon Eisenhower, Golda was asked how she had felt to be the first-ever woman foreign minister. Golda smiled. "I don't know. I was never a man foreign minister."

(10) Golda always insisted, in her negotiations with Arabs, on meeting her Arab counterpart face to face. A journalist suggested to her that such direct negotiations were unnecessary. "Even divorces are arranged without personal confrontation," the journalist argued.

Golda responded, "I'm not interested in a divorce. I'm interested in a marriage."

MEIR OF ROTHENBERG (c. 1215–1293)
German rabbi, teacher, and scholar.

(1) Rabbi Meir ben Baruch of Rothenberg was widely known in Germany for his scholarship. He was especially famous as the last of the supplementers, those rabbis who reconstructed the Talmud from memory after Pope Gregory had ordered the burning of all existing Talmuds.

The people turned to Meir in an hour of great need. In 1241, the Mongols had begun their invasion of Europe. German Christians accused Jews of being in collusion with the Mongols. Jews were subject to horrible attacks.

Rudolph became emperor of Germany in 1273. He tried to restrain his subjects in accord with a petition sent by Pope Innocent IV asking that Jews not be "unjustly tormented." Rudolph needed money, and he hoped that, in return for his protection, the Jews would provide that money to him. But Rudolph also needed to appease his people, so he issued several edicts barring Jews from public office and requiring them to stay in their houses during Easter week. Rabbi Meir was sent to talk to the emperor about these edicts, but their talks were not successful.

Many Jews began to flee the country. Their departure deprived the emperor of needed tax revenue. Meir himself had fled from Rothenberg to Lombardy.

One day, Meir was spotted. The local bishop ordered him sent back to Germany. Rudolph decided that he would make an example of Meir. Meir was immediately imprisoned in the fortress at Ensisheim.

A disciple came to visit him there.

"Master," the disciple called through the opening in the dungeon's door.

"I am here," Meir replied.

"I bring you good news."

"Has the Lord made Rudolph change his mind?"

"No, but soon you will be released."

Meir did not understand. "But if Rudolph's heart has not changed, and I am not dying, how shall I get out?"

"Twenty thousand marks of silver have been promised to release you. Not even Rudolph could refuse."

"I forbid you to do this," Rabbi Meir said sternly.

The disciple could not believe the answer. "It is for your ransom," he said.

The rabbi again said, "I forbid it." Then he continued, "If you pay such a huge ransom for me, Rudolph will arrest a hundred more Jews and hold them for ransom. Twenty thousand marks for Rabbi Meir will be even more for Rabbi Moses or Samuel the banker."

The disciple left, despondent at his master's answer. The next day the disciple returned. "I have spoken to all the leaders of our congregation, Rabbi. They say that they must deal with today's evil, not tomorrow's. Today this cell is evil. They wish to pay your ransom."

"As your rabbi, I beg you not to pay. As your teacher, I ask you to remember your people and forget the ransom."

The disciple left. He returned each day to see his teacher.

Rabbi Meir remained in prison for seven years until, in 1293, he died.

The question of ransom continued after Meir's death. Rudolph would not release the body, which he held for fourteen more years. Still, the Jews did not pay the ransom. Finally, in 1307, a Jew from Frankfort, Susskind Alexander Wimpfen, bought the corpse and buried it according to the laws of Judaism.

(2) In 1239, a renegade Jew who had become a Dominican monk denounced the Talmud to Pope Gregory IX. Nicholas Donin of La Rochelle accused the Talmud of blaspheming against God and the Christian faith. He claimed that it advocated views that were in conflict with biblical teachings. Donin made a tract of thirty-five articles of accusation and gave it to the pope. Particularly important to Donin was the charge that it was the Talmud, and only the Talmud, that caused Jews to refuse to accept baptism and become practicing Christians.

The pope received the tract and thought its accusations important enough to initiate an investigation. He asked that bishops in France, England, Castile, and Aragon seize all copies of the Talmud. A trial of the Talmud would then be held. Bishops in England and Spain simply disregarded the pope's request, but King Louis IX in France – St. Louis – ordered the papal orders to be carried out. On March 3, 1240, Jews were forced under threat of harm to surrender all known copies of the Talmud.

On June 24, a debate was begun in the French king's court. The disputants were Donin and four representatives of the Jewish people, led by Rabbi Jehiel ben Joseph of Paris. The judges were bishops and Dominican monks. Rabbi Meir was among those present to witness the debate.

The judges, not surprisingly, given their theological position, found the Talmud both blasphemous and harmful. All copies were ordered burned. The implementation of the sentence was delayed for two years.

Finally, though, on a Sabbath evening in June of 1242, twenty-four cartloads of Jewish books were set aflame in Paris.

Rabbi Meir was there, too, to witness the destruction. He composed an elegy, *Sha'ali Serufah ba-Esh*—"Ask, you who have been consumed by the fire, what has become of those who shed tears over your terrible lot." The elegy is included in the liturgy on Tisha B'av in the Ashkenazic service.

MENACHEM MENDEL OF KOTZK (1787–1859)
Hasidic teacher.

Menachem Mendel published none of his writings during his life. One day, a visitor came to see him and inquired about his famous refusal to publish his thoughts. Mendel provided his answer: "Who is it who would read my work? The scholars, the scientists wouldn't read it. They are more learned than I am. Only a person who believes he knows less than I do would be willing to read my work. And who is it who knows less? Only the poor peasant who must work hard. When could he ever have time to read a book? Only on the Sabbath, but even then, when? On Friday evening he wouldn't; he would be too tired. On Saturday morning he would be at services. After services, he returns home, has a good meal, sings, and then lies down on his sofa, finally at peace. Then he has a moment to look at a book. He picks my book up; he turns its pages. But he has eaten so much that he gets tired. Soon he is asleep. My book falls. Should I publish a book just to have that happen to it?"

Even on his deathbed, Mendel remained concerned that some of his writing might remain. He asked his friends to search everywhere, every hiding place, to make sure that all of the writing had been destroyed. They had, for only his story remains.

MENDELE MOCHER SEFORIM (1835–1917)
Hebrew and Yiddish writer.

Mendele, whose real name was Shalom Yaakov Abramovich, loved to play pranks and hated to be disturbed. He developed certain special tricks to avoid being bothered by those he disliked.

Once he was sitting with the Hebrew writer Ben Ami when the two heard a knock on the door. Ben Ami got up to answer, but Mendele held him back. "Sh-sh," Mendele said. "Sit still. That fellow is a terrible nudnick."

Ben Ami said, "How do you know who is knocking?"

Mendele responded, "Some time ago that man asked me if he could come to visit me. I told him that I was a very busy man, and to make sure that I would receive him, he should knock on the door in a certain way. That's how I know."

MENDELSSOHN, ABRAHAM (1776–1835)
Communal leader.

Abraham Mendelssohn was the son of Moses Mendelssohn. Abraham's son was the well-known composer Felix Mendelssohn. Abraham used to utter a constant complaint: "At one time I was known just as my father's son. Now I am known just as my son's father."

MENDELSSOHN, MOSES (1729–1786)
Leader of German Jewry and philosopher of Enlightenment.

(1) Mendelssohn was a close friend of King Frederick the Great. Once, walking on Berlin's main street, the two met.

"Where are you going?" the king asked.

Mendelssohn responded, "I don't know."

"You don't know. Aren't you bound for somewhere?"

"Yes," the philosophic Mendelssohn agreed, "but where I don't know."

The king thought that Mendelssohn was mocking him and ordered his arrest. On reflection, though, the king knew Mendelssohn as a wise man; perhaps he had intended a profound meaning to his words. The king went to visit Mendelssohn in the prison.

"Why did you trifle with me?" the king asked.

"I did not mean to trifle with you, Your Majesty. I really did not know where I was going. I intended to visit a friend, but ended in jail instead."

(2) Mendelssohn was walking on a busy street in Berlin. He was, as usual, deep in philosophic thought, so that he unintentionally bumped into a rather plump officer in the Prussian army. Mendelssohn began to apologize, but the officer was furious.

"Pig!" he shouted at the philosopher.

Mendelssohn gave a deep bow and said, "Mendelssohn."

(3) Mendelssohn spent part of his youth in Berlin working for a man who was ignorant of the philosophy young Moses was interested in studying. Furthermore, the employer was cruel. Later in life, one of Mendelssohn's friends said, "As a philosopher, you claim that you know all about the justice of God, but your employment proves the injustice of God."

Mendelssohn considered this. "On the contrary. My situation proves the justice of God. For if the opposite had been true and I had been an employer, what could I do with a boor like that?"

(4) One evening Frederick II hosted a dinner to which invitations were sent to a large number of well-known scholars, writers, and philosophers.

Mendelssohn arrived late for the gathering, and the emperor was exceedingly angry. When the famed philosopher finally did show up, Frederick took some paper and wrote out the following: "M. *ist Ein Narr* [M. is a fool]." The emperor signed it and had it sent to the thinker, who read it quickly and put it in his pocket.

The emperor was not satisfied. "Read it aloud," he ordered.

Mendelssohn took out the note and read it: "M. *ist* ein *Narr*; *Friedrich der Zweite* [M. is one fool; Frederick, the second]."

MENUHIN, YEHUDI (1916–   )
Violinist.

Rabbi Meir Kahane had organized the Jewish Defense League in part to protest the Soviet treatment of Jews. One particular target of their attacks was the impresario Sol Hurok, who had brought many Soviet cultural events to the United States.

One such event occurred on February 1, 1970, in Carnegie Hall. A recital was scheduled by visiting artists David Oistrakh and Sviatoslav Richter. The opening sonata was played without incident. But during the first movement of a Brahms composition, a young man attached to the Jewish Defense League charged down the aisle, jumped onto the stage, and shouted, "Soviet Russia is no better than Nazi Germany."

Oistrakh left, but Richter stayed by his piano. A police officer came toward the stage. Some audience members helped the officer mount the stage, where he took hold of the young demonstrator and escorted him off the stage. Oistrakh then returned. The Brahms piece was started from the beginning. It had just reached its final movement when a second young man raced toward the stage.

Yehudi Menuhin went backstage to comfort the artists who had left.

Richter was feeling all right, but Oistrakh felt terrible. His wife, Tamara, was upset. He had had two heart attacks, and the event had clearly unnerved him. Tamara turned to Menuhin and asked, "Yehudi, were those your Jews or mine?"

Menuhin said, "They were ours."

MOHILEWER, SAMUEL (1824–1898)
Rabbi and founder of religious Zionism.

The rabbi approached a wealthy man to seek funds for the Zionist movement. The man refused to make a donation, however, claiming that Israel's redemption could be ushered in only by the Messiah.

Rabbi Mohilewer asked the wealthy man if he would permit a story. The man readily agreed, and so the rabbi began.

"There was a student who regularly received money from home. The money was sent to a storekeeper, who then gave it to the student. One day, the student received a letter from his father asking why the student had not acknowledged the money that had recently been sent. The student showed the letter to the storekeeper, who claimed never to have received the missing funds. The student called for a rabbinical trial.

"At the trial, the rabbi in charge ruled that the storekeeper had a choice. Either he could swear that he had not received the money, or he could pay the missing amount. But the storekeeper chose to do both. First he gave the student a sum equal to the missing money. Then he swore that he had never received the money that the student's father had sent.

"Naturally, the storekeeper was then asked why he had done this, and he explained, 'If I had sworn but not given the money, some would say I had taken the money and lied. If I had paid and not sworn, some would say I had stolen the money but was afraid of the consequences of a sworn oath. Now I have done both, and nobody can suspect me.' "

The rabbi then turned to the wealthy man. "You also should make a contribution and then say why you are opposed to Zionism. Then nobody will doubt that you are sincere."

MOISHE OF KALENKOVITCH (nineteenth century)
Rabbi and scholar.

Rabbi Moishe was well known as an extraordinarily hospitable man, always willing to help visitors, especially the poor. One day two traveling preachers came to his home. One of them ate and drank to excess. The other, hoping to stop his traveling companion, turned to Rabbi Moishe. The preacher said, "In the Talmud it says that until age 40, a man gets more benefit from eating than from drinking, and after 40, from drinking more than from eating. I cannot see how my friend justifies his behavior. If he is under 40, why does he drink so much, and if he is over 40, why does he eat like a glutton?"

Rabbi Moishe pondered this and said, "We are also told in our Talmud always to judge others in the best possible way. I would suppose that your friend is just 40 today and can take advantage of both sides of this rule."

MONOBAZUS (first century C.E.)
King of Adiabene and convert to Judaism.

It was during a period of great famine. Despite the widespread hunger, Monobazus gave away all his wealth to the poor. His relatives were aghast at his behavior, and they told him that they thought he was squandering his wealth and possessions. He responded, "All our ancestors stored up treasures of money for this world. I, too, am storing up by giving away my money, but I have stored up a treasure for my soul."

MONTEFIORE, SIR MOSES (1784–1885)
British financier and philanthropist.

(1) A man was once talking to Sir Moses Montefiore at a reception. The two had a pleasant conversation until the man, forgetting to whom he was talking, made an uncomplimentary remark about the Jewish features of a woman passing them. Suddenly remembering how attached Montefiore was to Judaism, the man began to apologize. "I ask a thousand pardons. It was so stupid of me to forget. You look angry enough to eat me alive. I beg you not to devour me."

"Sir," replied Montefiore. "It is impossible. My religion forbids."

(2) Sir Moses was once asked how much he was worth. He answered, "I am worth 40,000 pounds."

The questioner was flabbergasted. "I thought you were worth millions."

Sir Moses smiled. "I do possess millions. But you asked me how much I am worth, and since 40,000 pounds represents the sum I distributed during the last year to various charitable institutions, I regard this sum as the barometer of my true worth. For it is not how much a person possesses, but how much he is willing to share with the less fortunate that determines his actual worth."

(3) Montefiore was a deeply religious man, at least in an ethical sense. Despite his lack of Jewish learning, he believed it a religious duty to do good every minute of his life. To aid him in his task, he hired a man whose sole job was to tell him every hour, "Moishe Montefiore, another hour of your life has passed."

(4) Montefiore was very anxious to see the inside of the Cave of Machpelah, in Hebron, where, according to Jewish tradition, the patriarchs and matriarchs are buried. The Arabs, who had control over the area, refused to permit any Jews or Christians into the cave.

In 1819, on a trip to the Holy Land, Sir Moses obtained a letter from the Sultan of Turkey which directed the Arab authorities to allow the distinguished visitor into the cave.

The Arab chieftains faced a dilemma. They could not disobey the sultan's order, and yet they did not wish to let any Jew into the cave. They finally told Montefiore, "The sultan's letter says we must admit you to the cave, but it does not say that we must let you out."

Sir Moses did not ever go into the sacred Cave of Machpelah.

(5) Sir Moses attended a dinner party at which he was seated next to a nobleman known to be an anti-Semite. The nobleman wasted no time. He began his conversation by saying, "I have just returned from Japan, and it's a most unusual country. Did you know that it has neither pigs nor Jews?"

Montefiore answered, "In that case, you and I should go there, so it will have a sample of each."

MOSES *(first half of thirteenth century B.C.E.)*
Law giver and major prophet who led the Jews on the exodus
from Egypt.

(1) While the Jews were wandering in the desert after their exodus from Egypt, there were those who challenged Moses's authority. Korah, the Levite, was among those challengers. Korah went among the twelve tribes and argued against Moses as a leader. He said that a real leader could have crossed the desert in a few months, not forty years, and that Moses wanted to doom the people by having them attack the Canaanites. He offered himself as a new leader.

Aaron, Moses's brother, heard of the plot and told Moses about it. Moses sent a message to Korah, who responded by asking whether Moses claimed to be a prince.

Moses decided to speak to Korah directly. Aaron was aghast. "It is demeaning for you to go to him. You're a prophet. He should come to you."

"It is not important who goes to whom," Moses said. "It is only important to avoid civil war." Moses then went to Korah. Aaron and Joshua accompanied the prophet. People watched as Moses approached his opponent.

Moses came to Korah's tent and called for him to come out. Korah did so, smiling as though to tell the assembled crowds that the great Moses had been shown to be a lesser man than Korah. Then Korah brought out a stool and placed it in the shade of the tent. Moses was not offered a stool. Although he was an old man, he stood in the sun.

Moses asked for peace. Korah simply shrugged his shoulders, so Moses continued, "We are in a strange land. Nations all around wish to slaughter us. We must remain together as brothers."

Korah would not relent. "Old man, you are too filled with age and fears. I do not fear those few who continue to follow you. They will accept me as leader or they will die."

Moses began to beg Korah. This begging shocked the crowds; they did not expect their leader and prophet to act in such a way. Then, most shocking of all, Moses got down on his knees. One in the crowd yelled, "Moses, you spoke to God Himself at Mount Sinai. Why, now, do you kneel before Korah?"

Moses responded, "It is because I saw God on Mount Sinai that I now kneel. It was there I learned that service to the people and to the will of the Lord is more important than pride."

Korah laughed at Moses.

Moses spoke in a rising voice, "I have asked you in the name of the Lord and for the sake of our people not to divide us. You continue in your efforts. Now I must call upon the people to forsake you. The vengeance of the Lord is on you."

The people supported Moses. Only Korah's chief lieutenants remained faithful to him.

According to tradition, these men were engulfed by a crack in the earth.

Moses wept, however, for Korah was a human, created by God, and therefore holy.

(2) One story about Moses is illustrative of how deeply the Jews believed that the way a person treats animals is a guide to the person's character.

When Moses was the shepherd for Jethro's flock, he used to let the young sheep loose first to feed on the tender grass while he held back the older ones. Then he'd let the old ones loose to eat the regular grass while he held back the strongest sheep. Only after the others had grazed did Moses let the strongest sheep eat the tough grass.

Once, a lamb ran away from the rest of the flock. Angry, Moses chased after the young sheep, but lost it. After a long search, Moses paused to rest by leaning against a tree. Suddenly he saw the kid drinking out of a pool of water. Moses walked over to the lamb and said, "I did not know that you ran awaybecause you were thirsty. If you were overcome by thirst, you must also be tired." Moses picked up the lamb and carried it back to the flock.

MOSES OF CRETE (fifth century C.E.)
Pseudomessiah.

Many of those who focused on the arrival of the Messiah interpreted various biblical passages as indicating that the Messiah would come in the fifth century.

A man named Moses appeared in Crete claiming to be the Messiah. He traveled throughout Crete and convinced most of the population of his authenticity.

Many Jews there, ready to receive the Messiah, reacted wildly. They abandoned homes and businesses, and prepared to be led to their promised land.

Moses, instead, led most of the Jews of Crete to a point overlooking the sea. Hundreds of people, most carrying all the possessions they could hold, followed him.

At the water's edge, he raised his arms. He ordered that the sea part. Then he told the people to march forward, armed with their faith in him. His followers began to march.

The sea failed to part, and many drowned. Fishermen in the area did save some. Survivors sought revenge, but Moses of Crete had vanished, never to be heard from again.

MOSES LEIB OF SASOV (1745-1807)
Hasidic rabbi.

Rabbi Moses Leib was known far and wide for his tolerance and learning.

One day Rabbi Moses heard a case involving a *shochet* (ritual slaughterer). Almost the entire community wished to have him dismissed. One man alone stood up in defense of the *shochet*. The trial proceeded, but at the conclusion, Rabbi Moses ruled that the *shochet* retain his post.

The community was shocked. A community leader called out to the rabbi: "How can you accept one man's word compared to the word of so many others?"

The rabbi considered this and replied, "When the Lord commanded our father, Abraham, to sacrifice his son, Isaac, did not Abraham listen to a single angel? God thought this just, despite the fact that Abraham opposed his will. God was just, because to order harm to another requires a decision from a high authority, but to rescue someone from harm requires a single word from even an insignificant man."

N

NACHMAN OF BRATSLAV (1772–1811)
Hasidic rabbi and leader.

(1) Rabbi Nachman was concerned that if he left his ideas in written form, they would become dusty tomes, never to be studied by future generations. He therefore told his disciples that he wished his ideas to be put in the form of prayers, which would convey his message every time they were spoken. He wanted all his written work destroyed. Just prior to his death, he again ordered that his words be put to the fire. His follower, Rabbi Nathan, who later wrote a biography of Nachman, did as his master wished, but Nachman's tales remain because they were passed on by Rabbi Nathan.

(2) Before Rabbi Nachman became close to Nathan, he had another friend, Reb Shimon. The two men studied together.

One day, Rabbi Nachman came to Shimon with a plan: The two would leave the town and settle in Hungary, where they would live as poor, unknown peasants. Rabbi Nachman complained that he was too famous, that people paid respect to him because of his family background; in Hungary, though, people wouldn't care if he were made to suffer. The journey itself never came to be, and Rabbi Nachman, on reflection, reconsidered the very need for such a move. He told Reb Shimon that there was, in fact, no real need to leave: He would be persecuted regardless of where he lived.

NAPHTALI OF ROPSHITZ (1760–1827)
Rabbi and founder of hasidic dynasties.

Even as a young boy, Rabbi Naphtali astonished adults with his quick, insightful replies. One day, a friend of Naphtali's father came for a visit and said to the

167

child, "Naphtali, I'll give you a gold coin if you can tell me where God can be found."

The boy immediately replied, "I'll give you two gold coins if you can tell me where He can *not* be found."

NETANYAHU, JONATHAN *(1946–1976)*
Israeli hero of Entebbe rescue.

It was during the very first hours of July 4, 1976, that Israeli commandos departed from Africa after having rescued more than 100 hostages at Entebbe Airport in Uganda. The raid itself entered Israeli history and created a hero for the Jewish people. That hero was, of course, Jonathan Netanyahu, field commander of the rescue force and the only casualty among the Israeli commandos.

The raid itself had been a model of military planning and precision. Yoni Netanyahu had flown in the leading Hercules aircraft. As the plane approached the Entebbe Airport, Netanyahu and nine other commandos crowded into the repainted Mercedes that would be the first vehicle to exit from the rear ramp of the plane after landing. All of the commandos had covered their faces and hands with a black coating. Even the pistols they used—ones like the pistols used by Ugandans, but fitted with silencers—were darkened. The flight had lasted seven hours. Its tension had been heightened by terrible lightning storms.

Netanyahu and his Mercedes were out and moving fast as the plane landed. The Ugandan security guards, clearly confused, saluted as the doors of the Mercedes flung open. The commandos opened fire, and the guards fell. Netanyahu and his men began to wipe the makeup off their arms and faces and to remove the shirts that made them look like Ugandan soldiers; they didn't want the other Israeli commandos to confuse them with the real Ugandans.

Netanyahu's men swung into action. One, code-named "Ilan," had been given a female German terrorist as his target. He found her. Others in his group made it into the airport lounge, where the hostages were kept. The commandos shouted in Hebrew for everyone to get down on the floor. These orders were followed by a minute and forty-five seconds of shooting; the terrorists were being systematically discovered and killed. Doctors came in to remove the wounded.

The Israelis sustained heavy fire from a control tower. Netanyahu's group led the way to end the threat. In the Israeli fashion, Netanyahu, the leader, was at the front. The Israelis fired bazooka shells and spat their machine guns at the guards in the tower. One of the guards found Netanyahu in his sights. He shot Netanyahu in the back, and the Israeli fell down, his face to the ground.

Medics were called in, but to no avail.

Netanyahu would live only in the memory of those who would learn about, or already knew of, his heroic deeds.

NILES, DAVID *(1890–1952)*
Aide to Presidents Roosevelt and Truman.

David Niles played a crucial behind-the-scenes role in the birth of Israel.

As an assistant to President Truman, Niles was a political troubleshooter and liaison to various minority groups, including Jews. Niles mirrored Truman's commitment to a Jewish state and therefore directed various political efforts to implement Truman's policy decisions.

The most important of those efforts involved the United Nations vote on partition in November of 1947. There were fifty-seven member states in the United Nations; a vote for partition of the land into a Jewish nation and an Arab nation would necessitate a two-thirds majority of those voting. Many nations clearly intended to abstain, however, so the mathematics of partition became extremely complicated. By most Zionist estimates, if the Arabs garnered fifteen votes, they could effectively block partition and thus prevent the formation of a Jewish nation. They had garnered thirteen votes in early voting decisions on related matters.

Both the United States and the Soviet Union, for very different reasons, supported partition. Nevertheless, the line-up of nations against a Jewish state looked ominous. There were the five Arab states as well as nations with large Muslim populations. The European nations couldn't choose between Arab oil and a sense that the Jewish claim had enormous moral and historical merit. One of the remaining battles was for Latin American support; Latin American nations formed fully one-third of the United Nations.

On Wednesday, November 26—the day before Thanksgiving—the Zionists were in a panic. They calculated that the Arabs had gathered more than their fifteen votes, and the final partition vote was about to take place. The American delegation, which might have exerted great pressure on wavering nations, was held in check by some members of the State Department. It looked as though Thanksgiving was going to be gloomy indeed for Zionist aspirations. The only solution was to attempt to delay the vote. In that way, perhaps, some votes could be changed.

Some Latin Americans who favored partition helped the Zionist cause by delivering long speeches, deliberately attempting to postpone the vote until Friday, the day after Thanksgiving. The Arabs, misjudging the political implications, reacted to the Latin American speeches with equally long speeches of their own. A recess was finally called.

The Zionists and their friends had forty-eight hours in which to change some votes and make history.

President Truman, prodded by the Zionists and friends in Congress, called in David Niles and told the political advisor that, if it would be helpful, more US pressure could be applied. Niles immediately saw the importance of Truman's statement and went to work. He focused on four nations—Haiti, the Philippines, Liberia, and Greece. It was judged that three of them would have to change their votes for partition to be accepted.

Niles turned first to the Philippines, which had flip-flopped in its vote. Niles called Supreme Court Justice Felix Frankfurter and apprised him of the situation. Frankfurter called fellow justice Frank Murphy, and the two of them visited the Philippines ambassador to the United States to make their case. Meanwhile, ten senators were quickly rounded up to sign a telegram to the president of the Philippines describing the potentially adverse effect of the negative vote. (At the time, a financial aid package was awaiting congressional approval.)

Niles correctly judged that Liberia was more than anxious to receive some direction from the United States. Niles heard from contacts that Liberia had not felt any pressure from the United States, so he assumed that the United States was indifferent. Niles called Robert Nathan, an economist familiar with Liberia. Nathan then called the Liberian delegate to issue a stern warning: Liberia would vote for partition, or former secretary of state Edward R. Stettinius would have to call Harvey Firestone, Jr., owner of the huge tire and rubber company which played a central role in Liberia's economy. Stettinius, in fact, called the Liberian president directly.

On the Wednesday prior to Thanksgiving, Haiti had announced that it was opposed to partition. To complicate the matter, however, the Haitian chief delegate at the United Nations announced that he was going to vote for partition. Niles called all his business contacts who had any connection to Haiti.

Niles next turned to Greece. He called an old friend from Boston named Tom Pappas. Pappas, in turn, contacted movie executive Spyros Skouras, and others. Telegrams and cables were sent.

After working on the four crucial countries, Niles turned to the still-wavering France. He spoke to financier Bernard Baruch, who, though previously unconnected to the Zionist cause, was swept up in the historic excitement. Baruch not only called his business contacts but, in person, told the French delegate that if France voted against partition, no more American aid to France would be forthcoming.

It was not to be until Saturday, November 29, that all the parliamentary procedures that had to be followed were concluded.

A vote could finally be taken.

Niles, the Jewish Agency, and all the numerous people who had worked for partition were still anxious. They knew that the Arabs had been busy exerting pressure as well. The political battle was about to be fought.

At shortly after 5:00 P.M., fifty-six votes were cast. (Only Siam was not present.)

The Philippines voted for partition. Liberia voted for partition. Haiti voted for partition. France voted for partition. Of the countries contacted during those crucial forty-eight hours, only Greece refused to support partition. In the final analysis, ten nations abstained, thirteen voted against, and thirty-three voted for partition.

The motion carried. Israel would become a nation.

Niles never became famous for his efforts. He always avoided publicity. Yet his political brilliance made a crucial difference in Jewish history.

NOAH, MORDECAI MANUEL (1785–1851)
American writer and Zionist forerunner.

On September 15, 1825, a Jewish nation was declared to exist as an asylum for persecuted Jews from around the world. This asylum, this Jewish state, was located on Grand Island, near Buffalo, New York. This attempt at founding a Jewish nation was made by a man subsequently known as the first American Zionist, Mordecai Manuel Noah.

Noah was a journalist, playwright, politician, and visionary. After realizing some writing success and some political success by defending the United States' fighting in the War of 1812, Noah was appointed American consul in Tunis in 1813. Two years later he was dismissed, falsely charged with mishandling finances. The charges were never proved, and Noah believed that he had been fired because of his religion.

His reaction to losing his job was one of anger and intensified religious identification. His analysis of anti-Jewish prejudice led him to a nationalist position, as it would for later Zionists as well. At first, Noah believed that the Turkish sultan would be removed and that the European powers would allow and encourage Jews to reestablish a Jewish nation. When such events failed to occur, Noah's eyes turned toward the United States.

In 1820, Noah petitioned the New York state legislature for an allowance to purchase Grand Island. The island, only eight miles long and six miles wide at its broadest point, was to be used to settle Russian Jewish immigrants who would farm the island's 17,000 acres. The bill did not pass, but Noah continued with his plan even after this legislative rebuff. Noah had wanted to subdivide the land into lots of 100 acres and allow 170 Jewish families to settle and farm the land. The legislature had told him that no survey of the land had been made and so no subdivision could occur. A survey did begin in 1824 and was completed the following year. Noah was then free to purchase land.

Noah arranged for Samuel Leggett, a non-Jew from New York City, to purchase more than 2,500 acres.

Late in August of 1825, Noah arrived in Buffalo determined to proclaim the founding of a new city on Grand Island, to be called Ararat (from the biblical site on which Noah's Ark had come to rest). Weather prevented Noah from crossing the Niagara River.

The ceremony in September to name the city was held in St. Paul's Episcopal Church in Buffalo, a site chosen because the church rector, Addison Searle, was so interested in the project. The day began in confusion. Crowds had gathered on the banks of the Niagara River, expecting the ceremony to occur on Grand Island and hoping to be provided with cake, ale, meat, and other food.

The ceremonies had begun at dawn, when a gun salute was fired in front of the Buffalo courthouse. At 10:00 in the morning a parade went from the Masonic Lodge to St. Paul's.

When the paraders reached the church, the ceremony began. Morning prayers were read first. Each prayer had been carefully chosen exclusively from Hebrew scriptures. Noah then spoke. He offered what he called the "Jewish Declaration of Independence." It actually had been previously published and sent out for world Jewry to see.

A cornerstone had been brought from Cleveland and was appropriately inscribed.

Noah left, apparently without having visited Grand Island. The foundation stone was put in the churchyard and was eventually moved to Grand Island's town hall.

Noah came to believe in the land of Israel as a more appropriate refuge for the Jews.

Although Grand Island never became a Jewish homeland, the project achieved considerable publicity, arousing the interest of many Americans. President John Quincy Adams, for instance, wrote Noah: "I really wish again in Judea an independent nation, for, as I believe, the most enlightened men of it have participated in the amelioration of the philosophy of the age."

NORDAU, MAX (1849–1923)
Author and early Zionist leader.

On November 17, 1895, Theodor Herzl came to visit Nordau. Nordau was by then world-famous for his rejection of modernist trends and the social conventions of so-called civilization. Herzl had already composed his pamphlet *Der Judenstaat* (The Jewish State). It had been written during June and July of that year, but it had not yet been published. Herzl very much needed support from such leading thinkers as Nordau, for the great Jewish philanthropists had already rejected Herzl's ideas.

Herzl came to Nordau on that November morning. The two had previously met, but were not yet close. Herzl's first words were "Schiff says that I'm insane." Herzl was referring to Friedrich Schiff, the Paris correspondent of the Wolff Telegraphic Agency, and a journalistic colleague of Herzl's and Nordau's. Schiff was also a doctor, and he had examined Herzl right after the pamphlet was written. Herzl had read the work to him, and Schiff had suggested that the product was the result of mental strain.

After that rueful introduction, Herzl began to read the work, originally written as an address to the Rothschilds, to Nordau. For three days Herzl returned to continue to read the pamphlet. Nordau listened, asked for explanations, and argued some points.

At the end, Nordau stood up and spread his arms in a gesture of welcome. He had indeed grasped Zionism's essence. Herzl was trembling. Nordau said, "If you are insane, we are insane together. Count on me!"

Nordau suggested that Herzl go to the Maccabean Club in London. The club had as its members various artists, writers, and Jewish intellectuals. Nordau said that he would provide an introduction to the famous English writer Israel Zangwill.

Thus, as Herzl hoped he would, Nordau provided Zionism with both moral authority and access to leading Jewish thinkers. It had been a fateful few days for Herzl and for his plan.

ONKELOS BAR KALONYMUS (second century C.E.)
Bible translator and famous proselyte.

Onkelos, the nephew of the Emperor Titus, embraced the Jewish people and became a Jew. Titus sent a group of soldiers to arrest his nephew and return him to the palace. Onkelos spoke to the troops about the Bible, and the troops converted to Judaism.

The emperor sent a second group of troops. They, too, all became Jews.

Angered, the emperor sent still a third group, ordering them not to converse with Onkelos.

The troops came and arrested Onkelos and were bringing him to the palace when they passed a Jewish home. Onkelos kissed the mezuzah on the house and laughed.

"Why do you laugh?" the leader of the troops asked.

"It is a rule in this world that the king stays in his palace and his servants stand outside and watch out for him. But in the case of Israel it is the reverse: The Almighty King stands outside and keeps guard over his servants."

The third group, too, became Jews.

The emperor stopped sending troops.

OSHRY, RABBI EPHRAIM (1914–)
Rabbi in Kovno.

A traditional Jew in the Kovno ghetto was greatly agitated and came to Rabbi Oshry, seeking advice. The man was compelled each day by the Nazis to perform acts of forced labor, and yet part of his daily prayer was "Blessed art thou, O

Lord, who has not made me a slave." The man asked the rabbi how he could be honest in speaking to God when he was, in fact, a slave.

The rabbi told him that the Nazis were the genuine slaves; they were slaves to a terrible wickedness. But, the rabbi went on, a human who could feel free in the middle of such a terrible situation to pray to God and to seek to do so honestly was not a slave at all, but a free person.

OZICK, CYNTHIA (1928–   )
American author.

Several years ago, before she became famous, Cynthia Ozick was invited to be part of a literary program at a university on Long Island. The hall for the lecture was very large, but the audience was quite small.

Ozick stepped behind the lectern and surveyed the scene. She took a quick mental count of the members of the audience. After finishing her silent count, she said, "There are thirty-six people in this room. The number thirty-six is very important in Jewish life. It represents the thirty-six righteous people living in the world in each generation, whose goodness prevents the world from being destroyed." Then she began her lecture.

In one sentence she had both demonstrated her brilliance and relieved the audience of any uneasiness about the small group in attendance.

PEERCE, JAN *(1904–1984)*
American opera star.

When Jan Peerce was in Kansas City, he was scheduled to meet with former president Harry Truman. First, though, Peerce went to the local synagogue to say the required prayers for his deceased parents. Because of the synagogue visit, he was late for his meeting with Truman. Peerce apologized for his lateness and began to explain.

Truman said, "I don't mind. The Lord won."

PERES, SHIMON *(1923–   )*
Israeli prime minister and political leader.

Shimon Peres almost missed greeting Anwar Sadat when the Egyptian leader made his historic landing in Israel.

It was Friday, November 18, 1977. Peres, then head of the Labor party, which was out of power, and his wife, Sonya, were in the United States on a lecture tour for the United Jewish Appeal. They had just landed in Los Angeles and were very tired. All Peres wanted to do was find his hotel and get some rest.

But just as he got off the plane, he was met by Israel's consul-general in Los Angeles. The consul-general informed Peres that Egyptian president Sadat was going to arrive in Israel on Saturday night and would speak to the Knesset the following day. The consul-general recommended that Peres return immediately to Israel.

Peres, of course, knew of the rumors that Sadat might visit, but the reality of it was startling. He never left the airport. Peres waited for an hour and boarded a plane to New York, thinking that he could get connections from there

177

on an Air France flight to Israel. Unfortunately, a runway accident at Kennedy
Airport forced Peres's plane to circle above the airport for three hours. Meanwhile, Golda Meir was on the Air France flight at Kennedy. She requested that
the plane wait for Peres. It did wait for an hour, but then departed.

Peres's plane finally did land, but by that time there were no flights to
either Israel or Europe that day. Peres was now certain that he would not be
home in time for Sadat's historic visit.

But Peres would not give up. He contacted an Israeli military delegation
then in New York. They checked and discovered that an El Al cargo plane
carrying industrial piping was scheduled to depart for Amsterdam at 3:00 in the
morning. Peres and his wife got on that plane. It was only after they boarded
that they discovered that the cargo plane had no seats. Blankets were spread out
on the floor of the fuselage. The plane reached Amsterdam, where Peres and his
wife boarded a regular El Al flight to Israel.

Peres's odyssey, which had already lasted thirty-six hours, was not yet
over. After arriving in Israel, he found out he was scheduled to give a speech at
the Knesset. He had to prepare the speech.

Peres called Yitzhak Navon, who was learned in Arabic, to give him some
help. In particular, Peres wanted a quotation from the Koran. Peres worked on
his speech and showed it to Navon, who concluded that no quotes from the
Koran were needed.

At 6:30 that night, Peres changed clothing and went to Ben-Gurion
Airport. Hundreds of security guards and police had already cordoned off the
airport. Peres took his place in the middle of the reception line.

Sadat stepped out of the plane at 7:58 P.M.

Peres returned to his home late that night. Although he had remained
awake for two days, he was so overwhelmed by the Sadat visit that he could not
fall asleep.

PERLMAN, ITZHAK (1945–   )
Violinist.

Perlman was being interviewed for a 1980 broadcast of "60 Minutes." Mike
Wallace, the interviewer, mentioned the names of several great violinists,
including Jascha Heifetz, Yehudi Menuhin, and Isaac Stern, as well as Perlman.
Then Wallace asked why so many great violinists were Jews.

Perlman, genuinely annoyed at the question, held up his fingers, moved
them, and said, "You see, our fingers are circumcised, which gives it a very good
dexterity, you know, particularly in the pinky."

PERLMUTTER, NATHAN (1923–1987)
National director, Anti-Defamation league of
B'nai B'rith.

Nathan Perlmutter spent his life combatting anti-Semitism. One day he came face to face with it and was surprised by his own reaction.

One Sunday morning, Perlmutter was walking to the store to get a newspaper. He lived in Yorkville, a section of New York with a large German population. His regular store was closed, so he continued to walk. He finally came across an older man carrying a paper, and he asked the man where he had bought the paper. Despite the cold, the man stopped and, in a thick German accent, gave him precise directions.

Perlmutter had barely started off when he spotted another, closer store. He turned to tell the man that there was another store close by.

The man said to him, "Don't go in there. It's Yiddish. Jews own it."

Perlmutter was stunned by the remark. He walked toward the older man and asked him to repeat the statement. The repetition was accompanied by open hatred. Perlmutter spoke forcefully to the man, "I'm Jewish, damn you, and if you weren't older than me, I'd punch you in the nose."

The man replied that Jews were filth and said that no Jew would be able to hit him, but Perlmutter could try if he wished.

Perlmutter wished. He punched the man once on the cheek and hit him with a left, and the man crumbled on the street. Perlmutter continued to punch him in the head.

A chorus of people yelled for someone to stop the fight.

Finally, Perlmutter got up to get his paper.

When he reflected on the morality of the incident, Perlmutter remained certain that he would have been more haunted had he failed to react.

PHILO (c. 20 B.C.E.–50 C.E.)
Philosopher of Judaism.

The Emperor Caligula ascended to the throne in Rome in the year 40 C.E. Unlike his predecessor, Tiberius, Caligula oppressed the Jews terribly. He ordered his governor, Flaccus, to set up a statue of the emperor in every synagogue in Alexandria. Mobs stormed the synagogue even before the order was carried out. Many synagogues were burned, and Jewish merchants were murdered.

The Jews were deprived of their Roman citizenship and then driven out of their two Alexandrian quarters. They went to the Delta area of the city, near the harbor, where they attempted to hold off the mob.

It was August, and the Egyptian heat was at its worst. Some Jews left to get food and water. The men who did were captured and crucified in sight of the barricades that the Jews had erected. Captured women were given pig meat to eat; those who refused were tortured.

The Jews realized that only the emperor could save them. They sent three leaders, with Philo as the head of the delegation.

Philo knew Caligula's reputation as a madman who really believed that he was a god. Philo thought that he was going to his death, and so he recited the appropriate prayers.

The delegation was met by Roman Jews, who offered to provide them with shelter. Philo refused, however, saying that in case the emperor intended to use the delegation as targets, he didn't want the Roman Jews also to get hurt. Instead, Philo and his delegation stayed at an inn.

Starting early the next morning, Philo began to stand in front of the palace gates waiting for permission to enter. Only in the evening did they leave. Each day they saw their Alexandrian enemy Apion go in to talk to the emperor, but they were not allowed to see the ruler. Finally, during the afternoon of the sixth day of waiting, they were ushered in to see the emperor.

The introductions did not go well. Caligula began by saying, "So you are the Jews who do not recognize me as god?"

Philo began to speak, but Caligula yelled at him, "Do you dare to interrupt god?"

Apion stepped forward and slapped Philo. "Silence before this god, the equal of Jupiter."

Caligula spoke a bit more calmly. He asked Philo, "Do you prefer worshipping that which is without name or form? All my other subjects accept that I am god."

Philo then said, "We have offered three different sacrifices on our altars to honor Caligula. We offered such sacrifices when you came to the throne, when you were victorious over the Teutons, and when you were ill."

Caligula misunderstood. He looked at Philo and asked, "You made sacrifices to me?"

Another in the delegation saw Caligula's confusion in thinking that the sacrifices were made to him as god rather than in his name to God. The delegate urged Philo to tell a lie in order to end the oppression and save their lives.

Philo refused to lie. "No, we made our sacrifices to the Lord, hoping that he would favor you."

Caligula became angry again. "You dare ask a favor for me? I am a god."

A soldier then moved behind Philo and pushed a spear into the philosopher's back. Caligula continued, "Now tell me, aren't I the equal of your God with no name?"

The soldier pressed the spear into Philo's back. Philo spoke up: "There is only one God. We are all mere mortals, even kings and emperors."

Caligula came forward and took out his dagger. He put it at Philo's throat and drew some blood. "Now," said Caligula, "don't you think I'm stronger than your God? I have the power of life and death over you. What can your God do for you now?"

"The Lord is all-knowing and all-powerful. If he causes you to kill me, it will be part of his design for the world and his mercy."

Caligula threw his dagger and stomped his foot. "No God can cause me to kill you. No God can force me to do anything."

Caligula walked away. Some of his courtiers laughed at the way Philo had handled their leader.

The delegation stayed on in Rome to attempt to accomplish their mission. Each day they returned to the palace gate. No audience was granted.

A few months later, in January 41, Cassius Chaeria, a Roman tribune, assassinated Caligula.

PHINEAS BEN YAIR *(second half of second century* C.E.*)*
Rabbi and scholar known for his goodness.

Two men carried a small number of sacks of barley. They came to Rabbi Phineas's house and asked to be allowed to leave their sacks there. Rabbi Phineas granted them permission. The men eventually left the town, but they had forgotten to retrieve their barley. When Rabbi Phineas saw that the men were not going to return, he sowed the grain in one of the fields that he owned. Then he reaped the crop, stored it in a barn, and sowed it again the following year. He did this each year for several years.

Some time later, the men returned and asked if their few sacks of barley were still available. Rabbi Phineas took the men to a barn and showed them an enormous pile of barley. Rabbi Phineas said to them, "This is yours. Get some mules or camels and remove it from here."

PICON, MOLLY *(1898–   )*
Actress active in Yiddish theater.

(1) Molly Picon was on tour. She listened to the gripes of other performers in the theatrical company about where they had to live. She interrupted them, "I never

complain about such things. My grandmother brought up eleven children in four rooms."

One of the actresses asked with surprised, "How did she manage?"

Molly replied, "She took in boarders."

(2) In 1929, Molly followed her Broadway debut with a performance at the Chicago Palace. After the performance, the theater's manager came backstage to tell her how successful the show had been. Molly was curious and asked whether Chicago's critics had been in the theater. The manager scoffed at that; he said that people more important than critics were there. In particular, the by-then world famous gangster Al Capone had attended Molly's performance, along with thirty members of his entourage.

One of Capone's men came backstage to see Molly and invited her and the cast back to Cicero to a cabaret that Capone controlled. Capone's reputation had preceded him; he was infamous for supposedly having ordered the beating of one of the Duncan sisters for refusing one of his "invitations." Molly and the cast decided to attend.

Molly remained apprehensive as she sat at her table in the cabaret. Capone was seated at a separate table. Then the same man who had come backstage came over to Molly. He asked her to sing a song from the show, a song that his boss had particularly liked, something called "The Immigrant Boy." Molly's husband immediately understood what the man meant. The song's actual title was "The Rabbi's Melody," and it was about a little boy from Poland who came to the United States, but is filled with homesickness.

Molly sang the song.

Capone sat and listened. Then he began to cry.

PINCHAS OF KORETZ (1726–1791)
Hasidic rabbi and kabbalist.

(1) An atheist approached Rabbi Pinchas and said, "Do you know what the great philosopher Spinoza wrote in one of his books? He wrote that humans are no higher than animals and that they have the same nature."

The rabbi said, "If that is the case, how is it that until now the animals haven't produced a Spinoza?"

(2) A disciple came to see the rebbe. The disciple was overcome with sadness. All he could see in the world was evil and torment and unhappiness. All humanity disappointed him. "I am overcome with doubt. I doubt the language of prayer, I

doubt truth, and I doubt faith. I don't know any longer who it is I am. My confusion overwhelms me. Please help me, Rebbe. Tell me what I should do."

The rabbi said to the man, "All you can do is study. The Torah has all the answers you need."

The disciple was not convinced, however. "Rebbe, I cannot even study. Uncertainty has so filled my mind that even when I open the Talmud to study, my mind strays from the holy words. My mind stays on the same page, on the very same problem."

The rabbi told his anguished visitor to come closer. "You know, what is happening to you also happened to me. I, too, struggled with the questions about human fate and the meaning of creation. I tried to study and to pray, but all to no avail. One day, I learned that the Baal Shem Tov would be speaking in our town. I was curious about him, so I went to the house of prayer where he was receiving his disciples. He was just finishing the Amidah prayer when I entered. He looked at me so directly, I thought he knew what was on my heart. Then I was able to go and study. You see, the questions remained, but they had led me to a rebbe, just as they have led you to me."

(3) The Hasidim were suspicious of the dangers of achieving fame. A famous Hasidic leader, the Grandfather of Shpole, used to tell his disciples about what he had lost when he became well known. For years, he had lived as a beggar, going from town to town and village to village.

Once, on a Sabbath evening, he found himself in the village of Koretz and attended services conducted by Rabbi Pinchas. After the service, Rabbi Pinchas greeted all the worshippers by shaking their hands. When it was Grandfather's turn, though, Rabbi Pinchas embraced him, even though the two men did not know each other.

Many years later, now famous, the Grandfather came back to Koretz to greet Rabbi Pinchas. Again Rabbi Pinchas greeted the strangers who had come to pray. When he came this time to the well-known Grandfather, Rabbi Pinchas said, "Who are you? Where are you from?"

Reflecting on this, the Grandfather of Shpole said, "It is not so good to be famous."

POOL, DAVID DE SOLA (1885–1970)
American rabbi and community leader.

The great rabbi's wife, Tamar, once came to her husband and told him that she had heard a professor claim that the Arabs had written the Ten Commandments. The rabbi said, "Yes? Well, let them *keep* them."

POTOCKI, VALENTINE (died 1749)
Polish count and martyred proselyte.

Potocki was studying in Paris. Once he was in a tavern with his friend Zaremba when he observed that the owner, an elderly Jew, was studying the Talmud. Potocki asked to learn more about Judaism. He and his friend took a vow that they would become Jews if they could be convinced that Christianity was in error. Zaremba, though, first married and left the city. Potocki continued his study of Judaism and finally decided to convert. Zaremba heard about the conversion, remembered his vow, and then took his family to Amsterdam, where he, too, converted. He then moved to the land of Israel.

Potocki, meanwhile, moved to Ilya, in Lithuania near Vilna, and lived as a Jew under the name Abraham ben Abraham. It was while there that he got into trouble with the authorities. He was praying one day in the synagogue when a small boy began to make noise. He yelled at the boy for bothering him while he prayed. The boy's father arranged for Potocki's arrest on the charge that he had abandoned Christianity, then a crime. Legend has it that the Gaon of Vilna visited Potocki in prison to persuade him to maintain his faith in Judaism and to assure him that he should not grieve because he would soon experience eternal bliss.

On the second day of Shevuot in 1749 (5509 on the Hebrew calendar), Potocki was burned at the stake near the fortress of Vilna. He died uttering the prayer "Blessed are thou O Lord . . . who sanctifies thy name before multitudes."

A Vilna Jew named Eliezer Ziskes, pretending to be a Christian, bribed some soldiers to obtain some ashes and a finger from the corpse. He buried the remains in a Jewish cemetery. A tree eventually grew over the burial spot. The area became known as the resting place of the Ger Tzedek, or Righteous Proselyte, and became a place for pilgrimages by Jews on Tisha B'av and the High Holy Days. Polish vandals eventually desecrated the gravesite.

PRIESAND, SALLY (1946–   )
Rabbi; first woman ordained in the United States.

It was on June 3, 1972, that Sally Priesand was ordained a Rabbi by the Hebrew Union College-Jewish Institute of Religion (HUC-JIR) in Cincinnati, the seminary that prepared Reform rabbis. The ordination was to take place in the Plum Street Temple. This historic site was appropriate because the ordination itself was historic.

Women had been facing barriers in traditional Judaism for several thousand years. Women were not counted as part of a minyan; they could not initiate a divorce; and in Orthodox and many Conservative synagogues they were still were separately seated. There were many other barriers as well to a woman leading a full Jewish life. On this day a major barrier—the ordination of a woman as rabbi—was about to be removed.

Rabbi Priesand had entered the HUC-JIR eight years earlier with no certainty (indeed no overwhelming probability) of being allowed to enter her chosen profession. She had been admitted as a rabbinical student by Dr. Nelson Glueck, the president at that time, but she knew it was possible that various professors would want to see her fail or that Reform Jews would not accept a female rabbi. Indeed, in her fifth year, when she was ready to serve as a student rabbi, some congregations refused to accept her.

After her eighth year of study, she went out to be interviewed, and again some congregations refused even to talk with her. Finally she received a position as assistant rabbi at the Stephen Wise Free Synagogue in New York.

As part of the ordination ceremonies, Rabbi Priesand publicly proclaimed herself committed to the survival of the Jewish tradition. Then the ordination—and history—took place.

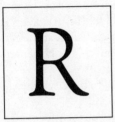

RABIN, YITZHAK (1922–   )
Israeli prime minister and politician.

Early on June 12, 1948, Menachem Begin, then chief of the Irgun, told Israeli officials that a boat, the *Altalena*, was carrying 5,000 rifles, 250 machine guns, and some antitank weapons—enough arms to equip ten battalions. The boat was due to dock in five days. (*Altalena* was the pen name of Vladimir Jabotinsky, founder of revisionist Zionism and spiritual founder of the Irgun.)

Prime Minister David Ben-Gurion was furious about the ship. He had declared a state just the month before, and the Arabs had invaded. The Irgun, which stood outside the provisional government, seemed to Ben-Gurion to be providing weapons to its own private army. Ben-Gurion, suspicious of Begin, feared that there would be several separate armies and perhaps even an overthrow attempt and civil war. (In fact, an overthrow attempt was being planned, but without Begin's knowledge.)

Ben-Gurion concluded that the boat could land, but that the weapons would be controlled by the army. Begin apparently either misunderstood those orders or chose to ignore them. He planned for the Irgun to maintain control of the weapons.

During the afternoon of June 20, the cabinet of Israel's provisional government took the decisive step of voting to seize the ship's weapons, by force if necessary.

Later that same night, the *Altalena* was anchored off Kfar Vitkin. Five hundred men were on the ship. They began to unload the weapons into smaller launches and even rowboats. Irgun members arrived from all around the country and worked through the night and on into the next day, unloading the weapons. Finally, a member of the Haganah, the regular army, issued an ultimatum to Begin. Either the Irgun had to surrender the weapons, or those weapons would be confiscated. Begin was given ten minutes to make up his mind, but he responded immediately, saying that he would not surrender the weapons. Ben-Gurion then gave the fateful orders: Force was now to be used.

Force was used. One member of the Irgun was killed. Begin was dragged back on board the ship by his supporters. The ship set sail for Tel Aviv.

On the morning of June 22, Ben-Gurion contacted Yigal Allon at the Ritz Hotel in Tel Aviv. The Ritz housed the headquarters of Palmach, the Haganah's strike force.

Meanwhile, Begin was off the Tel Aviv shore speaking to the city's citizens from the ship, asking for their help in unloading the weapons.

Yitzhak Rabin was scheduled to attend a meeting at Palmach headquarters. He was walking to the Ritz when he spotted the *Altalena* and two smaller boats. He also saw Allon. Allon decided that he had to go to Haganah headquarters, and Rabin, who had no knowledge of what had previously occurred, was put in charge.

Rabin had forty men under his command. Most of them had been wounded and were recovered at the Palmach headquarters; they were not looking forward to battling other Jews after having been shot by Arabs. Rabin set about organizing them. He handed out grenades. He quickly realized, with some horror, that he was facing what could be the opening battle in a civil war, that he might soon be ordering Jews to kill other Jews.

The *Altalena* was given another order to surrender; the order was refused. Rabin's men then fought with the Irgun supporters. Machine guns, rifles, and grenades were used by both sides. Rabin called for reinforcements. The battle raged for ten hours. Finally, a field gun firing from the beach set the *Altalena* bursting into flames. Irgun supporters in small boats began to evacuate those still alive. Begin wanted to be the last person to leave the ship, but some of his supporters threw him overboard, and one of the Irgunists in a smaller boat grabbed him and took him to land.

The Irgun supporters were arrested, but Begin escaped and spoke defiantly on the radio that evening. Ben-Gurion replied, "Blessed be the gun that set the ship on fire."

Meanwhile, Rabin considered his losses. The Irgun had evidently suffered significantly; fourteen of them were dead, and nearly one hundred were wounded. Rabin had lost one man and had several wounded. The Haganah was in control of the ship.

The next day, Rabin organized an elite Palmach unit, nicknamed the Desert Beasts, which would raid the Irgun's headquarters on King George Street in Tel Aviv. The raid was delayed. Instead, on September 20, 1948, the government issued one more ultimatum: The Irgun was given twenty-four hours to agree to obey all laws of Israel, to dismantle the separate army, and to serve in the regular army.

The Irgun accepted. Civil war had been averted.

RACKMAN, EMANUEL (1910–   )
Rabbi, Orthodox leader and chancellor of Bar-Ilan University.

Rabbi Rackman supplied the following anecdotes.

(1) It was early in June of 1944, a few days before the Allies crossed the channel. Rabbi Rackman was stationed at Randolph Field in Texas. All the soldiers were stuck on the base.

The rabbi walked into the office that he shared with the Protestant chaplain. The chaplain was going berserk.

"Henry, what's the matter?" Rabbi Rackman asked.

The chaplain said that he had just received a call from the base commander. A man had walked in and said that he was a believer in the Old Testament and had just gotten married. The man was requesting a year's furlough, claiming as his reason that Deuteronomy read that when a man married and hadn't had a chance to go on a honeymoon, he was entitled to leave the army for a year.

The base commander had become frightened that everyone on the base would ask for a furlough while the country was just on the eve of the invasion of France. The man was not Jewish, so the base commander had called the Protestant chaplain. Neither the commander nor the chaplain knew what to do. Rabbi Rackman spoke to his disturbed colleague, "Henry, listen, I think I know how to handle him. Let's meet him."

Soon after, the young man came to meet the rabbi. Rabbi Rackman told him how happy he was that someone else on the base took the Old Testament seriously. After they had spoken for forty-five minutes, Rabbi Rackman noticed that it was a quarter to noon. The rabbi suggested that the two get some lunch. The rabbi then asked the man where he usually ate. The man replied that he ate "anyplace."

Rabbi Rackman was surprised. "You eat anyplace? Do you eat everything?" The man replied that he did, and the rabbi continued, "Don't you know that in the Book of Leviticus there is a list of forbidden foods?"

The man was exposed as a phony. The base commander's panic quickly vanished.

(2) A Protestant chaplain attended a wedding at which a Reform rabbi and Rabbi Rackman officiated. The Reform rabbi, Max Eichhorn, had some difficulty explaining to the chaplain why Jews broke a glass at the conclusion of the wedding ceremony. He decided that instead of telling him about the destruction of the temple, which the non-Jewish chaplain might not understand, he would explain that it was a prayer that the marriage would last until something could bring all those glass particles together again.

About fifteen years later, Rabbi Rackman was on a trip through the southern United States with Rabbi Eichhorn, who was then field director for the Jewish Welfare Board. They came to a base where the Protestant chaplain served. "Max," said the minister, "I learned something from you at that wedding that I never forgot, and since then we break a glass at every Protestant wedding at which I officiate."

RASHI (1041–1105)
Rabbi aand major biblical commentator.

Many Jews who were forced to accept baptism during the Crusades later encountered tremendous hostility from unconverted Jews. Rashi demonstrated the need for tolerance in dealing with those forced into baptism.

Rashi, *Rabbi Shlomo ben Itzhak*, had finished his great commentaries on the Torah and Talmud in November of 1095. Two months later, Pope Urban II issued a call for the first crusade.

The crusaders rampaged toward Jerusalem. In one city after another they left Jews with a cruel choice: Accept baptism or die. Severe torture frequently accompanied their threats. Some Jews, under such unbearable duress, did accept baptism.

After the crusaders had left, many of those who had been forcibly converted sought to return to Judaism. But those who had remained Jews, and other Jews who had not been confronted by the crusaders, rejected the apostates.

Rashi was the rabbi in Troyes, France. One day, while walking in the marketplace, the rabbi spotted an apostate Jewish traveler going into the inn to seek shelter. At first the innkeeper was kind, but when he was informed of the guest's apostasy, he threw him out bodily. The traveler did not argue. He walked to another inn. The same thing happened. Rashi continued to watch as the stranger was refused cheese, baked goods, fruit, and wine, despite having money with which to pay. None of the merchants wished to serve an apostate. The stranger seemed resigned to such treatment. He began to walk to the city gates. Rashi stopped him and gave him the traditional greeting, "Shalom Aleichem."

The stranger returned the greeting, though he was not sure why the rabbi was being friendly.

Rashi invited the man to his house for food.

"Maybe you don't know, Rabbi," the man said, "but I'm an apostate. It was by force, but I accepted the cross. I would like to rejoin my people, but they will have nothing to do with me. I do not wish to bring you shame or harm."

"You are a stranger in this city. You need food and drink. It is a commandment to take care of you." Rashi then took the stranger to his house and gave him a meal and a place to sleep. He learned that the man was from Spires and that hot pincers had been used to make him accept baptism.

The rabbi took the man to the synagogue in the evening. The Jews of Troyes were outside waiting. Rashi entered the synagogue with the stranger, but no one followed them inside.

Rashi went out to remind the crowd that it was time for evening prayers. It was the innkeeper who spoke for them. "We will not go into the synagogue while an apostate is in there." Someone else called out that they would not follow a rabbi who stayed with an apostate.

Rashi explained to the stranger that the two of them would have to leave. "These Jews have a greater need to be near the Ark than we do. Maybe that is because they are so much nearer to sin."

Rashi and the stranger prayed in a field.

The rabbi did not appear at the synagogue the next day for morning or afternoon prayers. Near evening, the head of the synagogue, a man named Eliahu, came to find out why the rabbi had failed to appear at the house of worship.

The rabbi explained, "My guest was not made welcome in the synagogue. I, also, feel unwelcome."

Eliahu told Rashi that the people were angry at their rabbi. Rashi answered him, "I will accept their being angry at me before I will accept the Lord's being angry at me." Then he told Eliahu, "I will be in the court of the synagogue before evening prayers. Tell the people to come." Rashi asked the stranger to accompany him to the synagogue. The stranger begged not to go, saying that he could not bear to come between Rashi and the congregation. But Rashi insisted that he go, and so the stranger reluctantly accompanied him.

A large crowd had gathered in the synagogue's court. The crowd watched as Rashi climbed the steps. He turned and spoke to the people: "You who are gathered here are good Jews. You remain faithful to the commandments given to our people. I am your rabbi, and I know this. But what would happen if you were placed near a fire, with your feet feeling its heat? Would you be able to resist accepting baptism?"

People yelled out that they would be able to resist. Rashi looked at one of the men who had yelled out. The rabbi stared at him for several moments. The man finally said, "I think I could have resisted, Rabbi."

Rashi nodded. "I think so, too. And I think Eliahu would have gone through the torture. But I am not so sure of myself. I hope I would have, but I don't really know. That is why it is written that we must judge all people charitably, and that we shouldn't judge until we have been in that person's place." Rashi's voice grew louder. "Did you put yourself in this stranger's place before you judged him? Have you been charitable in that judgment?"

Rashi then extended his hand to the stranger. "Come, let us go into our house of prayer, where we may praise the Lord."

The stranger and Rashi started inside. The others slowly followed.

Later that week Rashi sent out a message throughout northern France and the Rhineland. He would hear those who were forcibly baptized but now wished to return to their Jewish faith.

Many came to see him.

REUBEN BEN ISTRUBLI *(mid-second century C.E.)*
Scholar.

The Romans issued a decree that made it unlawful for Jews to observe the Sabbath or to circumcise their sons. Reuben ben Istrubli resolved that somehow he would have these edicts revoked. He developed a careful plan.

First, he cut his hair in the same manner as the Romans did. Then he dressed himself as did the Romans. He used the disguise to pass himself off as a genuine Roman. Eventually, he became friendly with several important government officials.

One day he engaged these officials in conversation. He said to them, "If you had an enemy, would you want your enemy to become richer, or poorer?" They agreed that they would want their enemy to be poorer. "But you compel the Jews to work on their Sabbath. By doing this, you are making them richer." They admitted that he was right.

Reuben continued. "Now, would you like your enemy to grow stronger, or weaker?" They agreed that they wished their enemy to grow weaker. Reuben said, "The Jews circumcise their sons, and this causes them to grow weaker." The officials accepted this pagan belief and agreed.

The two edicts were soon revoked.

Unfortunately, when the Romans discovered that Reuben was Jewish, they reissued the edicts.

ROSENZWEIG, FRANZ *(1886–1929)*
German philosopher and theologian. Author of The Star of
Redemption, *among other works.*

Franz Rosenzweig's return to Judaism, dramatic in its own right, was fateful because of his later immense contributions to modern Jewish philosophy.

In his youth, Rosenzweig had studied and absorbed the philosophy of Hegel. He had even written his doctoral dissertation on Hegel's political views.

Over time, though, he found that his attachment to academic studies had weakened and had been replaced by a strong interest in religion. He discussed religious faith with two cousins who had become Christians and with friends. He was especially close to a Protestant friend, Eugen Rosenstock-Huessy, who convinced Rosenzweig that a religious view was an intellectually acceptable way to engage the world.

The two friends had an extended discussion on the night of July 7, 1913. Rosenzweig came to accept the need for a religious view. With little knowledge of Judaism, and fresh from the arguments of Rosenstock-Huessy and others, it seemed to Rosenzweig that he would have to become a Christian. He determined to prepare for his baptism but decided to remain faithful to Judaism until then. He picked out a godfather and continued his studies.

Rosenzweig underwent intense internal struggles over the next weeks and months as he sought to clarify his views and feelings.

Then, on October 11 — Yom Kippur — he attended a service in Berlin at a traditional synagogue. Somehow, as he sat there all through the day, Rosenzweig experienced the clear and present reality of God. Rosenzweig had not believed that such a clear spiritual encounter was possible within Judaism; he had thought that the Christian notion of Jesus as a mediator was necessary. His own experience was a great revelation.

By October 23, Rosenzweig had reached his theological conclusion, which he expressed in a letter to his mother; he had painfully found his way back to Judaism.

ROTHSCHILD, EDMOND DE (1845–1934)
Member of the famous banking family.

(1) Rothschild was frequently bothered by people seeking funds, favors, or employment. He quickly learned just how he could use his influence.

Once, a Jewish young man seeking to start a banking career came to Rothschild with a letter of introduction. Rothschild read the letter, which extolled the young man's honesty. The man had experience and now wished to become part of the House of Rothschild.

Rothschild invited the man to lunch at a well-known restaurant. Their interaction was most friendly. Rothschild talked intimately with the young man, held his arm, and generally proved to be a kind host. After the lunch, the man shyly asked whether he might expect the position he so wished to obtain.

"My dear fellow," Rothschild said, "I have done for you all that I could."

The young man was extremely disappointed, but he realized that he could not change the great banker's mind.

That afternoon the man went to a bank and was surprised to note that his presence was causing quite a stir. The president of the bank personally welcomed him.

"Didn't you have lunch with Baron Rothschild today?" the president asked.

"I did," said the young man.

"Is there anything I can do for you?" continued the banker.

"I am, in fact, looking for a position with your bank."

He was immediately hired.

(2) Baron Rothschild once entered involuntarily into an argument with a fervent socialist. The socialist passionately argued that it was unfair that one man should have so much money, while millions of people had so little. The socialist finished with a call for the baron to distribute his wealth.

The baron considered the argument. He then called in his secretary to determine the full extent of the Rothschild fortune. Once this was calculated, the baron consulted an almanac to figure out the world's population. Using simple division, the baron made his final calculation. He then turned to his secretary and said, "Will you give this gentleman sixteen cents. That is his share of my wealth."

ROTHSCHILD, LIONEL DE *(1808–1879)*
Member of the famous banking family.

Rothschild wished to break the barriers that prevented Jews from serving in the British Parliament.

Rothschild was elected to Parliament, but then he refused to take the oath of office on a Christian Bible. He was not allowed to serve. He ran again, however, and was elected again. Rothschild then repeated his refusal to take the oath on a non-Jewish Bible. He fought to serve for eleven years.

Then, on July 26, 1858, he was finally allowed to swear on a Jewish Bible and with his head covered. He then began his service in the House of Commons.

RUPPIN, ARTHUR *(1876–1943)*
Developer of Zionist settlements.

Arthur Ruppin was an energetic builder on behalf of the Zionist movement. He visited the land of Israel for the first time in 1907 on behalf of the Actions

Committee of the World Zionist Organization and the Jewish National Fund. He was at the time unofficially in charge of representing Zionist interests there.

Ruppin was also instrumental in fostering an interest in the sociology of the Jews. To aid him in his study of Jewish society, he decided to attempt to ascertain the exact size of Jerusalem's Jewish population.

He began his sociological quest simply by asking those he presumed knowledgeable to provide him with their estimates. These estimates varied widely, however. Ruppin decided, on the spot, to conduct a census, the first ever taken in Jerusalem since the time of Emperor Augustus.

Ruppin went to a Jewish school and requested the help of several of the older students. He divided the city into twenty-four districts and assigned one district each to twenty-four of the students. Unfortunately, several of the census takers were subsequently arrested. The local authorities then informed Ruppin that he would need the sultan's permission.

The first census attempt since Roman times had failed. A census would not be taken until the British conducted one in 1922.

RUTH (c. eleventh century B.C.E.)
Loyal proselyte.

Ruth, a non-Jew from Moab, had married Mahlon. Mahlon and his father, Elimelech, his mother, Naomi, and his brother, Chilian, had originally lived in Bethlehem, but had left because of famine. They had traveled to Moab, an area east of the Dead Sea, where the fertile highlands held out the promise of sustenance. Instead, Naomi's husband and two sons died there.

Naomi and her two daughters-in-law, Ruth and Orpah, were left. Naomi was old and tired and desired to return to where she had been born. Naomi advised her two daughters-in-law to return to their mothers; the two were young and could easily marry again. Orpah quickly agreed to do what her mother-in-law advised. Ruth, however, did not. She didn't see her mother-in-law as a burden to be discarded. She expressed her continuing love for her dead husband by maintaining loyalty to his mother, to the Jewish people and nation, and, finally, to God. When Naomi asked her to leave, Ruth said, "Do not try to persuade me to leave you, to turn back and not go with you. Wherever you go, I will go too. Wherever you stay, I will stay. Your people shall be my people, and your God my God."

SAADIA GAON (882–942)
Scholar and leader of Babylonian Jewry.

Saadia carried on the Jewish tradition of fairness even when such honesty was costly.

A prince stood to realize great financial gain as a result of a lawsuit concerning an inheritance. He made an unfair decision to get that inheritance and then sought signatures from various Jewish leaders to indicate the decision was correct.

The Jewish leader of Pumbeditha complied, but Saadia refused to ratify such an unfair decision. The prince argued with him and then threatened him, but Saadia responded, "You should not show any special respect, even for important people, when making a judgment." This, of course, greatly angered the prince.

Saadia was removed from his position and was forced to retire. Nevertheless, he had maintained both his own integrity and Jewish tradition.

SAFRA (*first half of fourth century C.E.*)
Rabbi and Babylonian scholar.

Rabbi Safra was widely known for his honesty.

The rabbi was once offered some merchandise for sale. Some men came to buy the merchandise and asked the price. The rabbi replied that the merchandise cost ten pieces of gold. The traders offered five pieces, but Rabbi Safra declined the offer.

The traders returned the following morning to raise their offer and found the rabbi at prayer. One trader said that he was prepared now to purchase the merchandise for seven pieces of gold. But the rabbi did not want to interrupt his praying, so he remained silent. The trader, believing that the silence signified displeasure with the offer, finally said, "All right. We will pay the ten gold pieces you ask."

The rabbi finished his prayers and said, "I could not answer because praying and business do not belong together. I had decided before you spoke that I would accept your offer of five pieces. I would be cheating you if my praying led to my accepting ten pieces."

SALANT, SAMUEL (1816–1909)
Chief rabbi of Jerusalem.

Rabbi Salant was one of the best known rabbis in Jerusalem, along with Rabbi Joshua Leib Diskin. He and Rabbi Diskin had some different ways. One of the differences was in their sleeping patterns. Rabbi Salant awoke very early and went to sleep early, which was the local custom, whereas Rabbi Diskin maintained his more familiar pattern of arising at a later hour.

A Russian Jew, Reb Shiya Dovid Komalinka, came to Jerusalem to spend his last days. He decided that he could do no better than to seek wisdom from Jerusalem's two famous rabbis.

He went late one evening to see Rabbi Salant, but he was told that the rabbi had already retired for the evening. Reb Komalinka, assuming that this was the local way, left. One morning he decided to see Rabbi Diskin. He went to the rabbi's house and was told the rabbi was not yet up, despite the lateness of the hour.

Reb Komalinka went home and told his wife, "It is shocking. The rabbis in the Holy Land spend all their time in sleep."

SALANTER, ISRAEL (1810–1883)
Rabbi and founder of the Musar movement, which emphasizes ethics in Jewish religious life.

(1) Rabbi Salanter's gentle humanity provided moral lessons for all who knew him. One such lesson came on a Yom Kippur eve. The synagogue was crowded. It was time to begin the Kol Nidre prayer. Suddenly it was noticed that Rabbi Salanter was missing. The shammes was sent to the rabbi's house to find the great man. But the rabbi was not at home either.

A group of congregants formed to search for their missing rabbi.

Finally, after a long search, the rabbi was found in a small, dimly lit house in a poor section of the town. The rabbi was rocking a baby to the tune of a religious melody.

Rabbi Salanter's followers were utterly puzzled. "What are you doing here?" one asked.

The rabbi responded, "I was on my way to the synagogue when I passed this house and heard a baby's cries. I supposed the family had gone to pray and had left the baby alone. So I went in to take care of the child."

(2) Rabbi Salanter was asked how best to prepare on Friday for the upcoming Sabbath. He told his disciples, "Help your wives with the housework and speak especially gently to them."

(3) Unlike many other well-known rabbis of his day, Rabbi Salanter poured only a very small amount of water over his hands as part of the required ritual washing of the hands prior to a meal. This seemed to be in contradiction to the talmudic advice to use as much water as possible. The rabbi was asked why he met only the law's minimum requirement with his sparse use of water. He responded, "I know that it is a mitzvah to use a lot of water, but the poor servant girl has to bring in the water from the well outside, even in the bitter cold. I am not anxious to be so pious at the expense of the poor girl's hard work."

(4) Rabbi Salanter was very strict about the baking of matzoh. He undertook to supervise the baking process himself.

He became ill, however, and needed to be taken home. His disciples were to take his place. Before they left for the bakery, they asked him which part of the process merited their greatest concern. Rabbi Salanter replied, "Take heed that you don't speak harshly to the kneader. She is a poor widow."

(5) Rabbi Salanter began serving in Kovno in 1848. One summer, some time after he had achieved fame there, a cholera epidemic broke out. At first only the poor were devastated, but the epidemic spread quickly until it had reached every area of the town. In just two weeks, most of the town had been infected. There was no place to house the ill, so Rabbi Salanter turned the synagogue into a hospital.

The community leader, who was against this decision, came to see the rabbi. Rabbi Salanter was busy cleaning the bed of a comatose man, and he didn't stop until it was time for the evening prayers. Finally, after hearing the leader's complaint, the rabbi said, "God would much prefer that his house be for the suffering and the poor than just a place where the rich can worship."

Rosh Hashanah arrived, and the epidemic continued to ravage the town. Two days before Yom Kippur, Rabbi Salanter toured the town with a physician. The rabbi wanted an assessment of how long the horror would last. He was told that in only a week or ten days the epidemic would finally be over.

"How, though, can we ensure the health of those still alive?" the rabbi wanted to know.

The doctor considered this. "Most of all they need food and rest and some sunlight."

"But it will be Yom Kippur in just two days," Rabbi Salanter said. "All the people will fast." The rabbi returned to his synagogue and prayed for a long while. When he finished, he put up a sign on the synagogue's gate announcing that, in order to maintain everyone's health, there would be no fasting.

The Jews of Kovno could not believe that the sign was genuine. They protested, claiming that they would rather die than break the fast.

On the evening of Yom Kippur, the cantor sang out Kol Nidre in a weakened voice. The small number of people who were still able to walk had assembled. They looked exhausted. Their bodies trembled. Some had become feverish.

Rabbi Salanter began to speak. "I am your teacher. It is my job to interpret the Law for you. This year it is no sin to eat."

Still, the people protested.

The rabbi raised his hands to quiet their outcry. "If you fast, you will die. How, then, can you serve God and fulfill his commandments?"

He saw their still-determined faces. Rabbi Salanter took out a small bag. The congregation was in turmoil. Rabbi Salanter withdrew a loaf of bread from the bag. He held the bread in both hands, said a prayer, tore the bread, and began to eat.

The people then prayed and ate.

The plague soon ended, and Kovno slowly recovered.

SALOMON, HAYM (1740–1785)
American patriot and financier.

High holy day services once had to be interrupted to save the American Revolution.

It was Yom Kippur in the year 1780. Haym Salomon arose and made his way to pray at Mikveh Israel. The congregation's leader, Rabbi Gershom Mendes Seixas, began the services. The room was filled with well-known people of the time: the Gratz brothers, Simon Nathan, Jonas Phillips, and Philip Moses Russell, who had been commended by George Washington for his work as a surgeon's mate at Valley Forge. The prayers continued throughout the day.

There was a sudden knock on the door. Everyone was shocked at such behavior on the Day of Atonement. The sexton called out for the person knocking to come inside. In a few minutes, the sexton made his way down the aisle to Salomon's seat. He told Salomon that a Gentile wished to see him. The sexton had told the man of the religious significance of the day, but the man insisted that it was urgent.

Worried about his family, Salomon moved to the back of the room. The young man was standing at the door. He told Salomon that there was a message from Robert Morris, the minister of finance for the colonies rebelling for their independence. Salomon slowly opened the note and read it. The finance office had been unable to raise sufficient money to cover two notes, which Morris enclosed. They totalled $20,000. Morris went on to say that even his personal sources of aid were exhausted. Immediate action was required. The fate of the revolution depended, at least in part, on its financial solvency.

Salomon was aghast that the request had come on Yom Kippur. If he waited for the holy day to end, it would be too late.

Salomon made his decision. He went forward to speak to Rabbi Seixas, explaining that he had received a message from Robert Morris and that he had to speak to the congregation. The rabbi was outraged. Discussing finances on Yom Kippur was forbidden. Salomon explained that both the Continental Congress and the army were in trouble. Salomon asked God's forgiveness.

Salomon then began to speak, but he was interrupted by congregants who were angry about the disruption of the service. Salomon continued to speak. He talked about the soldiers dying of starvation, and he spoke openly about the threat of mutiny against General Washington. He told of Morris's urgent plea. Salomon then had the sexton call Morris's aide in to record pledges. Salomon started by giving $3,000. A man named Samuel Lynn also begged God's forgiveness and pledged $1,000. It took only fifteen minutes for the $20,000 to be raised.

The aide left, and the congregation resumed the service.

SAMUEL BEN SOSRATI (*end of second century–mid-third century* C.E.)
Rabbi and scholar.

Rabbi Samuel risked death to prove his faith.

On a visit to Rome, he chanced upon some royal jewelry that the queen had lost. Before he had a chance to return the jewelry, the queen issued a proclamation offering a reward to anyone who returned the lost items within thirty days, but threatening with death anyone who waited more than the thirty days.

Instead of returning the jewelry immediately, Samuel waited until the thirty-day period had elapsed. He then went to the palace and returned the jewels.

"Weren't you in the city during these past thirty days?" the queen asked. Samuel replied that he had been in the city. "But didn't you read the proclamation ordering the return of the jewels within thirty days?"

"I did, indeed, read the proclamation," said Samuel.

The queen was mystified. "Why, then, did you wait to return my jewels?"

"I waited for the thirty days to pass so that you would not think that I returned your jewels because I feared either your power or the punishment you might give. I wanted you to know that God is the only ruler I obey."

SAMUEL HA-NAGID (993–c. 1055)
Spanish rabbi, statesman, and scholar.

Rabbi Samuel was serving as a minister in the court of the caliph. Because of the rabbi's high-ranking post, the caliph often gave him difficult jobs to do, and he was the object of other ministers' jealousy.

Once, another minister insulted Rabbi Samuel and spoke about him in a mean-spirited fashion. The caliph ordered that Rabbi Samuel cut out the tongue of the minister who had used that tongue so cruelly.

Several weeks later the caliph saw the offending minister once again and was shocked that the man still had his tongue. The caliph immediately ordered Rabbi Samuel to explain why the explicit order had not been carried out.

Rabbi Samuel said, "Your Majesty, I did obey your command. I got rid of his tongue. With kindness and warmth I gained his sympathy, respect, and friendship. Indeed, he no longer has his vile tongue."

SAUL OF TIKTIN (eighteenth century)
Russian rabbi.

Rabbi Saul was once called upon to be a modern-day Solomon.

Two women came to see the rabbi. Both were holding an end of a five-ruble note. Each claimed that the money was hers. The rabbi questioned each woman carefully, but he could not determine which one really owned the money.

Finally he went to the next room, being careful to leave the door slightly open. He spoke to his wife. "This is a very difficult problem. I have no evidence, but there is a clue. You see, one corner is a bit torn, and neither woman has yet mentioned it as a sign of identification. I'm not sure what I am going to do."

One of the two women was listening near the open door and heard what the rabbi had said. When he returned, she called out to him, "Rabbi, that five-ruble note is mine, and I just remembered how I can prove it to you."

"How can you do that?" the rabbi asked.

"Just look at the corners of the bill. One of the corners is a little torn."

"If that is your claim, then you must have very good ears indeed." The rabbi turned to the other woman. "This is obviously your money. There is clearly no torn corner on the bill, so it cannot belong to the other woman. Therefore, it must be yours."

SCHECHTER, SOLOMON (1847–1915)
Rabbi, scholar, and leader of Conservative Judaism.

Schechter once met a young woman from the Salvation Army who told him that she was "collecting for the Lord."

Rabbi Schechter looked at her and said, "I am much older than you are and certainly will see the Lord before you do. I will pay my debts to Him personally."

SCHEINDELE (eighteenth century)
Rebbitzin of Vashilishock.

Scheindele was well known throughout the Jewish world for her wisdom. She was always considered more learned than her distinguished husband, Reb Velvele.

One day the rebbitzin and her husband were involved in a familiar argument. The rabbi, frustrated at his wife's reputation as a wiser person than he, finally said, "Now you listen, Scheindele, dear. You are a rabbi's wife. You are only a rebbitzin because I am a rabbi."

"Yes," she said, "that is certainly true, but nothing could stop me from being the rebbitzin of the largest Jewish community in the world. It is only through you that I am rebbitzin of such a small place as Vashilishock."

SCHIFF, JACOB (1847–1920)
American financier and philanthropist.

Although he was a follower of Reform Judaism, Jacob Schiff had great respect for more traditional Jews and was a major donor to all Jewish causes, whatever the particular religious group.

One day a young man from Yeshiva University met with Schiff about the construction of an Orthodox synagogue. Schiff had made a substantial contribution, and the young man wanted to know why a Reform Jew would help the Orthodox.

Schiff said to him, "My dear young man, if there were no Orthodox Judaism, there would be nothing to reform."

SCHREIBER, SIMON (1850–1944)
Hungarian rabbi.

The rabbi once had to think fast to evade the trap of an anti-Semite.

Besides being a scholar, Rabbi Schreiber served as a member of the Austrian Parliament. He once received an invitation from Emperor Franz Josef to visit the palace on a Sabbath afternoon. When the rabbi arrived, the emperor gave him a cigar. The rabbi felt that he had to take the cigar so that he would not insult the emperor, but he decided that since Jewish law forbade lighting or handling a fire on the Sabbath, the sensible thing to do was simply to hold on to the unlit cigar.

Graf von Pfuffendorf, an infamous anti-Semite, was also at the palace and saw a chance to embarrass the rabbi. Von Pfuffendorf lit a match and came over to the rabbi. "I know you like to smoke, Rabbi. Can I offer you a light?"

"No, thank you," the rabbi responded politely.

Von Pfuffendorf was not finished, though. "Perhaps, Rabbi, the emperor's cigar is not good enough for you. In that case, His Majesty will order some better ones."

The emperor looked over at the rabbi. Schreiber considered his situation. He could simply have told the emperor that it was the Sabbath, a day on which he was forbidden to smoke. But he didn't wish to use the Sabbath as his reason, because to do so would suggest that the emperor had been tactless in the first place by even offering a cigar. Instead, the rabbi turned to von Pfuffendorf and said, "Why, my dear Graf, would you really think it right for me to let a present from His Majesty vanish in smoke?" The rabbi then carefully put the cigar in his pocket. "I will keep it as an everlasting remembrance of this visit."

The emperor smiled. Von Pfuffendorf was left speechless.

SELIGMAN, JOSEPH (1819–1880)
American financier.

Joseph Seligman, a prominent banker, was involved in a famous anti-Semitic case.

He worked through the spring of 1877 on a plan to help the government of the United States pay off its war debt. Treasury Secretary Sherman finally approved Seligman's plan over the others that had been submitted. By the summer of 1877, Seligman was tired; he decided to go on a vacation.

Without question, the most popular of American resorts at the time was Saratoga Springs, in upstate New York. The Grand Union was the best hotel in Saratoga Springs. It was at the time one of the largest hotels in the world. It covered 7 acres and had 834 rooms. It had 12 miles of red carpeting and room for 2,500 people. The hotel had been owned by Alexander Stewart, a rival of Seligman's. After his death in 1876, his various enterprises—including the largest department store in Manhattan—were managed by Judge Henry Hilton.

Seligman took a train upstate. He arrived at the hotel on June 19, right after lunch. He went to the front desk, expecting simply to be given the key to the suite the Seligmans always rented.

According to the *New York Times* account, the manager of the hotel approached Seligman and said, "Mr. Seligman, I am required to inform you that Mr. Hilton has given instructions that no Israelites shall in the future be permitted to stop at this hotel." Seligman was obviously taken aback. He was silent for a while and then asked why this rule was being applied. He asked about the Jews, "Are they dirty, do they misbehave, or have they refused to pay their bills?" The manager said that none of those statements was true. Rather, business had fallen off, and Judge Hilton had concluded that the Christian clientele was not coming because of the presence of Jews. Seligman was furious. He and those with him stormed out of the hotel lobby and returned to New York.

Seligman was faced with two choices: He could ignore the incident or make it public. Previous cases of anti-Semitism in the United States had not been publicized, so the question was genuinely difficult. After much reflection, Seligman decided to go public.

He wrote a bitter letter to Judge Hilton and released the scathing attack to the papers. The Manhattan department store being operated by Hilton was boycotted. Hilton released his own letter; he remained unapologetic. He wrote, "I know what I have done and am fully prepared to abide by it." Hilton went on in the letter to justify the exclusion of Jews.

The debate over this refusal took on a life of its own. Religious figures, newspapers, politicians, and ordinary citizens took sides. Henry Ward Beecher, then one of the most important ministers in the nation, attacked Hilton's actions.

The feud had its effects. Hilton was eventually forced to sell the department store. For the first time, whatever the consequences, a Jew had decided to face anti-Semitism and fight it in the open for all the world to see.

Some of the effects were not favorable for Jews. The times, it turned out, were seemingly on Hilton's side. Seligman's encounter turned out to be but the first skirmish in a war carried on by native anti-Semites. The emerging era was to be one of restrictions and quotas designed to keep Jews out of hotels, clubs, universities, businesses, and many other places in American life.

SENESH, HANNAH (1921–1945)
Fighter and martyr.

Hannah Senesh gave her life to fight the Nazis.

By the summer of 1942, a decision was made by the Haganah's leadership to send *shlichim*, messengers, into Nazi-occupied Europe. These messengers were to reveal the Nazi horrors and the inevitability of death and destruction if there were no resistance. They were to arouse and organize that resistance. The messengers were to be parachuted into Europe. Hannah Senesh was among the first to volunteer to be such a messenger.

Hannah had been born in Budapest, Hungary. At the age of 18 she went to Israel and enrolled in an agricultural school. She also continued the diary she had begun as a child. Eventually she became involved with the Haganah. She trained for her new mission by parachuting over the Egyptian desert.

On March 13, 1944, Hannah was dropped over Yugoslavia. On June 9 she was to cross over into Nazi-controlled Hungary. At the border, before she crossed, she turned to Reuven Dafne, another parachutist, and said to him, "If I don't return, give this to our people." She handed Reuven a copy of her poem "Blessed is the Match," which she had written on May 2.

Hannah made contact with the Hungarians who were supposed to be her guides. But these men were actually spies, and they led her to the police. The police saw the radio she carried and knew that if they learned the necessary codes, they could lead the entire intelligence network into capture.

The police were not gentle with Hannah. They tore her blouse and described in detail the tortures that would be inflicted upon her if she did not reveal the code. Hannah refused to speak. At one point she was struck hard in the kidney and fell over. Still she remained adamant. She maintained her silence throughout the following days of torture.

The police switched tactics. They brought in Hannah's mother to see her daughter in a prison cell; Mrs. Senesh had not even known that Hannah was in Hungary.

After the visit, Hannah was again confronted by the Fascist authorities. They threatened that if she did not reveal the code in an hour, they would torture and kill her mother.

She gave them her answer after the hour had elapsed: "I am certain that my mother would want to die rather than have me betray my people."

Hannah was given a "trial" on the following day and was condemned to death.

On November 7, the prosecuting officer entered cell 13. He asked whether she wished to request clemency. She responded that she wished to appeal her conviction. The captain told her that that was impossible. She replied that she would never request mercy from murderers. She was given an hour in which to prepare to die.

During that hour Hannah wrote farewell letters, but they never reached their destinations. At 10:00 in the morning, the captain returned to the cell. Two soldiers took Hannah to the courtyard. There was a sandbox next to a gray brick wall. A post was driven into the sand. Hannah was strapped to the post, her hands behind her back.

An officer stepped forward with a blindfold. She shook her head sharply, refusing it. Three men fired their rifles.

Hannah Senesh is sometimes called the Israeli Joan of Arc. Every Israeli schoolchild knows by heart her poetic gift, "Blessed is the Match."

SHAMIR, YITZHAK (1915–   )
Israeli prime minister and politician.

Menachem Begin once persuaded Shamir not to carry a gun.

The two major underground groups fighting the British, the Irgun, headed by Menachem Begin, and the FFI (Fighters for the Freedom of Israel), headed by Avraham Stern (until his death) had different views about the advisability of carrying weapons after Stern's death. The FFI was now headed by a triumvirate that included the commander, then known as Yitzhak Ysernitsky. (Ysernitsky would later grow a long black beard and call himself "Rabbi Shamir." Still later, he would accept the name Shamir and go on to become Israel's prime minister.)

The FFI developed a rule that all its members had to carry weapons day and night. They were to fight to the death to avoid being captured. This decision, Ysernitsky explained to Begin at a meeting, was made because the FFI members did not want to be the captives of the same British who had so brutally murdered their leader, Avraham Stern. In contrast, members of the Irgun kept their weapons hidden and never carried them except on an operation. Begin never even had a bodyguard.

All during the spring of 1944, FFI members, true to their vow, resisted when they met British troops. Several FFI members were killed by the larger British forces.

During Passover in 1944, Begin met with Yitzhak Ysernitsky in a tiny room on the roof of a house in Bnei Brak. They were there to discuss the policy of carrying weapons. Begin argued forcefully that it was more harmful than useful to carry weapons, that unexpected confrontations interfered with taking the initiative in planning, which was the underground's best weapon. Begin then told Ysernitsky what had happened to Yaacov Meridor a few days earlier. Meridor had once headed the Irgun and was still one of its leaders. He and another man had been on their way to visit Begin. They had reached his house when British police surrounded them and demanded their identification cards. The cards were in order, but the police nevertheless proceeded to search the two men. The police found no weapons, and the men were freed. Begin then asked, rhetorically, what would have happened had weapons been found.

Soon after, the future Prime Minister Shamir led the FFI in changing their point of view.

SHARON, ARIEL (1929-   )
Israeli soldier and politician.

Sharon was responsible for facilitating the peace process at Camp David.

Menachem Begin and his aides engaged in diligent, difficult bargaining at Camp David in an attempt to reach peace with Egypt. Key matters fell into place. The Sinai airfields were bargained away for new airfields in the Negev. The Egyptians' selective use of the text of United Nations Resolution 242 was removed. Prime Minister Begin finally, after considerable discussion, agreed to include language that recognized "the legitimate rights of the Palestinian people."

It looked as though the entire agreement would fail, however, because of the Jewish settlements in the Sinai. The matter of the settlements was a deeply emotional one. Begin also had political questions about whether enough of his supporters in Israel could accept evacuation of the settlements. Begin simply could not be persuaded. Suddenly this last, large impediment to a peace treaty threatened to doom the talks.

It was at this point that General Avraham Tamir, the head of military planning for Minister of Defense Ezer Weizman, had an idea. He wanted to call General Ariel Sharon to get Sharon to call Begin and urge the prime minister to evacuate the settlements. Weizman did not believe that such a call to Begin from Sharon was likely. "Arik" Sharon was known throughout Israel, indeed throughout the world, for his hawkish views. In particular, he had always been a leading proponent of settlement activity. But Weizman realized that there was absolutely nothing to lose. He told Tamir to place the call.

Several hours later, Begin called the Israeli delegation together. He told them that he had received a call from Arik Sharon. Begin said Sharon agreed to evacuation if that meant that a peace treaty could be signed. Begin quoted Sharon as saying that he saw "no military objection to their evacuation."

Begin remained skeptical, but with Sharon's unexpected blessing, the prime minister found the political courage to sign the Camp David Agreement.

SHCHARANSKY, NATAN (ANATOLY) *(1948–   )*
Activist on behalf of Soviet Jews. Former prisoner in the Soviet Union.

On October 13, 1973, as the Yom Kippur War raged in Israel, a 22-year-old woman named Natalia Shtiglits joined hundreds of other young Jews outside a synagogue on Arkhipova Street in Moscow.

It was extremely cold. All the Jews were discussing the fighting in Israel and seeking out the latest news about the war. Young Natalia's brother had applied to immigrate to Israel and began protesting after his and other applications were refused. He was in prison serving a brief sentence. His sister had prepared a package of clothing for him, in which she included a note in Hebrew about Israeli progress in the war.

The problem was that there were several prisons in Moscow, and Natalia didn't know which one held her brother. She decided to ask someone in the crowd for advice. She saw a group of Jews demonstrating on the steps of the synagogue and began to approach them. They reassured her about her brother's fate.

One young man approached her. He was shivering and evidently had the flu, but he asked about her, her work, and her desire to immigrate to Israel. She knew that he was only trying to help her to keep her mind off her brother, but she appreciated his efforts nevertheless.

The young man was named Anatoly Shcharansky, but even then he told her that his real name was Natan, the name he planned to call himself when he reached Israel. He told the young woman that if she ever planned to live in Israel, it was important that she study Hebrew.

A few days later she went with him to her first Hebrew lesson. Later she would adopt the Hebrew name Avital, and eventually she and Shcharansky would marry.

Later, Avital would lead the worldwide efforts to free her husband from prison.

SHIMKIN, YITZHAK *(1905–1977)*
Member of Haganah.

Yitzhak Shimkin decided to kill Hitler.

Shimkin had been born near Odessa and had settled in the land of Israel in 1921. He had studied at the Herzliya Gymnasium and joined the Haganah, the Jewish community's organized defense group.

Shimkin was in a movie theater one day in 1938. He saw a film of Hitler's entry into Vienna, Austria.

Shimkin went to his Haganah group with a plan of action. He wanted a squad of men who would volunteer to assassinate Hitler. The group discussed the plan and considered its merits, but finally rejected it. The group concluded that the idea was worthy but simply not possible.

Yitzhak Shimkin was not satisfied with the rejection. He remained troubled for weeks. Finally, he decided that he could not simply stay and hope for Hitler's death. He told his family that the Haganah was sending him overseas on a mission. He packed his bags, carefully including two guns and some ammunition.

Shimkin first took a train to Lebanon. From there he traveled to Syria and then to Turkey, Greece, and finally to Vienna. He found a cheap hotel. He would have to wait ten days until Hitler's scheduled visit.

Hitler was scheduled to lead a parade down Vienna's main street. Shimkin intended to place himself in the front row of spectators and shoot the German dictator. In newsreels of parades that Shimkin had seen, Hitler stood up in an open car and waved to the crowd. Such a target was relatively easy for someone with Shimkin's experience with weapons. Shimkin fully expected that carrying out his plan would cost him his own life.

The ten days passed. Shimkin arrived very early to line up for the parade. As he had hoped, he found a position in the front. He checked to make sure that the sun would be behind him. He checked the two guns sticking in his belt.

The parade began. Bands strode smartly by the crowd. People cheered. Shimkin then heard in the distance what he had hoped he would. The crowd gave a great roar. Hitler's car was approaching.

Shimkin carefully put his hands on his weapons. The sweat poured out of his body. The car was there.

But it was not at all as Shimkin had imagined. Hitler was riding in a closed, bullet-proof car, seated in a way that made him barely visible. Shimkin's plan was foiled.

Shimkin returned to his hotel, packed his bags, and went back to his kibbutz.

He never forgot his lost chance.

SHNEUR ZALMAN (1745–1813)
Rabbi and founder of Chabad movement in Hasidism.

When he was about 20 years old, Rabbi Shneur Zalman felt the urge to leave his home to search for a spiritual guide. In particular, his choice was narrowed to two possibilities. Either he could go to Vilna to study with Gaon Elijah at the famed Talmudic Academy, or he could go to Miezricz to study with Rabbi Dov

Baer, a leader in the still-new Hasidic movement. Rabbi Shneur determined that he had already seen talmudic study, but not Hasidic discipline. He decided to go to Miezricz.

This decision infuriated his father-in-law, who cut off all financial support to his daughter and Shneur. But Rabbi Shneur's wife remained steadfast in her support. She asked only that he restrict his stay to no more than a year and a half. She then obtained some money and purchased a horse and cart.

After Passover in the year 1764, Rabbi Shneur departed, accompanied only by his brother, who had come without his wife's agreement. They had traveled no further than fifty miles when the horse died. Shneur suggested that his brother return home; he intended to continue on foot.

Shneur finally arrived and met Dov Baer. He watched the Maggid of Miezricz, as Dov Baer was known, and his disciples at work. Shneur was initially disappointed because the amount of time preparing for prayer and actually in prayer left that much less time for the study of the Torah. Rabbi Shneur was intellectually drawn to the study of texts. He was sure that Dov Baer would not be his spiritual guide, and, for his part, the Maggid made no effort to change Shneur's mind.

Rabbi Shneur Zalman decided to leave. As he was going, he suddenly recalled that he had left something in the Bet Midrash. He went there to retrieve what he had left. As he entered, he heard Dov Baer discussing a complex Halachic question. The discussion was so brilliant that Shneur decided that he should stay at least for a while.

Shneur slowly became very attracted to the ways of Hasidic life. His final "conversion" to Hasidism came soon after. The senior disciples, known as the Holy Society, were discussing the kabbala. They discussed the state of awe and love in which the Divine was experienced. The disciples became so caught up in the subject that they began to enter the rapturous state they were discussing. For the first time, Shneur Zalman truly felt the mystical bond with the Infinite. They stood waiting for Dov Baer. He came in and spoke in an intellectual fashion so that his disciples drew back from their ecstatic state. Shneur Zalman suddenly saw what he had been searching for: the deepest ecstasy combined with a calm intellect. At that moment in his mind he knew he would become a Hasid.

SILLS, BEVERLY (1929–   )
American opera singer.

In 1970, Beverly Sills was invited for the first time to sing in Israel with the Israeli Philharmonic Orchestra. Her mother, as proud of the Jewish state as Beverly was, told her to do the concerts for free because "no nice Jewish girl takes money out of Israel." Abe Cohen, the Philharmonic's manager was, of course, very pleased when Beverly announced her intention to donate her services.

Beverly was scheduled to sing a total of eight performances.

It was while waiting for these performances to commence that Beverly went for a walk through Tel Aviv. She saw posters that advertised the concerts. She examined the posters carefully. Her name was in English, but the rest was in Hebrew, which she could not read. She did notice, though, that her name was printed more than eight times.

Later, she asked Abe Cohen about the number of concerts listed on the poster, reminding him that she had agreed to do eight concerts. He told her that she was scheduled for fourteen. She asked why that was so. He simply said, "The price was right."

SILVER, ABBA HILLEL (1893–1963)
American rabbi and Zionist leader.

The image of Jews, and especially rabbis, in heartland America was sometimes drawn from biblical reading rather than from reality.

Rabbi Silver was to appear before the National Association of Women's Suffrage in Bluefield, West Virginia, an area without a significant Jewish population. The association was holding a mass meeting and wanted the distinguished rabbi and orator to deliver a powerful speech.

Rabbi Silver was told that he would be met at the train by a committee of women from the organization, but he found no group when he arrived. He began pacing up and down along the railroad platform. Finally, a woman hesitated and then approached him. "Pardon me, but did you just get off the train? I am supposed to meet here a certain Silver, but he is not around."

"I am Rabbi Silver," he told the woman.

"You are! But where is your beard?"

SIMEON BEN SHETAH (first century B.C.E.)
Rabbi, major scholar of the Second Temple period.

Moral behavior was always the highest guiding principle for the rabbis. There are many stories about honest and ethical rabbis.

One famous story of such behavior is told about Rabbi Simeon ben Shetah. The rabbi once bought a mule from an Arab. After he brought the mule back to his house, the rabbi's students found a very valuable diamond on it. The students were excited about their new wealth. But Rabbi Simeon said, "The diamond is not ours. I purchased a mule, not a diamond. We must return the diamond to the Arab tradesman."

He returned the diamond that very day.

SINGER, ISAAC BASHEVIS (1904–   )
American Yiddish author. Winner of the Nobel Prize for literature.

(1) An interviewer asked Singer whether he had become a vegetarian for religious reasons or out of concern for his health. Singer told him, "It is out of consideration for the chicken."

(2) Singer was asked whether, in all his philosophical musings, he had reached any conclusion about whether humans have free will or whether their actions are determined. His answer was, "We have to believe in free will. We've got no choice."

(3) Singer often faced difficult financial circumstances when he was an unknown, struggling writer. Once, almost down to his last dollar, Singer went into a restaurant to call his editor. Without the $50 or $60 he got for a story, he would not be able to pay the rent or eat. Such a fee would pay his rent for about three months.

The thought of suicide crossed his mind. He made his call, believing for certain that the editor would not be in.

But the editor's voice came on the line. Singer's voice trembled as he identified himself. The editor gruffly told him that his story would be published that Sunday, and then the editor asked for still another story. Singer was overjoyed as he hung up the phone. Just as he did so, a dollar's worth of change came spilling out. Thinking that the phone company would not get the money back, and assuming that someone less needy than he was would find it, Singer accepted this second miracle of the last few minutes.

(4) When Singer came to the United States for the first time, one of the many novelties he encountered was that American eating institution, the cafeteria. The first time he entered one, he thought that the cafeteria was a normal restaurant. He saw people getting trays and thought to himself, "Why do they need so many waiters?" Singer kept signalling to the people, who he thought were waiters. Some smiled at him but ignored his waving hands. It felt like a dream to him.

Singer eventually mastered the mysteries of cafeteria life. The cafeterias at which he ate became his second home and the background for many of his stories.

(5) Singer was very embarrassed by the failure of his first novel, one about Jacob Frank. Ashamed to show his face, he delivered his new writings at midnight, putting his stories in a little box. He wanted to wait until he was prouder of what he had written before he showed himself.

(6) It was because of a crowd that Singer discovered that he had been awarded the Nobel Prize for literature in 1978. He was walking back to his house and saw a large group of reporters and photographers. The only questions they asked him were, "Were you surprised?" "Were you happy?" Rather than argue with them about the meaning of happiness, he simply said yes, he was surprised and happy. This kept up for several minutes.

Ten minutes later, a reporter came in and asked again, "Were you surprised? Were you happy?"

Singer said, "How long can a man be surprised and how long can a man be happy? I have already been surprised and I have already been happy. I'm still the same shlemiel that I was before."

SLEPAK, VLADIMIR (1927–   )
Soviet Jewish activist.

After Slepak was denied an exit visa, he was visited by a KGB member. Slepak asked why his visa request had been denied. The KGB officer told him that the government considered Slepak's work to be secret.

Slepak had been an electronics engineer, but he told the KGB officer that his work for the Soviet Union was twelve to fourteen years behind similar research being done in the West.

The KGB officer answered, "That is the secret."

SLONIMSKY, HENRY (1884–1970)
Philosopher and writer.

The following anecdote was supplied by Rabbi Adam D. Fisher, who was a student of Henry Slonimsky's at Hebrew Union College.

The word was that it was important to take at least one of his classes while at HUC-JIR. He taught just after lunch, and I remember one prematurely warm, early spring day having eaten a little too much and having trouble staying awake despite his passion and eloquence.

I awoke in a startle hearing him thunder, "Isn't that right, Fisher?" I mumbled an apologetic, "Yes, sir," and, mercifully, he continued with his lecture. During the break between the two hours of his class, he called me aside and apologized for embarrassing me. He said, "If you fell asleep you must have been tired."

SOKOLOW, NAHUM (1859–1936)
Hebrew writer, president of the World Zionist Organization.

When Sokolow was serving as editor of *Ha-Zifirah*, the Hebrew daily, a young man came to see him to submit a poem for publication.

Sokolow read the poem, stared at the young man, and asked, "Did you write this poem yourself, or did someone else write it?"

"I wrote it myself," said the young man.

"If that's the case, then I am delighted and amazed to see you."

The young man was puzzled by this comment. "Why?" he asked.

Sokolow looked and him and said, "Because I was under the impression that Judah L. Gordon, the author of this poem, had been dead for ten years."

SOLOMON (tenth century B.C.E.)
Third king of Israel and builder of the Temple.

(1) The most famous of Solomon's judgments involved a prostitute's child.

Two prostitutes lived alone in the same house. By coincidence, they both had babies within a three-day period. One of the babies died. The dead baby's mother stole the other baby while its mother was sleeping and substituted the dead child.

The switch was noted immediately, but the prostitute whose child had died refused to surrender the baby. The women came before King Solomon.

The king ordered his officers to bring a sword and cut the baby in two so that each woman would get half.

The real mother called out to give the child to the other woman and not to kill it.

The false mother asked that it be divided.

Solomon then knew who the real mother was, and he ordered the baby to be reunited with her.

(2) King Solomon built the Temple with great care. He imported only the very finest stone and wood from all over the world. He obtained beautiful tapestries and the most lustrous gold and silver ornaments. The entire Temple was a great and beautiful symbol of goodness.

But King Solomon kept one room cleared of any ornaments. He called the room "The Chamber of the Silent."

The room was entirely empty except for charity boxes. People entered and left the room undisturbed. There were no guards and no observers to see how much money was left. Just as the money was collected anonymously, it was similarly dispersed. Some entered the room to give and some entered the room to get, but they were indistinguishable.

(3) It was a year of famine. A wealthy man had a poor neighbor with nine hungry children. The wealthy man lent nine boiled eggs to the poor man.

Twenty years later, the wealthy man asked for a very large sum of money from the poor man. He argued that eggs produce hens, and new hens lay eggs, which eventually also become hens. The poor man could offer to return only nine eggs.

The argument eventually came before King David, who, after listening to both sides, agreed with the wealthy man and awarded him 300 gold dinars.

The poor man did not know what to do. He had to sell his children as slaves. This provided 200 dinars. He then mortgaged his house and got 10 more dinars, but he still owed money.

After hearing his father's judicial decision, Solomon went to see the poor man and told him to sow his field with cooked peas. King David was told of his son's strange advice and came to him saying, "How can you expect anything to grow from cooked peas?"

Solomon responded, "And how can hens come out of boiled eggs?"

SOLOVEICHIK, JOSEPH BAER (1820–1892)
Rabbi and talmudist.

(1) Even strange requests can provide insight into Jewish wisdom.

Rabbi Joseph once invited a traveling preacher to stay for the Sabbath. Late on Friday afternoon, he asked the preacher for a loan. The preacher gladly provided the money. As soon as the Sabbath was over, Rabbi Joseph returned the crown.

The traveling preacher was mystified. "Rabbi, why did you borrow this money when it's clear you never needed it?"

Rabbi Joseph said, "I kept wondering how you, as a man who wanders, could perform the mitzvah of lending money to others, since nobody is likely to request money from someone who goes from place to place. I wanted to give you a chance to fulfill this great commandment."

(2) A poor man came to Rabbi Joseph's house. The man said that he had come to ask a question regarding the sacred rituals of Passover. He told the rabbi that he could not affort to buy wine, so he wished to know if he could fulfill the obligation to drink four cups of wine during the seder by drinking four cups of milk. Rabbi Joseph said that no Jew could fulfill this important religious commandment with milk. The rabbi then gave the man twenty-five rubles with which to buy wine.

After the man had gone, the rabbi's wife went to her husband with a question. Why, when wine cost two or three rubles, had the rabbi given the man twenty-five?

Rabbi Joseph smiled and said, "When a poor Jew asks if he can use milk at his seder because he cannot afford wine, it is obvious that he cannot afford meat either."

SONNEBORN, RUDOLF (1898–1986)
American business executive and Zionist.

An American businessman secretly helped arm the Jewish state.

It was July of 1945. The European war had finally been won. Hitler was dead. The Japanese were on the verge of surrender. David Ben-Gurion, the leader of the Jews in their effort to forge a nation, had been in New York for a month. He had one mission: to raise money for the Jewish army, the Haganah. Money was especially needed for new groups set up underground. One group, Bricha, would smuggle concentration camp survivors to the land of Israel in defiance of the British blockade that prevented Jewish immigration. Rehesh, the other group, was to obtain weapons and military equipment for what was shaping up to be a life-or-death battle with the Arabs.

Ben-Gurion was concerned. He had to be especially careful not to call on American citizens to break the laws of their land. He needed some guide to those American Jews who would be willing to help.

On June 25, Ben-Gurion met at a hotel with Henry Montor, executive vice-president of the United Jewish Appeal and a man who was intimate with American Jewish leaders, and Rudolf Sonneborn, a wealthy industrialist who was then chairing the United Jewish Appeal's finance committee. Ben-Gurion asked them to set up a private meeting with a dozen or so discreet, committed Jews. They would, Ben-Gurion said, be asked to undertake a mission that might determine the fate of the soon-to-be-born Jewish nation.

Sixteen invitations were issued in Sonneborn's respected name. All were contacted by phone, so that no information was in writing. Each invitee was told only the date, time, and place of the meeting, and its urgency was emphasized. No one—even a spouse—was to be told.

On July 1, 1945, the heat was so oppressive that, as Sonneborn arose early to prepare for the meeting, he heard on the radio that 50,000 people had slept on the beaches the night before. He was therefore surprised when all sixteen invitees actually showed up. The sixteen were in the apartment along with Sonneborn, Montor, Ben-Gurion, and four others from the Jewish agency.

The group met at 9:30 A.M. There was a rabbi and five lawyers; the remainder were business people. Ben-Gurion, open-shirted as usual, but still perspiring, no doubt as much from the enormity of his task as from the heat, sat and watched as each man was introduced to the others. Ben-Gurion then spoke at length, providing what turned out to be a remarkably acute analysis of the Jewish situation. Ben-Gurion predicted exactly how the British and the Arabs would act. He soberly analyzed the desperate need for weapons for self-defense. Yaacov Dori, who was with Ben-Gurion and who served as the Hagana's chief of staff, noted that the end of the World War would mean that there would be enormous amounts of surplus war material available at very low prices. Reuven Shiloah, chief of Hagana's intelligence, outlined how the weapons could be obtained and smuggled into Jewish hands.

Ben-Gurion was careful not to directly solicit pledges. But in essence, without directly saying so, he was asking for the creation of an American arm of the Hagana. These men had the money and the access to weapons. Carefully, indirectly, Ben-Gurion tried to tell them what was at stake.

The Sonneborn Institute was created out of that meeting. In the early fall of 1945, Ben-Gurion sent Sonneborn the message he'd been waiting for: "The time has come." The insititute began its work on the following day. Over the next two and a half years, the institute, working always against time, was responsible for the purchase of eighteen vessels, including the famous *Exodus 1947*. These ships transported more than 75,000 "illegal" Jews to the Jewish homeland. The institute raised millions for the purchase and shipment of desperately needed materiel. They worked with the Hagana and with a nation-wide network of Jews and non-Jews to provide for the security of the new state of Israel.

SPEKTOR, ISAAC ELHANAN (1817–1896)
Rabbi.

(1) The rabbi was widely recognized for his saintliness and his learning. His tolerance was also noted, for he counted among his friends a chemist in Kovno. The chemist was an atheist.

One day Rabbi Spektor was very ill. He refused all visitors, but he agreed to see the chemist.

The young atheist was surprised at the honor of being the only one allowed to see the sage and asked why the rabbi had agreed to see him.

The rabbi responded sadly, "You see, in heaven I am certain to meet all my friends again. But this may be the last chance I have to see you."

(2) Rabbi Spektor was visited one day by a young, well-dressed man. The young man had come to ask the sage to solve a vexing religious problem. The man did not believe in any religion, but he remained unsure about whether he should also discard his belief in God.

"I am glad you came," the rabbi said. "You say you don't believe. Tell me, have you mastered the Bible?"

"I can't claim that I have. I did read some parts of the Bible as a child, but recently I have concentrated on my studies at the university."

"Perhaps the Talmud?" the rabbi inquired.

The young man looked surprised. "Rabbi, you don't expect me to waste time on anything like that."

"Okay, you know nothing about the Talmud. How about the great Jewish philosophers? What have you read of Maimonides, ibn Gabirol, or Moses Mendelssohn?"

"I haven't read a word any of them have written."

"Young man, you call yourself an unbeliever, yet you know nothing about Jewish literature. At least call yourself by your right name—you are an ordinary ignoramus."

SPINOZA, BARUCH (1632–1677)
Dutch philosopher, excommunicated for heresy.

Spinoza was known to hold heretical views about Judaism. Two students who attended synagogue classes with him decided to expose his views. They asked him his opinions on whether angels exist, whether God has a body, and whether the soul is immortal. Spinoza replied quickly, only sketching out his answers. He promised to elaborate on his views at a later time. But the two students had heard quite enough. Spinoza's views, even briefly expressed, were distinctly at odds with the teachings of Judaism. The students went directly to the synagogue authorities.

The authorities already knew that Spinoza was studying Latin with Francis Van den Ende, a Catholic free thinker. They also knew that Spinoza did not perform many of the ceremonies and observances common to Judaism. The leaders responded. They gave Spinoza a choice: They would provide him an annual fee of 1,000 florins in return for his conformity to synagogue rules, or he would face excommunication. He was given thirty days in which to make up his mind.

Spinoza did not answer the synagogue authorities. One report has it that an attempt was made on his life. At any rate, Spinoza left Amsterdam to stay with friends. The excommunication was finally pronounced. Spinoza was then barely 24 years old. Spinoza heard of the ban and sent back a reply in which he staunchly maintained his dissident beliefs. Spinoza never again referred to himself as either Jew or Gentile, though he changed his first name to Benedict.

STEINBERG, MILTON (1903–1950)
Rabbi, philosopher, Zionist, and author of such books as Basic Judaism.

Milton Steinberg's novel *As A Driven Leaf* is about a rabbi in the first century of the Common Era. This story of Elisha ben Abuyah was of a struggle for faith in a pagan world filled with temptations. Actually, in some ways, Rabbi Steinberg's novel was a substitute for an unfinished dissertation on that era in Jewish history.

Steinberg had worked very hard on the novel. He had spent three years researching the subject; he had organized the sections of the book; he had completed the first draft.

One evening he decided to show the manuscript to his wife, Edith. He said, "Here. It's finished," and quickly left to let her read. She had the worst of all possible feelings toward a book—that it wasn't good enough, that the hero's character was insufficiently defined, and that the women in the book were simply not portrayed accurately at all. Rabbi Steinberg disagreed with his wife and forwarded the book to his publisher. It was returned. The publisher had found it "too intellectual."

It was then that Steinberg realized how valuable his wife was to his writing, so he established a routine. Edith Steinberg read every passage out loud, almost acting it out to make it sound right. Rabbi Steinberg asked that she be present whenever he wrote.

Despite the pressure, Edith Steinberg refused to allow a bad passage to be retained. The struggle to find the right words led to more than one verbal battle. Yet the dependence of the brilliant and famous rabbi on his wife somehow strengthened the marriage. They kept at it. Two drawers were filled with discarded materials.

Finally, they delivered the manuscript. It was published, to resounding critical praise, in January of 1940.

STEINSALTZ, ADIN *(1937–   )*
Rabbi and talmudic scholar.

(1) Rabbi Steinsaltz was teaching a class. He was only 25 years old at the time, and he realized that some in the class were great thinkers, the best in the nation. Some were three times his age. As he thought about it, he became embarrassed at the thought that *he* should teach *them*. Suddenly he realized that there was only one way he could justify his teaching. He decided to tell himself that these great minds, his elders, were listening to Adin Steinsaltz not as an individual, but as a representative of a tradition. In that sense, he was 5,000 years old and teaching 75-year-old babies.

(2) Steinsaltz was awarded the 1988 Israel Prize, that nation's highest honor, for his numerous achievements, the most significant of which are his on-going translations with commentaries of the Babylonian and Jerusalem Talmuds. The brilliance of the translation and the structure of the Talmuds have made these classic texts of Jewish religious thought accessible to a wide variety of Israelis for the first time. The success of the books was so overwhelming that an English translation will be prepared. Rabbi Steinsaltz, though, does not share in the adulation the nation feels. When he heard about the prize, he said, "Gee, one gets that a year before one dies."

STRAUS, NATHAN *(1848–1931)*
Merchant and philanthropist.

Money is valued in Judaism for the good it can do and the evil it can fight.

Lakewood, New Jersey, was a favorite spot for wealthy vacationers. The Hotel Lakewood, in particular, was considered a desirable place to stay. One day, Straus attempted to register at the hotel. But the clerk, noting Straus's name and his general appearance, told him that Jews were not allowed to stay at the famed hotel.

Straus left without a word. Several weeks later, however, Straus came back and told the clerk to get out. Straus had purchased the hotel and was dismissing its bigoted staff.

SUKENIK, ELAZAR *(1889–1953)*
Israeli archaeologist.

Elazar Sukenik was responsible for making the Dead Sea Scrolls available to the world.

Sukenik was a professor of archaeology at Hebrew University. It was 1947, and the Jews and the Arabs were poised for war.

One day, Sukenik received a call from an Armenian friend who was an antiques dealer. The dealer requested that Sukenik examine a newly found leather parchment, in order to determine its age. Sukenik agreed.

Sukenik looked at the object and immediately recognized that the writing on it was about 2,000 years old. Trying to calm himself, Sukenik inquired about whether there were other, similar pieces of parchment. The dealer told him about an Arab merchant in Bethlehem who had complete scrolls.

On November 29, Sukenik took a bus trip with the Armenian into the Arab-controlled area and went to the Arab's house. The Arab took the archaeologist up into the attic and showed him three scrolls. Sukenik asked where the Arab had obtained the scrolls and was told that they had been found in a cave near the Dead Sea by a Bedouin shepherd boy as he searched for a lost member of his flock.

Sukenik read some lines; he knew the Hebrew words, but not the text. He agreed to buy the scroll and the jars in which they had been found for his University if the Arab would let him examine them to determine their value. The Arab allowed Sukenik take the scrolls home for several days.

That evening, Sukenik sat down in his house in Jerusalem to make sense of the Dead Sea Scrolls. In the next room, Sukenik's son Mati was listening to the radio. A historic event was taking place: The United Nations was voting on whether the land should be partitioned, thereby creating a Jewish state. Sukenik continued his translation, interrupted by his son's report of the voting. Just as Mati came in with the news that a two-thirds majority allowing partition had been reached, Sukenik was working on a prophetic passage: "I was driven from my home like a bird from its nest . . . I was cast down, but raised up again." The hymn was preceded by the phrase, "I give thanks to Thee, O Lord." The scroll was subsequently named *The Thanksgiving Hymns*.

SYRKIN, MARIE (1899–1989)
American author, Zionist, and educator.

At the end of December in 1944, Marie Syrkin was to participate in a ceremony at which a ship would be named after her father, Nachman. The Jewish National Workers Alliance had purchased more than $2 million in war bonds and thus could – with the government's approval – name a liberty ship. The alliance chose to honor Nachman Syrkin. Marie Syrkin mentioned this honor to her non-Jewish friends. One asked what exactly her father had done that a ship would be named after him. She told the man that her father had been a leading Zionist. The man suddenly seemed to understand. "Ah, a scientist."

Further explanation ensued.

SYRKIN, NACHMAN (1868–1924)
Leading theorotician of Socialist Zionism.

Nachman Syrkin committed his life to forging a vision of Zionism that fused Jewish nationalism with socialism. Few contemporaries in Syrkin's youth shared this then-novel vision, but slowly Syrkin came to have enormous influence on Zionist and Israeli leaders. When Syrkin's body was transferred for reburial in Israel on September 3, 1951, Ben-Gurion said at the end of the service, "Syrkin, *hazonkha yitkayem,* your vision will be fulfilled." This influence grew as much from Syrkin's biting wit as from his ideas.

One of the famous stories about him involved the on-going debate between Jewish Socialists and Nationalists, who struggled for the intellectual souls of the young.

One day Syrkin attended a lecture given by Parvus, who was then a Social Democrat, but who later achieved fame as a Trotskyite and Marxist theorist. Parvus was feared by the Nationalists because of his great debating skills.

Parvus spoke loudly about the meaninglessness of nationalism. He argued theoretically and abstractly, when suddenly he realized that he needed a more concrete line of reasoning. He pointed to his coat and shouted, "The wool in this coat was taken from sheep that were pastured in Angora; it was spun in England; it was woven in Lodz. The buttons came from Germany; the thread, from Austria. Isn't it clear that our world is an international one, and that even this coat is made up of the labor of different peoples?"

The argument was having a visible effect on the audience. People began to applaud. But Parvus's coat was too small, and that, combined with his vigorous gesticulation, finally caused the right elbow of the coat to rip. A piece of white shirt was visible to the audience. Syrkin was sitting opposite Parvus. Syrkin jumped up and shouted, "And the rip in your sleeve comes from the pogrom in Kiev." Syrkin had undone the entire argument, and the audience applauded him.

SZOLD, HENRIETTA (1860–1945)
Founder of Hadassah and leader of Youth Aliyah.

(1) Henrietta Szold applied her love of people to all aspects of her life.

She became especially well known later in her accomplishment-filled life for her work in organizing Youth Aliyah. (Youth Aliyah worked to save Jewish youth from persecution and to educate them in Israel. See *Freier, Recha.*)

Although fluent in English and German, Szold had a very difficult time expressing her thoughts in Hebrew. She nevertheless always spoke in Hebrew to

Dr. Chanoch Rinott, the first youth leader in Youth Aliyah. One day, Rinott told her how well she spoke Hebrew, and he wondered why she always berated herself. He claimed that she was easy to understand. She smiled at him and responded, "How do you know what I have *not* said?"

(2) Her interest in language extended to her warm feelings toward nature and toward children. One day she was on a visit to Mishmar Ha'emek. She decided to go for a walk in the woods with Rinott and her assistant, Hans Beyth. Because it was a bright spring day, many flowers were in bloom. Along the way, she would gaze at a flower that she didn't recognize and ask the two men whether they knew its name. They rarely did. Rinott, growing impatient, asked, "Why must you know the name? I enjoy their beauty just the same."

Szold gave him her best grandmotherly smile. "If you meet a person to whom you are attracted, wouldn't you like to know the person's name?"

Her response evoked in Rinott the memory of his first meeting with Szold. She had been in Haifa greeting new youngsters. He remembered that she had asked each one his name and where he had come from. She had had a personal interest in each child.

TALNER, DOVID'L (1808–1882)
Rabbi and scholar.

A poor Hasid came to Rabbi Talner with a series of complaints about his lot in life. "I have a wife and ten children, and we all live in only one room. Life is just unbearable. Pray for me, Rabbi."

Rabbi Talner pondered the situation. "Do you own a goat?" he asked the man.

The surprised Hasid said yes, he did own a goat.

The rabbi advised the man to move the goat into the house. A few days later, the Hasid was back, complaining even more bitterly; now, with the goat, he could not even put his head down to rest.

Instead of offering the expected solace, Rabbi Talner asked the man, "Do you own any chickens?"

The startled Hasid responded, "Yes, I own chickens."

"Take them into the house as well."

The Hasid was greatly confused by this advice, but still, remembering Rabbi Talner's learning and reputation, the Hasid could not disobey.

But just a few days later the Hasid was back. "Rabbi, I just can't stand it any more. It is beyond human endurance."

Rabbi Talner told the man, "Now go and send out your goat and chickens."

Several days later the Hasid returned for the last time. He was now a happy man. "Rabbi, you have saved us. With the goat and chickens gone, we are so comfortable."

TRILLING, LIONEL *(1905–1975)*
American critic and author.

Lionel Trilling exemplified the Jewish fight against the genteel anti-Semitism then prevalent at major American universities.

In 1938 and 1939, Trilling was teaching and working on his doctorate at Columbia University. He aspired to be the first Jew ever appointed to the position of assistant professor in the English department.

It was necessary for the awarding of his doctorate that Trilling's dissertation be published. W. W. Norton finally agreed to publish it—but only after Trilling paid a subsidy to the publishing house. Trilling borrowed the money and paid the subsidy, and his book was published.

One day, Trilling met Irwin Edman, a philosopher and one of the few Jews then on Columbia's faculty. Edman asked whether Trilling had yet sent a copy of the book to Nicholas Murray Butler, Columbia's almost legendary president. Trilling replied that the thought had never crossed his mind. Edman then informed the young scholar of Columbia's academic protocol. Trilling was first to write to Butler through the campus mail seeking permission to send the work. Without waiting for the reply, which, in any case, would never be sent, Trilling should, two days later, send the book, appropriately inscribed. Trilling found this process a bit ridiculous, but he followed Edman's suggestions.

Butler invited Trilling to dinner in the early spring of 1939. Trilling rented tails and a white tie. This dress turned out to be somewhat inappropriate, but Trilling carried on with the dinner. In the library after the meal, the president, a wide variety of important guests, and Trilling gathered for brandy and cigars.

Butler began to speak. He talked to those assembled, including the dean of the college and the chairman of the English department, about the correspondence he had been having with the chancellor of the University of Berlin. The two universities had planned to exchange philosophy professors. Butler had suggested Felix Adler. The chancellor had responded that Adler would not be acceptable because he was Jewish. Butler then stared at the important leaders of Columbia. "I wrote back," he told them, "that at Columbia, we recognize merit, not race."

A few weeks later Butler appointed Trilling to the position of assistant professor of English.

TROTSKY, LEON *(1879–1940)*
Russian revolutionary and Communist leader.

Leon Trotsky learned that even revolutions don't always change anti-Semitism. Not long after the end of the successful Russian Revolution in 1917,

Trotsky reportedly returned to Ivanovka, the small town where he had been born. The town's chief rabbi recognized the Bolshevik hero as Lev Bronstein and greeted the famous visitor with his original name.

Trotsky returned the greeting. "It's Trotsky now, not Bronstein. We've made a revolution and everything is different now, even the names. Czarist Russia is now the Soviet Union, the first workers' state in the world."

The elderly rabbi considered this and answered, "Yes, but be careful. It's the Trotskys who make the revolutions and the Bronsteins who pay the bills."

TRUMPELDOR, JOSEPH (1880–1920)
Soldier and early Zionist advocate of armed self-defense.

Joseph Trumpeldor's name has become a symbol for the Jewish people's struggles against its Arab enemies. He led the defense of Tel Hai, a Jewish settlement under attack by Arabs.

In late 1919 in the upper Galilee, there were armed confrontations between the French and the Arabs. In April of that year, the League of Nations had awarded France a mandate over Syria. The French wished to dispose of any Arab kings who might interfere with their rule. In June, they deposed King Faisal. The Arabs reacted angrily, believing that the French were acting in a concerted plot with the British to allow more Jews to enter. The upper Galilee region, in what was then still Syria, became the scene for marauding bands of Arabs who attacked both the French and the growing number of Jewish settlements.

Jewish leaders dispatched defenders to the north so that these outposts could be protected. All the Jewish fighters knew that the defense was going to be difficult. They would require a remarkable leader. Joseph Trumpeldor was appointed to be that leader. Trumpeldor was already famous. He had been in the Russian army during the Russo-Japanese war, and as a result of a battlefield injury, his left arm had been amputated. He had an extraordinary reputation for military skill and for bravery in the face of overwhelming odds.

On January 1, 1920, Trumpeldor arrived in Tel Hai, which, along with other settlements such as Kfar Giladi and Metullah, followed his leadership and began fortification. On March 1, 1920, a large Arab force attacked Tel Hai. The defense held.

Negotiations with the Arabs were under way when fighting again broke out. Trumpeldor was shot in the stomach during the battle. As evening approached, he was carried to a nearby settlement, but he died before reaching it. Trumpeldor's last words, famous throughout Israel, were a call to continue the struggle: "It is good to die for your country."

TWERSKY, NACHUM (1880-1968)
Rabbi; member of Hasidic dynasty.

Nachum Twersky was John F. Kennedy's rabbi.

After Rabbi Twersky fled the Nazis, he lived in Chelsea, Massachusetts. As a widely respected figure in the Boston area, Rabbi Twersky met a large number of influential Jews and non-Jews, one of whom was Joseph P. Kennedy. At the time of the second meeting between the two men, Kennedy brought along his son Jack, who was then 12 years old. Kennedy asked the important rabbi to give a blessing to young Jack. The rabbi noticed the boy's bright eyes, his good looks, and his alertness, and he gave the blessing.

The young boy remembered the meeting, and so when he decided to run for Congress, Jack Kennedy again sought out Rabbi Twersky to request another blessing and perhaps also to influence Jewish voters. After that, every time Jack Kennedy ran for office, he requested, and received, a blessing from Rabbi Twersky.

Kennedy continued this contact even after his election to the presidency. He sought Rabbi Twersky's prayers after Joseph Kennedy suffered a stroke; he visited the rabbi's synagogue on Israel's tenth anniversary; and he invited the rabbi to the White House.

Once Rabbi Twersky was going to visit Israel, but first he came to see the president. The rabbi voiced concern for Israel's safety, but the president reassured him. The president asked that the rabbi pray for him at King David's tomb in Jerusalem. As the rabbi rose to leave, the president gave him a present, a walking stick, and told him that as surely as Moses turned his stick into a serpent, this stick was to serve as a reminder that the rabbi's fears would be turned into shrivelled twigs.

WAHL, SAUL (1541–c. 1617)
Polish merchant and community leader.

Saul Wahl was the only Jewish king of Poland—even though his power lasted only one day.

Stephen Bathori, the king of Poland, died on December 12, 1586. Several people, including Archduke Maxmillian of Austria and the Duke of Ferrara, claimed a right to the throne. The two major Polish families, the Azmoiskis and the Zborowskis, were split about a successor.

It was both law and custom to gather together on a specified day to select a new ruler. The day for the election was August 18, 1587, but by nightfall, after a long day of bickering among the nobles, no agreement could be reached.

Legend now takes over. Prince Radziwill, seeing no compromise and therefore no clear way to obey the law, is supposed to have recommended Saul Katzenellenbogen (later known as Saul Wahl; *wahl* meant "choice" in the vernacular Polish of the day) to be *rex pro tempore*, or the temporary king of Poland.

The Jewish Saul was widely known and widely respected as a business agent and court advisor. Prince Radziwill had been his patron. The nobles unanimously agreed to Saul's election and even toasted him: "Long live our Lord, the King."

Again according to tradition, Saul did not waste his royal night. It was customary for each ruler to add laws that he thought were wise. Saul took the various rolls of laws from the royal archives and added a number of enactments and decrees that would benefit the Jews, including one that a Gentile who murdered a Jew would be subject to the death penalty rather than being able to ransom his way to freedom, as had been the case.

On the next night, August 19, the Polish nobles elected Sigismund III, son of the king of Sweden, who was crowned that year.

And so the reign of the Jewish king of Poland for a day had ended.

WALLENBERG, RAOUL (1912–?)
Swedish diplomat who risked his life to save Jews from the Nazis.

Raoul Wallenberg was a non-Jewish Swedish diplomat who was in charge of distributing Swedish passes to Jews who wanted to leave Hungary. He learned that a Polish Jew named Boris Teicholz was counterfeiting Swedish passes. Wallenberg arranged a secret meeting with Teicholz.

The meeting was held in Gerbaud's coffeehouse in Budapest. Wallenberg entered the cafe, made sure that he was not being followed, and went into the small room in the back of the cafe.

Teicholz was waiting for him there. Teicholz was then in command of more than 300 Jewish partisans. His group smuggled Jews into Rumania, built bunkers to hide Jews, and stole and forged useful documents such as baptismal certificates, German and Hungarian passports, and neutral passes, especially those from Sweden, which were highly prized. Blonde Jews in Teicholz's group would dress in the green uniforms of the Arrow Cross (the Fascist party in Hungary) and would charge into soup kitchens where Jews gathered and put passes into everyone's hands.

Wallenberg did not really object to Teicholz's activities. The limited number of government-issued passes were given to Jews who could prove some connection to Sweden, and to the wealthier and better-educated Jews. Teicholz's group distributed the passes more equitably, and Wallenberg secretly admired that. Wallenberg also knew that he would not be allowed to increase the number of legitimate passes. But Wallenberg did have one serious concern: that Teicholz's activities would jeopardize all the passes.

Both men were understandably anxious about meeting. Teicholz was sure that the Gestapo was trailing Wallenberg wherever he went, and Wallenberg feared that he would be expelled from the country if seen with Teicholz.

Wallenberg started the conversation by telling Teicholz that he knew about the counterfeiting. Teicholz admitted his illegal activities and then waited silently. Wallenberg said, "I don't care." Teicholz couldn't believe the words. Wallenberg then asked Teicholz to swear that the passes were not being sold. Teicholz assured Wallenberg that the counterfeit passes were given away free to everyone who requested them.

Wallenberg promised to confuse the police if they tried to check up on the counterfeiting. He agreed to talk to the Swiss consul and the nuncio, the representative of the pope, so that they wouldn't complain to the authorities. Wallenberg also asked Teicholz to print fewer passes at a time.

Stunned, Teicholz agreed.

He left Gerbaud and instructed his assistants to go ahead and print 15,000 additional Swiss passes.

WEISGAL, MEYER (1894–1977)
Zionist leader.

Weisgal was a very successful fund-raiser who specialized in knowing exactly how much each potential donor could give to the Zionist cause.

Once, Weisgal invited a wealthy man to lunch. The man was a reluctant donor, but Weisgal knew how to talk to him. After lunch, the man took out his checkbook and wrote a check for $25,000.

Weisgal looked at the wealthy man and tore up the check. He said, "Thanks a lot, but the meal has already been paid for."

WEIZMANN, CHAIM (1874–1952)
First president of Israel, president of the World Zionist Organization, scientist.

(1) Early in his life, Weizmann was imbued with the idea of advancing culture in the land of Israel by establishing a Hebrew university in Jerusalem. To seek help in this endeavor, he journeyed to Paris to discuss his plans with Baron Edmond de Rothschild.

Rothschild was interested in the idea, but he was concerned about its practicality. "It is an excellent idea," he said. "But where will you get the right kind of instructors? What Jewish scientist is going to give up the glory and financial security of a professorship at Heidelberg or the Sorbonne and accept a precarious position at this embryonic Hebrew university? Here is what I am going to do. If you can interest Dr. Paul Ehrlich, the biologist who led the fight against syphilis and who was awarded the Nobel Prize for medicine in 1908, in the project, I will give you my financial support."

The very next day, Weizmann set out on a trip to Frankfort, Germany, to meet with Dr. Ehrlich. Weizmann faced a series of difficulties in even getting to see the famous scientist. Finally, Ehrlich agreed to see the young chemist. Their discussion lasted for two hours, and Weizmann got what he had come for. Ehrlich agreed to head a committee to advance the idea of a Hebrew university. Ehrlich noted the length of the their meeting, and said, "Mr. Weizmann, I admit that you represent a worthy cause. But what right did you have to take up two hours of my precious time when so many notables—barons, dukes, and princes—have been waiting for weeks to have a five-minute audience with me?"

Weizmann smiled. "They can wait. *They* are merely seeking an injection from you, whereas *I* have given *you* an injection—the injection of an ideal which I hope you will keep and cherish."

(2) It was the fall of 1917. The Feast of Tabernacles was approaching. Lord Allenby was in Egypt preparing for an assault on the Holy Land to free it from Turkish control. In Jerusalem, the Jews had no *hadasim* (myrtles) to use with the *lulav*, which they needed for the holy day.

Three Sephardic Jews called on Weizmann, seeking his help in procuring the much-needed myrtles. But Weizmann had sad news for them. "I am sorry," he said, "but I cannot do anything for you. I am just leaving for Egypt. Here is a message from Lord Allenby."

"No," the three Jews cried out. One said. "Do you mean you are going to leave us when there is not a single myrtle in all Jerusalem?"

Their arguments were to no avail. Weizmann journeyed to Egypt. He found Allenby reading a long telegram signed by hundreds of people.

"Glad you came," Allenby greeted Weizmann. "I have here a telegram informing me that the Jews of Jerusalem are facing a dire calamity, and that it is imperative that I proffer succor immediately. But I'll be damned if I know what they want me to do. They ask for a carload of *hadasim*. What the hell is it, anyhow?"

(3) When Weizmann was a young chemist during World War I, he was asked by the British government to develop a synthetic that could be used as a substitute for acetone, a substance vital to the production of explosives. Weizmann worked hard, and, using some unusual ingredients, including horse chestnuts, he finally discovered a useful synthetic.

David Lloyd George, the British leader, subsequently offered Weizmann a high honor. Weizmann is reported to have instead requested a "national home for my people."

(4) A government official called on Weizmann and found the president of Israel shining his own shoes. The official was astonished and said so. Weizmann looked up. "Did you expect me to shine somebody else's shoes?" he asked.

(5) Weizmann's election as the first president of Israel greatly interested the government of Burma, which became quite excited about the return of Jews to political history. The Burmese wished to provide a gift to the new president.

They proposed that the gift be a rather large Indian elephant, which weighed several tons.

Weizmann asked Abba Eban, then his assistant, to write a courteous letter saying that in the village of Mottele, the town near Pinsk in which Weizmann had been born, there had been a proverb among the Jewish farmers: "Never accept a present that eats."

(6) Nettie Cohen-Cole was offered a post in Weizmann's presidential office. This led to several visits to his home. One prominent American Jewish leader heard of this and asked her to help him get Weizmann's autograph on a book of photos about Weizmann's life.

On her next visit to Weizmann's home, she raised the subject. Weizmann knew the man who had requested the autograph, but he didn't like him very much. He said, "I'll make a deal with you. I'll autograph a book if you will keep him from visiting me." The deal was struck.

(7) Weizmann was a chemist serving at Manchester University in England in the early 1900s. He was represented in Parliament by Arthur Balfour. At the time, the crucial question in Zionist life was whether or not to establish a Jewish homeland in East Africa, as the British suggested, or hold out for the ancient homeland, the land of Israel.

An acquaintance arranged for Weizmann to meet Balfour. Weizmann's purpose was to convince the politician that East Africa was not acceptable. To make his point, Weizmann used an image that a loyal British leader would understand. "Just suppose, Mr. Balfour, that I were to offer you Paris instead of London. Would you accept it?"

Balfour reacted strongly. "But, Dr. Weizmann, we already *have* London."

Weizmann responded, "And we had Jerusalem when London was a marsh."

(8) Weizmann resented the limited, almost exclusively ceremonial, job of president of Israel. He longed for the combative, political life he had once led. He knew that he was at an advanced age, but he still missed the excitement.

One day he was reviewing a parade of the Israeli defense forces. He dropped his handkerchief. A brigadier general sitting nearby retrieved the handkerchief and returned it.

Weizmann praised the general for several minutes for this gesture. The general appreciated the gratitude but was surprised by it. "All I did was to return your handkerchief, Sir."

"Yes," Weizmann said. "But you don't understand how valuable it is to me. You see, it's all that's left for me to stick my nose into these days."

WEIZMANN, VERA (1882–1966)
Zionist, co-founder of Women's International Zionist Organization, wife of Chaim Weizmann.

Vera Weizmann saw a 12-year-old boy, the son of a Weizmann Institute scientist, riding his bicycle on the Memorial Plaza. She instructed the boy not to ride there. She had spoken to him in English because she couldn't speak much Hebrew. The boy immediately noticed this and asked her, "Don't you speak Hebrew?"

She said that she didn't.

Even after her admission, the boy would not stop. "Aren't you ashamed of yourself?"

Mrs. Weizmann thought about this and finally said, "It is easier to be ashamed than to learn Hebrew!"

WELLS, LEON (1925-   )
Holocaust survivor and author.

Wells was taken to the Janowska concentration camp in 1942, when he was 17 years old.

One day while at the camp he became extremely ill and could not even get out of his bed for the morning lineup. He was suffering from typhus and double pneumonia. He was taken out to be shot, along with 180 others.

No mass grave had been dug, so the guards gave shovels to those who would be killed and told them to dig their own graves. The guards shot the inmates in pairs. Each pair would then be covered with a bit of earth and be followed by two more people. All Wells could think of was that he wanted to be shot quickly. He had horrible thoughts. It struck him that if he were shot he'd have blood in his mouth and therefore something to drink.

Wells was about to be shot when he was sent back to the barracks. A man had been shot there, and Wells was to drag the man to the graves. Instead, Wells fled into a crowd of inmates. The guard, fearing for his own life, reported that all 180 inmates were dead.

Wells later became a *sonderkommando* (member of the death brigade) and had to dig up bodies. In November of 1943, the brigade of 120 people fought back against the Nazis. Only 6 members of the brigade, including Wells, survived. Wells and a friend found their way to the home of a Polish Catholic farm family, who hid them. Along with 21 other Jews, Wells lived underground, underneath a pig sty. They stayed there for eight months, until the liberation.

Later, after the war, Wells met the farmer's wife. Wells asked her why she had risked her life. She replied, "Leon, it was the first time I could do something for which I could respect myself. Until that time I was nobody."

WIDREVITZ, HAIM JACOB (1795-1854)
Rabbi and scholar.

Winning a Jewish argument can sometimes be difficult.

There was once a rabbi from a small town in Russia. He was given a monthly salary and allowed to live in a residence owned by the community. After many years of service, the town's Jewish dignitaries decided that he should be removed from his job. They discharged him and asked him to leave the house. He refused to go, and the case came before the Russian court. A judge there sent it to Rabbi Widrevitz.

The rabbi listened carefully to both sides and decided that the ousted rabbi had done nothing offensive, but that for the sake of the community, he should be discharged. He told the Jewish leaders that he had decided in their favor.

"But, he's still living in the house owned by the community," one said. "How can we get him to leave?"

"Compulsion is not a good idea," the rabbi said.

"What shall we do then?"

"There is a peaceful way. All of you should move from the town and leave him alone. That is my advice."

WIENER, NORBERT (1894–1964)
American mathematician and developer of cybernetics.

Norbert Wiener was 16 years old when, to his surprise, he found out that he was Jewish.

Wiener's father, Leo, had been the first professor of Slavonic language at Harvard University and was a man with a set view on how to educate his children. Norbert was taught the alphabet at the age of 18 months. He could both read and write by the age of 3. By 6 he knew arithmetic, algebra, and geometry. He went on to higher education and got a doctorate from Harvard when he was 19. This intense academic training was the key, but not the only significant element, in Wiener's upbringing. His parents determined that he would not discover that he was Jewish. Evidently they did this not from shame (his father, after all, had written *A History of Yiddish Literature*), but from a sense that it was a social handicap to be Jewish, and that therefore a child who grew up without knowing he was Jewish would be healthier.

Young Norbert had some hints about his background. His grandmother always read a paper printed in Hebrew characters. This fact didn't fully register, however; Norbert believed that some non-Jews used Hebrew characters in their writing. His cousin Olga had told him that they were Jews. He then went to his mother, but she told him that they weren't, and he believed her.

At age 16 he won a scholarship to Cornell University and planned to spend an academic year there. At the end of the summer before the semester he was to begin at Cornell, Norbert and his father took a trolley ride to Ithaca. They contacted Professor Thilly. Norbert was to stay at the Thilly's house; the professor and his wife had promised to look after the young scholar.

One evening, before his father left, the elder Wiener and Thilly reminisced about their student days at the University of Missouri. As the talk rambled on, Thilly casually mentioned that he remembered discussion of a famous philosopher in the Wiener family named Maimonides. Leo Wiener said that he had heard those rumors about his being descended from Maimonides, but that his father had lost the papers that had documented the family history.

Norbert listened, fascinated by the discussion. He had never heard that rumor, nor had he ever heard of Maimonides. It didn't take him long to locate an encyclopedia. He read the extensive entry about the great philosopher, whose real name, he discovered, was Rabbi Moses ben Maimon.

Norbert then realized, at age 16, that he was Jewish.

WIESEL, ELIE (1928–   )
Holocaust survivor, author, winner of
Nobel Peace Prize.

(1) Monroe H. Freedman, law professor at Hofstra University, served as director of the US Holocaust Memorial Council. As director, he helped organize an observance of Holocaust Remembrance Day in the East Room of the White House on April 30, 1981. Professor Freedman has supplied the following anecdote.

Prior to the observance, there was a great deal of negotiating between members of the Holocaust Memorial Council and representatives of the White House about the content and length of the ceremony. At one point, it was agreed that the Workmen's Circle Choir would sing. Later, the White House representatives said that the choir would have to be omitted because of time constraints.

Some of the council representatives inferred, correctly or incorrectly, that the real reason for the cancellation was the realization that the choir was going to sing in Yiddish. The council members believed that some people in the White House felt that Yiddish was inappropriate for a ceremony in the White House.

Professor Freedman cannot say whether the inference was correct, nor did Elie Wiesel, also speaking that day, ever express a view on the subject to Professor Freedman. When Professor Freedman mentioned the concern, Professor Wiesel commented, in a soft but firm voice, "Yiddish will be heard in the White House."

On the day of the ceremony, Elie Wiesel rose to speak. He ended his talk by reciting a poem in Yiddish that had been written by a boy who had died in the Holocaust. The language of the poem was haunting and expressive. Wiesel did not translate the poem.[1]

(2) Wiesel was teaching a course on the Holocaust at City College in New York. Students in one class session were particularly concerned about how to transmit the story of the Holocaust to the next generation. One student thought that children in the future simply would not believe what had happened. Another added that because of its very unbelievability, the Holocaust would be forgotten within several generations.

Wiesel did not agree, citing Rabbi Irving Greenberg's theory that the Jews of the Exodus did not realize the historical impact that their flight was to have.

But the students remained insistent. They felt caught in a paradox. Their teacher, Elie Wiesel, like many survivors, believed that those who had not personally experienced the camps could never understand them. If that were true, one student pressed, how could he tell others about the Holocaust?

Wiesel said that they could not comprehend all, but they could know of single incidents. "One tear"—that, he suggested, was what could be told. He then repeated a Hasidic legend.

According to the legend, the founder of Hasidism, the Baal Shem Tov, had a method for averting impending disaster. The Master of the Good Name would go to a particular spot in the woods, where he would light a candle and say a prayer. This would prevent the disaster.

Later, one of the Baal Shem Tov's disciples faced a disaster. The disciple knew where the place in the woods was, and he knew how to light the candle that had to be lit, but he did not know the correct prayer that had to be recited. Still, the disaster did not occur. Later, still another disciple was faced with an impending disaster. He knew the spot, but he knew neither how to light the

---

[1] The address and the poem, in English translation, can be found in Irving Abrahamson's *Against Silence*, vol. 3, p. 175.

candle nor the prayer to be recited. Still, the disaster did not take place. Finally, a later disciple also faced an impending disaster. He did not know where in the woods he could find the spot. He did not know how to light the candle. He did not know the prayer to recite. All he could do was to tell the story. This, too, averted the disaster.

After telling the legend, Wiesel continued by telling his students to say simply that they heard the story. To remember was what was important; it remained vital to tell the stories.

WIESENTHAL, SIMON (1908–   )
Holocaust survivor and pursuer of Nazi criminals.

The following anecdote was provided by Mr. Wiesenthal.

"Two Israeli journalists asked me in the course of a discussion in my office, "Mr. Wiesenthal, please tell us what would be gratifying for you. But we will not accept it if you were to say that you feel satisfaction when a Nazi criminal you have been looking for for a long time is finally caught, or when he is put on trial. This kind of success bears too much blood, too many tears and painful memories to give you a deep, humane feeling of satisfaction. So, what would give you real satisfaction?"

I felt in a way that they were right and thus I started trying to think of an occurrence that would show what gave me satisfaction. After a while I told them the following: "The kind of satisfaction I sometimes feel, no other person in this world can feel, neither Jew or non-Jew." Obviously the journalists became interested.

I continued. "When two Nazis quarrel, one threatens the other with 'I'll go to Wiesenthal and tell him everything about you!' "

The journalists began to laugh, and I said, "And believe me, some of them really come to me and give me some important information."

WIGODER, DEVORAH (born c. 1914)
Author and proselyte.

Devorah Wigoder's name at birth was Jane Frances MacDwyer. Later in life, she sought to convert to Judaism and to marry the learned rabbi Geoffrey Wigoder. The rabbi, a Conservative Jew and a man prominent in the Conservative movement, was delighted to marry someone he loved who was a sincere convert, but others questioned the propriety of so important a rabbi entering into such a marriage.

Devorah decided to go to various prominent faculty members of the Jewish Theological Seminary to seek their approval and to avert any future criticism of the marriage.

Rabbi Abraham Joshua Heschel gave his immediate, warm assent. But it was decided that the final test would be the approval of the marriage by Professor Saul Lieberman, the world-renowned talmudic scholar.

One night, after all the classes had finished, Devorah went to Lieberman's office door. She had dressed completely in black as a symbol of the solemnity of the occasion.

Lieberman opened the door. Devorah greeted him in Hebrew, realizing only later that she had used the feminine forms. Lieberman answered her in French. She looked at him and said, "Give me one advantage over you. Let's speak English."

He agreed, staring at her with his deep blue eyes.

Devorah began to talk with him. She told Lieberman how deeply attached she was to the Talmud. Then she stated her awe toward the Hebrew language and discussed her theory that gravity had affected many letters in the Hebrew alphabet. Professor Lieberman then asked her whether she had read books on the Hebrew alphabet. She admitted that she hadn't. He offered her some advice: "Good. Then *don't!* Keep working on your own ideas about the alphabet and one day write your own book."

After talking some more, Rabbi Lieberman told Devorah a story about a very learned rabbi who met a shepherd. He asked the shepherd how the simple keeper of sheep went about praying. The shepherd, clearly embarrassed because he was unlettered and in the presence of a rabbi, responded, "To tell the truth, I just say 'Dear God, I do love You so much. If You had sheep to tend, I would tend them for You for nothing.'" The rabbi was shocked at this informal approach to praying. He immediately provided some instructions to the simple shepherd about the appropriate prayers. For many days and nights after that, however, the rabbi could not put out of his mind the simple and honestly direct prayer of the shepherd. He was struck by the sense of closeness the shepherd felt to God. One morning he returned to the shepherd and said, "Forget what I taught you, good man. All these formal words are meaningless beside your own natural vocabulary with God. Pray as you did."

Then Professor Lieberman offered to write to Geoffrey Wigoder's father, who opposed the marriage. Lieberman called Devorah a "genuine convert."

Eventually Devorah and Geoffrey married and moved to Israel.

WISE, ISAAC M. (1819–1900)
American rabbi and Reform pioneer.

Rabbi Wise was a powerful proponent of Reform Judaism. His views often led him into conflict with Jewish leaders as well as with his own congregation. He seemed to the Orthodox to deny that a personal Messiah would come or that the dead would be resurrected. Such views were pure heresy at the time.

In 1850, Wise was serving the congregation Beth El in Albany, New York. In July of that year the divided congregation was shocked when Wise demanded from his pulpit that all members of Beth El's board observe the Sabbath. One member in particular annoyed Wise, and the rabbi demanded that the man either close his store on the Sabbath or resign from the board. The president of Beth El, fearing that Wise would publicly denounce the shopkeeper, forbade the rabbi from preaching at the following service. The irony of all this was not lost on Wise. His opponents denounced him for his Reformist ways while his congregation became angry when he asked the board to obey a fundamental Jewish law.

The president of Beth El finally preferred charges against Wise. The rabbi was fired on the morning of the eve of Rosh Hashanah. Wise refused to accept this dismissal, however. He went to the service. A riot broke out, necessitating that the police be called. On the following day, Wise and his supporters held services at his house. Wise soon started a new congregation—the fourth Reform congregation in the United States.

WISE, STEPHEN (1874–1949)
American rabbi and Zionist leader.

(1) Rabbi Wise was scheduled to speak at an anti-Nazi rally in Brooklyn. The rabbi had received several letters warning him to stay away from the meeting or risk being shot. But Rabbi Wise was not easily intimidated. Soon after the meeting began, he was called upon to speak. He stood up, spread his arms, and began his speech this way: "I have been warned to stay away from this meeting under pain of being killed. If anyone is going to shoot me, let him do it now. I hate to be interrupted."

(2) Every policeman in Manhattan knew Rabbi Wise. One day, Rabbi Jonah Wise (who, like Stephen, had once been the rabbi in Portland, Oregon), the son of Isaac Mayer Wise, came to New York. While still getting used to the city's ways, Jonah Wise crossed at a red light, only to have a police officer stop him. Jonah said, "I'm Rabbi Wise." The officer replied, "Yeah, and I'm Jesus Christ."

(3) The following anecdote was supplied by Zeldon Cohen:

> As a local leader in the American Jewish Congress in 1948, I met the
> great Stephen S. Wise and took him to his hotel room, where I was
> alone with him for about one hour until others arrived.
>
> Wise, in my presence, called Nahum Goldmann in New York
> and sought to have him use his influence as Jewry's ambassador to the
> world to have the new state named "Judea." Apparently Goldmann
> resisted because I can still hear that big, booming voice of Wise's saying,
> "No, no, Nahum! Judea, Judea!" Soon Wise hung up the phone. He was
> agitated.

(4) Rabbi Wise was attending a huge rally when he was introduced to a politician
not noted for his honesty or ethics. The politician was running for an important
office. "You don't have to introduce me to Rabbi Wise," said the politician to the
man standing between them. "After all, I should know who he is; he's denounced me often enough from his pulpit."

Rabbi Wise, an enemy of all politicians he considered unfit for office,
responded, "You're wrong, sir. I've denounced you often, but not often
enough."

(5) Rabbi Wise once opened a speech with these words: "When I make a speech,
I actually make three speeches. The first is the one that I prepare before I even see
my audience, and I somehow feel that that is not the right speech. So I tear up
my first speech and deliver an impromptu one. There again it's a wonderful
speech. Then comes the time for me to go home and think of what I should have
said. That is the best speech of all. So, if you want to hear a good speech, walk
home with me tonight."

(6) It was during the initial shock of the 1929 stock market crash that Rabbi Wise
was called upon to give advice to many who had lost all their money. One man
came to the Free Synagogue with an especially sad tale. He talked of all he had
once owned that was now gone. The newly impoverished man concluded that
suicide was his only option, for that at least would leave insurance money for his
family. He asked for the rabbi's advice.

Rabbi Wise contemplated for a moment. Finally, he offered his suggestion.
He advised the man to gather his family for a meeting and to ask their opinion
about whether or not he should commit suicide."If they argue against your
taking your life," the rabbi said, "you'll know they would rather have you keep
living than get the insurance. If they approve of your proposed suicide, however,

I'd go on living just to spite them. Surely you wouldn't want to sacrifice your life for such a family."

(7) Wise's wife Louise managed a child adoption service. She once received a letter from a woman who wished to adopt a child. The letter included this passage: "We have tried four times to have children of our own, but have always been unsuccessful." When Louise Wise told her husband about the letter, he made the observation "What an impatient lady!"

(8) Wise had many close friends in high office, one of whom was Woodrow Wilson. Wilson frequently called upon Wise for advice, especially on Jewish matters.

One of those Jewish matters involved the Balfour Declaration. In October 1917, the British government sent President Wilson a draft of the proposed declaration, which would be, in effect, the recognition of Zionism.

At the time, the land of Israel was under the control of Turkish authorities, and the United States had not issued a declaration of war against Turkey. Therefore, the text of the declaration had to be transmitted in the utmost secrecy so as not to jeopardize the United States' neutral status. The president turned to Louis Brandeis and Rabbi Wise to assess the document.

The proposed text included the idea that Great Britain would favor "a national haven for Jews." This phrase bothered Wise. He wanted some way to strengthen Zionism's claim to national legitimacy and yet not upset the British. Wise finally had an idea. He suggested to Wilson that the phrase read "a national home for the Jewish people." Wilson liked the idea and transmitted the suggestion to the British, who adopted it. (Wise's foresight was remarkable. The change did turn out to be an important one.)

Wise thanked Wilson, who was proud of what he was doing to help restore the Jews to their ancient homeland. He evidently saw his election to the presidency as the work of God, and believed that part of the reason he was elected was to help the Jews.

Wise and Brandeis both warned him that his support of the Balfour Declaration would trigger letters of protest from prominent non-Zionist members of the Jewish community. He told them, "My wastebasket is big enough to take care of all such matters."

(9) Wise traveled to Israel on a number of occasions. He took his third trip there in 1935, during a time that would include Passover.

Once he arrived, Wise decided to go to the Jordan River to immerse his hands in the well-known sacred site.

When Wise arrived at the river, he encountered a group of Russian peasant pilgrims. As Wise bent down to put his hands in the water, an old peasant woman yelled at him in Russian. His guide translated the woman's angry words: "Zhid, how dare you put your Jewish hands in our Christian River?"

Wise told his guide to translate his response. He wanted the woman to know that his Jewish ancestors had been bathing in the Jordan River for hundreds of years before her Russian ancestors had adopted the practice of bathing at all.

WOLF OF ZBARAZ (1708–1788)
Rabbi and community leader.

(1) Rabbi Wolf was widely known as the fairest of judges. Justice was extremely important to him, and he could not be corrupted.

One day his own wife accused her maid of having stolen a very valuable object. The servant, who was an orphan, began to cry, and then she denied having stolen the object. The wife decided that a rabbinical court was needed to decide the case.

When the rabbi saw his wife preparing to go to the court, he put on his Sabbath robe, so that he might go as well. His wife was surprised. "It's not dignified that a man of your standing should go to the court with me. I am very capable of pleading my own case," she told him.

The rabbi said, "Oh, I am sure that you are. What I am concerned about is who will plead the case of your maid, who is a poor orphan. I am going to make sure that she is treated justly."

(2) The rabbi met with some men who came to denounce card players. The protesters wished the rabbi to condemn the players for engaging in a frivolous activity that took time away from serious study. But the rabbi refused to do so. "The card players fight sleep. That's good. They concentrate deeply on their game. That, too, is good. Eventually they will cease to play cards. But a discipline of mind and body will remain. In time they will place this discipline in the service of God. Why, then, should I condemn them?"

WOLFSON, HARRY A. (1887–1974)
Historian of philosophy.

Lessons from a boy's yeshiva education can last a lifetime.

There were continuing problems for Jewish students as they walked to the yeshiva in Wolfson's hometown of Bialystock. Non-Jews taunted the students and sometimes fought with them. To ease the problem, the rabbi suggested to his pupils that they arrive at the yeshiva earlier than they were supposed to, in order to avoid the anti-Semites. To encourage arrival before dawn, the rabbi would send notes written in gold letters to each boy who arrived before the sun rise. The latecomers also received notes, but with black letters.

Young Harry learned to be the first there.

He sustained this practice throughout his life. At Harvard University, he would arrive before the library opened. Each evening, as the library was about to close, a custodian would rap on Wolfson's door to let him know that it was time to leave.

YAAKOV YITZHAK OF PRZYSUCHA (1766–1814)
Rabbi and hasidic leader.

Rabbi Yaakov Yitzhak's wife was given to nagging. He endured this mostly by maintaining a steadfast silence. One day, however, he ended his silence and responded to her continual nagging with some sharp words of his own. His disciple, Rabbi Bunam, heard Rabbi Yaakov's reply and was greatly surprised. "What suddenly made you talk back to your wife, Rabbi?" he asked his teacher.

The rabbi responded, "It would have been cruel not to answer her. What irritated her more than anything else was the fact that I did not respond to her nagging."

YADIN, YIGAEL (1917–1984)
Israeli archaeologist and second chief of staff of the Israel Defense Forces.

(1) Yadin served as the commander in chief of the Israeli army in the War of Independence. After the defeat of the Egyptian army in the battle for the Negev Desert, Yadin was asked whether he deserved credit for devising the victorious strategy.

"I don't know. All I can say is that if we had been defeated, the blame would have been placed on me."

(2) Yadin was often mistaken for Moshe Dayan. The two had thin, angular faces and looked alike, although Dayan wore his famous eyepatch to cover a war injury. One day, Yadin was walking along a street in Jerusalem. He paused, waiting for a traffic light to change, when a tourist bus pulled alongside him. The

245

guide on the bus spotted Yadin and told his passengers that a former chief of staff of the Israeli army was standing there. All of the cameras came out of their cases. One tourist rushed out of the bus, touched Yadin's arm, and said, "Sir, you can't imagine how overjoyed I am to see that your bad eye has been cured."

YECHIEL OF OSTROWCE (1851–1928)
Rabbi and scholar.

A group of rabbis were gathered at a celebration. They began to discuss their well-known rabbinic ancestors. Rabbi Yechiel had to say, "I'm the first eminent ancestor in my family." The collected rabbis were very surprised to hear this comment.

The conversation naturally turned to the Torah. Each rabbi began to explain a text by using the teachings and sayings of one of his rabbinical ancestors. Finally it was time for Rabbi Yechiel to speak. He got up and said, "My father was a simple baker. His teaching was that only fresh bread tastes good, and so I should avoid stale bread. This is also true of learning."

YEZIERSKA, ANZIA (1885–1970)
American author.

Anzia Yezierska had come to the United States in 1901. She worked in a tailor's sweatshop and as a waitress, a cook, and a teacher. By 1918 she had become a writer. Her first collection of short stories, *Hungry Hearts*, was published in 1920. In those stories she described immigrant life on New York's East Side. Like many Jews of her day, she was excruciatingly impoverished. She escaped this poverty only when her book was sold to the movies.

Anzia was living in a rooming house on Hester Street. It was 1920. One afternoon she was drinking tea, glad that the landlady was not around to nag her again for the rent. Suddenly she heard her name called. She was convinced that she was being evicted.

She went to her door to find a group of people surrounding a Western Union messenger. The messenger handed Anzia the yellow telegram. In the ghetto, a Western Union message usually meant that someone had died. Everyone waited. Anzia opened the envelope and read:TELEPHONE IMMEDIATELY FOR AN APPOINTMENT TO DISCUSS MOTION PICTURE RIGHTS FOR HUNGRY HEARTS.

After her neighbors left, Anzia reread the telegram. She was perplexed. The message was signed by R. L. Giffen, an important agent. *Hungry Hearts* had not sold well. She had received $200 in royalties from the book, and she had spent it long ago. She couldn't understand why a movie producer would be interested in her book.

Gradually she began to panic. She needed a nickel to make the phone call and a dime for carfare. She'd have to pawn something for the fifteen cents. She spotted her mother's shawl, which she used as a blanket and a cover for her cat. The shawl filled Anzia with memories, but she grabbed it and ran to the pawnshop. The pawnbroker dismissed the shawl as an old rag, but finally, and not without much haggling, he offered her a quarter. Reluctantly, she took the quarter.

She was at the agent's office a half hour later. He told her that several Hollywood producers wanted her book. He said they'd offered $5,000, but he was holding out for $10,000. He told her that if they settled with Samuel Goldwyn, as he wanted to do, Anzia would go to Hollywood to collaborate on the script.

Excited but very hungry, Anzia asked if the agent could advance her a dollar. He smiled and handed her a $10 bill. She walked out of his office.

Child's Restaurant was across the street. She had often stood outside the restaurant, staring at the food being thrown away and wishing she could have it. She went in and ordered the most expensive steak on the menu. She ate half of the food on her plate. She could not finish the meal. Tears came to her eyes. She thought of her hunger and of how her deceased parents would react to her success, and she wondered whether they had forgiven her for having run away from home to establish her own identity. A waitress came over, preparing to remove the dishes.

Anzia grabbed the plate. She wasn't hungry, but she couldn't let go of the uneaten food. She waited until no one was looking and then took out her handkerchief. She put the meat and potatoes in it, covered it with a newspaper, and left.

At home, she fed the steak to Lily, an alley cat.

YITZHAK, MEIR (1900s)
Rabbi and scholar.

A member of the Teamster's Union came to Rabbi Yitzhak with a religious problem. The man was in a quandary because his occupation frequently made it difficult or impossible for him to attend Sabbath services. He asked the rabbi about the appropriateness of such a job. The rabbi asked him, "Do you carry poor passengers free of charge?"

"Yes," replied the hard-working man.

"Then you serve the Lord in your occupation just as faithfully as I do when I am in the synagogue."

YOHANAN BEN ZAKKAI (first century C.E.)
Important rabbi and scholar after the destruction of the Second Temple.

(1) Yohanan ben Zakkai is credited by many with saving Judaism.

In the year 70 C.E., the Romans had surrounded Jerusalem and were preparing to attack. A Jewish group known as the Zealots controlled the capital. Some of the Zealots believed that Jews who did not fully agree with them were on the Romans' side and should be killed. The patricians who were pro-Roman opposed the Zealots. Many Jews were in the middle; they worried about Judaism's fate beyond Roman control.

Yohanan ben Zakkai was among those in the center.

The Romans attacked at Passover and Eliazer ben Simon, leader of the Zealots, asked Yohanan to choose sides. Yohanan simply said, "I stand with the Lord, not with any man."

Yohanan called his disciples together. They asked him what was to be done. He responded, "We must build a temple where it cannot be destroyed by any earthly power." The disciples were confused by this. "Where is that, Rabbi?" they asked.

"The temple must be rebuilt in the hearts of the people. After our holy city is destroyed, we must have scholars who can preserve the Law."

The disciples reminded Yohanan that the academies outside Jerusalem lay in ruin, and that after Jerusalem's destruction, there would be no scholars.

Yohanan faced a difficult decision. He decided to flee the city in order to preserve the Law. He knew that the Zealots and some others would think him cowardly, but he determined that saving the Law was more important than his reputation.

Yohanan's disciples spread the story that the rabbi was dying of cholera. For many days Yohanan lay still, practicing so that he could lie without moving a muscle. He learned to breathe without moving his chest. When he was ready, his disciples told everyone that the revered rabbi had died.

The disciples planned to sneak the rabbi out of Jerusalem. They put Yohanan in a prayer shawl and lay him in a wooden box. A disciple told Eliazer the Zealot that the rabbi's last wish was to be buried outside the walls of Jerusalem so as not to profane the holy city with his corpse. Eliazer provided an order permitting such a burial.

After Eliazer left, Yohanan rapped at his coffin. He told his disciples to find a rotten, smelly piece of meat and place it under the shawl. The rabbi knew that a dead body would reek in the heat. The meat was placed in the coffin as requested.

The disciples carrying the coffin reached the city gates, where they were stopped by the sergeant of the guard. The sergeant read the order, but he hesitated; after all, this wouldn't be the first time he had encountered people pretending to be dead so that they would be able to escape the city. "How do we know he's dead?"

A disciple said, "Just look at him and smell him."

One guard bent down and decided that the rabbi was indeed dead. But a second guard was more cautious. He said, "Stick him with your dagger. He won't care if he's already dead. If he isn't yet dead, he will be."

Yohanan didn't move. The sergeant removed his dagger and began to raise his arm, but a disciple stopped him. "This is the body of Rabbi Yohanan ben Zakkai. Do not mutilate the corpse of our greatest scholar."

The sergeant put his weapon away. "He smells too bad not to be dead. Take him away."

At nightfall, Yohanan left the coffin and came before Vespasian, the general who was made emperor during their talks. Rabbi Yohanan asked permission to establish a small academy for the purpose of teaching the Law to children. Vespasian agreed.

Rabbi Yohanan went to Yavneh and there established a place where, after Jerusalem's destruction, the Temple was rebuilt in Jewish hearts.

(2) When Rabbi Yohanan fell ill, he was visited by his disciples, who were greatly distressed by his illness. The disciples asked the rabbi to bless them. Yohanan agreed and said, "May you fear God as much as you fear people."

The disciples were surprised. One asked, "Is that only how much we are to fear God?"

Rabbi Yohanan said, "I wish you feared God even that much. Whenever people sin, they say 'I just hope nobody sees me.' "

(3) The talmudic rabbis always believed that education was far more desirable than wealth.

One day, while Rabbi Yohanan was walking with his friends, he pointed to a nearby vineyard. The rabbi said, "That vineyard was once mine. I sold it to help the poor. In that way, I no longer had to care for it and could instead devote my time to the study of Torah."

They walked some more until they came to a large field. The rabbi said, "That field, too, was mine. I sold it also, so that I could devote myself to study." They passed still another field, and the rabbi told the same story.

Finally, the rabbi's friends asked how he had provided for his old age.

The rabbi said, "Don't be troubled. I was glad to give up all this. I will be rewarded in eternity."

YOSE BEN HALAFTA (mid-second century C.E.)
Rabbi and talmudic scholar.

(1) A Roman woman, curious about Judaism, came to the rabbi and asked, "It took the Lord only six days to create the world. What has He been doing since then?"

Rabbi Yose replied, "The Holy One sits and makes ladders. Some go up on their ladders, some down." Then he looked at her. "On which rung of the ladder are you?"

(2) A Roman woman asked Rabbi Yose, "Can anyone who wishes to draw near to your God?"

Instead of responding, the rabbi offered the woman a basket filled with figs. She selected an especially ripe one and ate it. Then the rabbi said to her, "You know how to choose. God knows even more about choosing. God chooses all those who live righteously, and He draws them to Him."

ZANGWILL, ISRAEL (1864–1926)
British author and Zionist.

(1) Israel Zangwill was widely considered one of the greatest wits in England. Many stories are told about his clever comments.

One story is about an exchange he had with Theodor Herzl, the founder of Zionism.

Herzl was in a hotel room with Cyrus L. Sulzberger, Harry Friedenwald, and Zangwill. While Herzl spoke, Zangwill sat with his eyes closed, as he habitually did. Herzl looked at Zangwill and said, "Don't go to sleep, Israel."

Zangwill shot back, "The God of Israel slumbereth not, nor sleepeth – but Israel himself sometimes does both!"

(2) In 1903, Zangwill shocked London Jewish society by marrying Edith Ayrton, then a well-known literary figure, and a non-Jew. Zangwill was widely called a traitor to his people.

Not long after the marriage took place, Zangwill was scheduled to speak before a large Jewish audience at Albert Hall. Zangwill was prepared to endure heckling. Despite that, he came to the hall accompanied by his new wife.

Zangwill walked to the podium and began to speak. "Fellow Jews, I trust you will be courteous to Mrs. Zangwill, and that you will not do or say anything that might offend her. While I may deserve censure for marrying a Gentile, Mrs. Zangwill deserves nothing but praise. For she married a Jew."

(3) Zangwill was once riding on a London subway. Two well-dressed women sat opposite him. As the train stopped, a poor Jewish peddler carrying a pack on his back boarded the train and sat next to one of the ladies. The woman turned to her companion in disgust and said, "Do you know of a place where there are no Jews?"

Zangwill answered for the lady. "You might try going to hell, Madam."

ZOLEL *(eighteenth century)*
Cantor in Odessa.

Sadly, the cantor Zolel did not have a very good voice. He was a wonderful composer, however, and a gifted conductor.

Zolel and his choir once traveled to the city of Sadagora to appear before Rabbi Abraham Jacob. Zolel conducted the Sabbath services, and after the services the cantor said to the rabbi, "How did you like the way we prayed?"

"I was delighted by the choir's praying," said the rabbi. "But why are you so cheap?"

"Cheap?" exclaimed Zolel. "I pay members of the choir enormous amounts of money for their services."

"Ah," said the rabbi. "Then why not spend a little more and hire a cantor as well?"

ZUSYA OF HANIPOLI *(died 1800)*
Hasidic rabbi and preacher.

(1) Rabbi Zusya was asked whether an ordinary person without great accomplishment should fear the judgment day. Rabbi Zusya said that he himself was just an ordinary person, and he believed that on judgment day, God would not ask him why he had not been Moses or why he had not been Rabbi Akiba. Rather, God would ask whether he had been Rabbi Zusya.

(2) Rabbi Zusya was staying at an inn. A wealthy guest mistook him for a beggar and treated him without respect. The guest later learned the rebbe's true identity and asked for Zusya's forgiveness.

"Why do you ask me to forgive you?" Rabbi Zusya said in response. "You haven't done anything to Zusya. You insulted not Zusya, but a poor beggar. I suggest you go out and ask beggars everywhere to forgive you."

ZYGELBOIM, SHMUEL *(1895–1943)*
Polish Jewish leader.

Shmuel Zygelboim used the only weapon he had to alert the world to Nazi horrors.

Zygelboim was an organizer for the Jewish Social Democrat party, the Bund. He had been a member of the municipal councils in Warsaw and Lodz. After the Nazis took Warsaw in September 1939, twelve public leaders were to be given to them to serve as hostages. Shmuel volunteered and served as a member of the Judenrat. He opposed the Nazi demand that the Judenrat establish a ghetto.

In September 1940, Shmuel left Poland at the request of the Bund and went to the United States. From there he went on to London, where he served on the national council of the Polish government in exile. He spoke out on the radio and in the press about the Nazis. As a Jewish leader, Shmuel heard first-hand the almost unbelievable stories emerging from Europe. He tried unsuccessfully to arouse action by various governments. He was particularly depressed by the failure of a Conference on Refugees held in Bermuda in April 1943, and by the crushing of the Warsaw ghetto uprising.

Shmuel concluded that he had no weapons with which to fight public indifference to the fate of the Jews except his life. He made the cold calculation that perhaps his suicide would alert the governments of the world to the true horrors of Nazism.

Therefore, on May 12, 1943, in an act of desperation and of protest, but even more important, as an act to evoke the conscience of the world, Shmuel Zygelboim committed suicide. Shmuel left a letter saying that he could no longer live in a world in which Jews were annihilated. His letter ended with the words: "I wish to express my vigorous protest against the apathy with which the world regards and resigns itself to the slaughter of the Jewish people."

SOURCES

Aaronsohn: Cowen and Gunther, *Spy*, pp. 3–6, 56–58.
Abele: Neches, *Tales*, p. 34.
Abrabanel: Netanyahu, *Abravenel*, pp. 53ff.; and Schwarz, *Memoirs*, pp. 46–47.
Abraham: (1) Author; (2) Richman, *Jewish Wit*, pp. 220–221; (3) Midrash.
Abraham, Reuel: *Jewish Digest*, February 1970, pp. 47–48.
Abram: Abram, *Day is Short*, pp. 145ff.
Abulafia: Philip Alstat, *Jewish Week*, August 30, 1975.
Adler, Cyrus: Adler, *Days*, pp. 270–280.
Adler, Hermann: Fadiman, *Anecdotes*.
Adler, Jacob P.: Richman, *Jewish Wit*.
Agnon: Rosten, *Yiddish*.
Ahad Ha'am: Simon, *Ahad Ha'am*, p. 9.
Akiba: (1) Finkelstein, *Akiba*; (2) Mandel, *Treasury*; (3) *Jewish Digest*, December 1970, p. 76; (4, 5, 6) Talmud.
Aleichem: (1) Novak and Waldoks, *Book*, p. 144; (2) Richman, *Jewish Wit*; (3) Ausubel, *Treasury*.
Allon: Allon, *House*, pp. 77ff.
Alter: Correspondence.
Amnon: Ausubel, *Treasury*, pp. 147ff.
Amram: Talmud.
Angel: Polner, *Rabbi*, pp. 204–205.
Anieliewicz: Gilbert, *Holocaust*, pp. 564ff; and Kurzman, *Battle*, pp. 363ff.
Arendt: May, *Arendt*, pp. 109ff.
Asch: (1) correspondence; (2) Richman, *Jewish Wit*, p. 188.
Ashi: Gersh, *People*, pp. 129ff.
Asimov: *Jewish Digest*, January 1980, p. 51.

Note: Page numbers have been provided only for those anecdotes that are not readily located in the sources cited.

Baal Shem Tov: (1) *Jewish Digest,* March 1970; (2) Ausubel, *Treasury;* (3) Rywell, *Tears,* p. 110; (4, 5) Levin, *Tales,* pp. 113–114.

Baeck: Friedlander, *Baeck,* p. 48.

Bar Kappara: Reizenstein, *Wisdom,* pp. 66–67.

Bar Kochba: Josephus, *War.*

Baron: Shenker, *Coat,* p. 184.

Baruch: Author

Baruch of Medzeboth: (1) Wiesel, *Four Hasidic Masters,* pp. 29–31; (2) pp. 52–53.

Begin: (1) Begin, *Revolt,* pp. 212ff; and Katz, *Days,* p. 98; (2) Fadiman, *Anecdotes;* (3) correspondence; (4) Silver, *Begin,* pp. 201ff.

Beilis: Samuel, *Blood,* pp. 60–62.

Belkind: Miller, in Chissin, *Diary,* pp. 5–8.

Bellow: Bellow, *Jerusalem,* pp. 1–5.

Ben-Gurion: (1) Kurzman, *Ben-Gurion,* pp. 19ff; (2) *Jewish Digest,* December 1970; (3) *Jewish Digest,* March 1970; (4) Phil Miller, personal communication; (5) Humes, *Treasury;* (6) Sitewell, *Golf Digest,* April 1977; (7) *Jewish Digest,* May 1972.

Ben-Yehuda: (1) Chomsky, *Hebrew,* pp. 236–237; (2) St. John, *Tongue,* pp. 76–77.

Ben-Zvi: (1) Humes, *Treasury;* (2) Rywell, *Tears,* p. 204.

Benjamin: Butler, *Benjamin,* p. 434.

Benny: *Jewish Digest,* September 1977.

Berlin: Mendelsohn, *Ring,* p. 36.

Bernhardt: Fuller, *Anecdotes.*

Beruriah: (1, 2) Talmud.

Bialik: (1) Phil Miller; (2) Fadiman, *Anecdotes;* (3) Richman, *Wit.*

Blitzer: Blitzer, *Hadassah,* October 1987, pp. 14–15.

Borochov: Cohen, in Borochov, *Struggle,* p. 1.

Brandeis: (1) Urofsky, *Zionism;* (2) Urofsky, pp. 111–113; (3) Mandel, *Treasury.*

Breitbart: Ausubel, *Treasury.*

Brod: Correspondence.

Buber: (1) Author; (2) Buber, *Between Man and Man,* pp. 22–23.

Cahan: Film *Isaac in America.*

Carmel: Carmel, *Path.*

Caro: Werblowsky, *Karo,* pp. 138–139.

Chagall: Chagall, *Life,* pp. 44ff.

Chissin: Chissin, *Diary,* pp. 36ff.

Cohen, Elie: Author.

Cohen, Henry: Richman, *Wit.*

Cohen, Hermann: Roth, *Judaism*, pp. 185–186.
Cowan: Cowan, *Orphan*, pp. 179–180.
Cresson: Eichhorn, *Folklore*, pp. 97–98; and Epstein, *Zion's Call*, pp. 106–107.

David: (1) Mandel, *Treasury*; (2) Rywell, *Tears*, p. 180; (3) Reizenstein, *Wisdom*, pp. 73–74.
Davis, Jr.: Gross, *Almanac*, pp. 274–275.
Dayan: (1, 2) Dayan, *Life*, pp. 45ff.; 15ff; (3) Fadiman, *Anecdotes*.
Disraeli: (1) Fadiman, *Anecdotes*; (2) Mandel, *Treasury*.
Dov Baer: Braude, *Handbook*.
Dreyfus: Halasz, *Dreyfus*, pp. 54ff; and Elon, *Herzl*, pp. 128–129.

Eban: (1) Raphael Danziger; (2) Eban, *Abba Eban*, pp. 429–434.
Eger: Neches, *Tales*, pp. 47–48.
Einstein: (1) Humes, *Treasury*; (2) Wallace, *Significa*, p. 36; (3) Author; (4,5) Fadiman, *Anecdotes*; (6) Golden, *Humor*; (7) Richman, *Wit*; (8) Copeland, *Jokes*.
Eliezer ben Hyrcanus: Braude, *Handbook*.
Eliezer ben Yair: Josephus, *War*.
Elijah: Midrash
Elijah ben Solomon Zalman: (1) Ausubel, *Treasury*; (2) Jacobs, *Belief*; (3) Ausubel, *Treasury*; (4) Neches, *Tales*, pp. 25–26.
Elimelech: Ausubel, *Treasury*.
Ephraim ben Sancho: Ausubel, *Treasury*.
Eshkol: (1) *Jewish Digest*, October 1971; (2) Fadiman, *Anecdotes*.
Eybeschuetz: (1) Richman, *Wit*; (2) Mendelsohn, *Laughs*, p. 142.

Fackenheim: Correspondence.
Fox: Richman, *Wit*.
Frank: Gies, *Frank*, pp. 112–114.
Frankfurter: Baker, *Frankfurter*, p. 19.
Frankl: Frankl, *Search*, pp. 42–43.
Freier: Dash, *Jerusalem*, pp. 279ff.
Freud: (1) Eichhorn, *Folklore*, pp. 145–146; (2) Jones, *Freud*, p. 22.

Gamaliel: (1) Braude, *Handbook*; (2) Richman, *Lore*; (3, 4, 5) Talmud.
Gebihah ben Pesisa: Richman, *Wit*, pp. 225, 226.
Ginzberg: Shenker, *Coat*, p. 201.
Glueckel: Schwarz, *Memoirs*.
Goode: Eichhorn, *Folklore*, pp. 184–186.
Gordis: Conversation and correspondence.

Gratz: Author.
Greenberg: Shenker, *Coat*, pp. 96–97.
Grodner: (1–4) Ausubel, *Treasury*.

Harif: Neches, *Tales*, pp. 58–59.
Hart: Hart, *Auschwitz*, pp. 61–62.
Hartman: Hartman, *Heart*.
Hecht: *Jewish Digest*, December 1976.
Heifetz: Fadiman, *Anecdotes*.
Heine: (1) Author; (2) Braude, *Handbook*.
Hertz: Ausubel, *Treasury*.
Herzl: (1) Herzl, *Diaries*; (2, 3) Elon, *Herzl*, p. 234, 236, 247; (4) *Land and Life*,
    Summer 1987; (5) Mendelsohn, *Ring*, p. 149.
Hesil: Neches, *Tales*, p. 27.
Hillel: (1, 2, 4) Talmud; (3) Reizenstein, *Wisdom*, pp. 1–2.
Hirsch: Author.
Hobson: Fadiman, *Anecdotes*.

Imber: Kabakoff, *Hope*, pp. 78ff.
Israel Meir Ha-Kohen: (1) Correspondence; (2) Jacobs, *Belief*, p. 207.
Isserles: Shenker, *Coat*, p. 145.

Jabotinsky: Schechtman, *Jabotinsky*, pp. 73–74.
Jacob David: Richman, *Laughs*.
Jacob Joseph: Wiesel, *Souls*, pp. 40–41.
Jacobson: Grose, *Israel*, pp. 272ff.
Javits: Javits, *Javits*, p. 156.
Jeremiah: Author.
Job: Author.
Jose Dumbrover: Neches, *Tales*, pp. 46–47.
Joshua ben Hananiah: (1, 2) Talmud.
Judah Halevi: (1) Richman, *Wit*; (2) Author.
Judah Ha-Nasi: (1) Richman, *Laughs*; (2) Richman, *Wit*; (3, 4) Talmud.

Kafka: Crawford, *Kafka*, pp. 44–45.
Kahane: News reports.
Kalir: Mendelsohn, *Laughs*, p. 30.
Kaplan: Parzen, *Architects*, pp. 198 ff.
Kaufman: (1) Fadiman, *Anecdotes*; (2) Teichmann, *Kaufman*.
Koch: Koch, *Mayor*, pp. 262ff.
Kohen: Author.
Kohut, Alexander: Neches, *Tales*, pp. 67–68.
Kohut, Rebekah: Kohut, *Portion*, pp. 192–210.

Kollek: Slater, *Pledge*, pp. 301–302.
Kook: (1) Richman, *Wit*; (2) Mendelsohn, *Laughs*, pp. 137–138.
Korczak: Mortkowicz-Olczakowa, *Massacre*.
Kovler: Neches, *Tales*, pp. 50–51.
Kovner: Pinchas Peli, "The Other Side of Joy," *Jerusalem Post International Edition*. October 10, 1987, p. 22.
Krantz: Ausubel, *Treasury*.
Kurzweil: (1) Kurzweil, *Generation*, pp. 19–28; (2) Lecture, YM-YWHA, Commack, NY, September 27, 1987.

Lamm: Correspondence.
Landau: (1) Richman, *Laughs*; (2) Mendelsohn, *Laughs*; (3) Author; (4, 5) Rabbi Sholom Klass, *Jewish Press*, October 7, 1988, p. 6.
Lazarus: Cowan and Cowan, *Blessings*, p. 74.
Lebensohn: Mendelsohn, *Laughs*.
Levenson: *Reader's Digest Treasury*.
Levi Yitzhak: Richman, *Wit*.
Levin, Meir: Levin, *Search*, pp. 14–18.
Levin, Shamaryahu: (1) *Jewish Digest*, October 1978; (2) Richman, *Wit*.
Levin, Zevi Hirsch: Author.
Lindheim: Lindheim, *Quest*, pp. 47–55.

Luria: Ausubel, *Treasury*.

Maimonides: (1) Gersh, *People*, pp. 164ff; (2) Author.
Malbim: (1) Mendelsohn, *Laughs*.
Manasseh: Epstein, *Zion's Call*, pp. 11ff.
Mansoor: Braude, *Handbook*.
Marcus: (1, 2) Eichhorn, *Folklore*.
Marx, Harpo: Gross, *Almanac*, pp. 272–273.
Marx, Karl: Padover, *Marx*, pp. 81ff.
Matlin: Joseph Aaron, "Cheers for Marlee," *Jewish Week* (NY), April 17, 1987, p. 2.
Mattathias: Gersh, *People*, pp. 74ff.
Meir: (1) Bildersee, *History*, p. 22; (2) Reizenstein, *Wisdom*, p. 184.
Meir, Golda: (1) Meir, *Life*, pp. 203–206; (2) *Jewish Digest*, December 1970; (3) *Jewish Digest*, December 1969; (4) *Jewish Digest*, January 1970; (5) *Jewish Digest*, January 1974; (6) *Jewish Digest*, January 1971; (7) *Jewish Digest*, August 1971; (8) Eichhorn, *Folklore*; (9, 10) Fadiman, *Anecdotes*.
Meir of Rothenberg: (1) Gersh, *People*, pp. 188ff; (2) Keller *Diaspora*, pp. 224–225.
Menachem Mendel: Wiesel, *Souls*, p. 232.
Mendele Mocher Seforim: Richman, *Wit*.

Mendelssohn, Abraham: Richman, *Wit.*
Mendelssohn, Moses: (1, 4) Richman, *Laughs;* (2) Mendelsohn, *Laughs;* (3) *Jewish Digest,* August 1970; (5) Fadiman, *Anecdotes.*
Menuhin: Menuhin, *Journey,* p. 285.
Mohilewer: Richman, *Wit.*
Moishe: Neches, *Tales,* pp. 48–49.
Monobazus: Tosifta.
Montefiore: (1) Author; (2) Mandel, *Treasury;* (3, 4) Richman, *Laughs.*
Moses: (1) Bible; (2) Exodus Rabbah.
Moses of Crete: Siegel and Rheins, *Almanac,* pp. 584–585.
Moses Leib: Ausubel, *Treasury,* p. 82.

Nachman: (1, 2) Wiesel, *Souls,* p. 172, 176.
Naphtali: Wiesel, *Four Hasidic Masters,* p. 108.
Netanyahu: Stevenson, *Entebbe,* pp. 109ff.
Niles: Grose, *Israel,* pp. 250ff.
Noah: Adler and Connolly, *Ararat,* pp. 6ff.
Nordau: Nordau and Nordau, *Nordau,* pp. 120–121.

Onkelos: Richman, *Wit.*
Oshry: Jacobs, *Belief,* p. 153.
Ozick: Author.

Peerce: *Jewish Digest,* May 1970.
Peres: Golan, *Peres,* pp. 206ff.
Perlman: Fadiman, *Anecdotes.*
Perlmutter: Perlmutter, *A Bias of Reflection,* pp. 35–39.
Philo: Gersh, *People,* pp. 94ff.
Phineas ben Yair: Talmud.
Picon: (1) Fadiman, *Anecdotes;* (2) Picon, *Molly,* pp. 54ff.
Pinchas: (1) Ausubel, *Treasury;* (2, 3) Wiesel, *Four Hasidic Masters,* pp. 1–3; 10–11.
Pool: Author.
Potocki: Jacobs, *Belief,* p. 42.
Priesand: Priesand, *Judaism,* pp. xiii–xvi.

Rabin: Slater, *Rabin,* pp. 75–76; and Kurzman, *Ben-Gurion,* pp. 292ff.
Rackman: Correspondence.
Rashi: Gersh, *People,* pp. 146ff.
Reuben ben Istrubli: Richman, *Wit.*
Rosenzweig: Glatzer, in Rosenzweig, *Redemption,* pp. xi–xii.
Rothschild, Edmond de: (1) Richman, *Laughs;* (2) *Reader's Digest Treasury.*

Rothschild, Lionel de: Goldberg, *Connection*, p. 2.
Ruppin: Ruppin, *Memoirs*, pp. 82–83.
Ruth: Bible.

Saadia: Bildersee, *History*, p. 65.
Safra: Talmud.
Salant: Neches, *Tales*, pp. 38–39.
Salanter: (1) Richman, *Laughs*; (2, 3) Jacobs, *Belief*; (4) Mendelsohn, *Ring*; (5) Gersh, *People*, pp. 250ff.
Salomon: Milgrim, *Salomon*, pp. 67–74.
Samuel ben Sosrati: Author.
Samuel Ha-Nagid: Mandel, *Story*, p. 113.
Saul: Neches, *Tales*, pp. 53–54.
Schechter: Richman, *Wit*.
Scheindele: Neches, *Tales*, pp. 35–36.
Schiff: Richman, *Wit*.
Schreiber: Neches, *Tales*, pp. 27–29.
Seligman: Birmingham, *Crowd*.
Senesh: Senesh, *Life*, pp. 366ff.
Shamir: Begin, *Revolt*, pp. 106–107.
Sharon: Silver, *Begin*, p. 197.
Shcharansky: Gilbert, *Shcharansky*, pp. 29ff.
Shimkin: Gross, *Jewish Week*, August 13–20, 1977, p. 13.
Shneur: Mindel, *Shneur*, pp. 35–39.
Sills: Sills, *Bubbles*, pp. 185–187.
Silver: Mendelsohn, *Ring*, p. 212.
Simeon ben Shetah: Talmud.
Singer: (1, 2) Fadiman, *Anecdotes*; (3, 4, 5, 6) *Isaac in America* (film).
Slepak: *Jewish Digest*, November 1986.
Slonimsky: Rabbi Adam Fisher.
Sokolow: Richman, *Wit*.
Solomon: (1) Bible; (2) Mandel, *Story*, pp. 77–78; (3) Richman, *Wit*.
Soloveichik: (1) Richman, *Wit*; (2) Author.
Sonneborn: Slater, *Pledge*, pp. 11–19; and Levy and Postal, *Congress Monthly*, February 1978.
Spektor: (1) Richman, *Laughs*, (2) Mendelsohn, *Ring*.
Spinoza: Ratner, *Spinoza*, pp. xvff.
Steinberg: Steinberg, *Faith*, pp. 50ff.
Steinsaltz: (1) Sainer, "Steinsaltz," *Midstream*, December 1985, p. 33; (2) Richard N. Ostling, "Giving the Talmud to the Jews," *Time*, January 18, 1988, p. 64.
Straus: Richman, *Wit*.
Sukenik: Goldberg, *Jewish*, pp. 21–22.

Syrkin, Marie: Syrkin, *Syrkin*, pp. 229ff. Syrkin, Nachman: Syrkin, *Syrkin*, p. 9, 34.

Szold: *Youth Aliyah Bulletin*, Jerusalem, November 1980, p. 5.

Talner: Neches, *Tales*, pp. 42–43.
Trilling: Shahen, *Trilling*, pp. 38–40.
Trotsky: *Long Island Jewish World*, July 30–August 6, 1987, p. 3.
Trumpeldor: Silberberg, *Jerusalem*, pp. 115–117.
Twersky: Eichhorn, *Folklore*, pp. 49–50.

Wahl: Rosenstein, *Chain*, pp. 16ff.
Wallenberg: Werbell and Clarke, *Hero*, pp. 51ff.
Weisgal: Novak and Waldoks, *Book*, p. 142.
Weizmann, Chaim: (1, 2, 4) Richman, *Wit*; (3) Goldberg, *Jewish*, pp. 20–21; (5) Abba Eban, speech at Brookings Institute, Washington, D.C., June 24, 1987; (6) Correspondence; (7) Fadiman, *Anecdotes*; (8) Braude, *Handbook*.
Weizmann, Vera: *Jewish Digest*, March 1977.
Wells: Shenker, *Coat*, pp. 300–301.
Widrevitz: Neches, *Tales*, pp. 22–23.
Wiener: Wiener, *Ex-Prodigy*, pp. 143–155.
Wiesel: (1) Correspondence; (2) Kurzweil, *Generation*, pp. 129–130.
Wiesenthal: Correspondence.
Wigoder: Wigoder, *Hope*, pp. 115ff.
Wise, Isaac M.: Knox, *Rabbi*, pp. 51ff.
Wise, Stephen: (1) Braude, *Second Encyclopedia*; (2, 3) Correspondence; (4) *Jewish Digest*, June 1970; (5) Braude, *Handbook*; (6) Richman, *Wit*; (7, 8, 9) Eichhorn, *Folklore*.
Wolf: (1) Ausubel, *Treasury*; (2) Wiesel, *Souls*, p. 51.
Wolfson: Shenker, *Coat*, p. 175.

Yaakov Yitzhak: Ausubel, *Folklore*, p. 345.
Yadin: (1) Richman, *Wit*; (2) *Jewish Digest*, October 1971.
Yechiel: Ausubel, *Folklore*, p. 51.
Yezierska: Yezierska, *Ribbon*, pp. 25–30.
Yitzhak: Braude, *Handbook*.
Yohanan ben Zakkai: (1) Gersh, *People*, pp. 100 ff; (2, 3) Talmud.
Yose ben Halafta: (1) Rywell, *Tears*, p. 170; (2) Reizenstein, *Wisdom*, p. 20.

Zangwill: (1) Haber, *Zionist*, p. 42; (2) Richman, *Wit*; (3) Author.
Zolel: Neches, *Tales*, pp. 56–57.
Zusya: (1) Author; (2) Wiesel, *Souls*, p. 120.
Zygelboim: Gilbert, *Holocaust*, p. 565.

REFERENCES

Abram, M. (1982). *The Day is Short: An Autobiography.* New York: Harcourt Brace Jovanovich.

Adler, C. (1941). *I Have Considered the Days.* Philadelphia: Jewish Publication Society.

Adler, S., and Connolly, T. E. (1960). *From Ararat to Suburbia: The History of the Jewish Community of Buffalo.* Philadelphia: Jewish Publication Society.

Allon, Y. (1976). *My Father's House.* New York: W. W. Norton.

Ausubel, N. (1948). *A Treasury of Jewish Folklore.* New York: Crown.

Baker, L. (1969). *Felix Frankfurter.* New York: Coward-McCann.

Begin, M. (1977). *The Revolt.* New York: Nash.

Bellow, S. (1976). *To Jerusalem and Back.* New York: Viking.

Bernstein, F. A. (1986). *The Jewish Mothers' Hall of Fame.* Garden City, NY: Doubleday.

Bildersee, A. (1918). *Jewish Post-Biblical History Through Great Personalities.* Cincinnati: Union of American Hebrew Congregations.

Birmingham, S. (1967). *"Our Crowd": The Great Jewish Families of New York.* New York: Harper & Row.

Borochov, B. (1984). *Class Struggle and the Jewish Nation,* ed. M. Cohen. New Brunswick, NJ: Transaction Books.

Boxer, T. (1987). *The Jewish Celebrity Hall of Fame.* New York: Shapolsky.

Braude, J. M. (1957). *Braude's Second Encyclopedia of Stories, Quotations, and Anecdotes.* Englewood Cliffs, NJ: Prentice-Hall,

_____ (1963). *The Speaker's Desk Book of Quips, Quotes, and Anecdotes.* Englewood Cliffs, NJ: Prentice-Hall.

_____ (1971). *Speaker's and Toastmaster's Handbook of Anecdotes by and about Famous Personalities.* Englewood Cliffs, NJ: Prentice-Hall.

Buber, M. (1947). *Between Man and Man.* London: Routledge and Kegan Paul.

Butler, P. (1980). *Judah P. Benjamin.* New York: Chelsea House.

Carmel, A. (1977). *So Strange My Path.* New York: Bloch.

263

Chagall, M. (1960). *My Life*. New York: Orion.

Chissin, C. (1976). *A Palestine Diary: Memoirs of a Bilu Pioneer, 1882–1887*. New York: Herzl Press.

Chomsky, W. (1957). *Hebrew: The Eternal Language*. Philadelphia: Jewish Publication Society.

Copeland, L., and Copeland, F. (1940). *10,000 Jokes, Toasts, and Stories*. Garden City, NY: Doubleday.

Cowan, P. (1982). *An Orphan in History*. Garden City, NY: Doubleday.

Cowan, P., with Rachel Cowan. (1987). *Mixed Blessings*. New York: Doubleday.

Cowen, I., and Gunther, I. (1984). *A Spy For Freedom: The Story of Sarah Aaronsohn*. New York: Lodestar Books.

Crawford, D. (1973). *Franz Kafka: Man Out of Step*. New York: Crown.

Dash, J. (1979). *Summoned to Jerusalem*. New York: Harper & Row.

Dayan, M. (1976). *Moshe Dayan: Story of My Life*. New York: William Morrow.

Eban, A. (1977). *Abba Eban: An Autobiography*. New York: Random House.

Eichhorn, D. M. (1981). *Joys of Jewish Folklore*. Middle Village, NY: Jonathan David.

Elon, A. (1975). *Herzl*. New York: Holt, Rinehart and Winston.

Epstein, L. J. (1984). *Zion's Call*. Lanham, MD: University Press of America.

Fadiman, C., ed. (1985). *The Little, Brown Book of Anecdotes*. Boston: Little, Brown.

Finkelstein, L. (1976). *Akiba*. New York: Atheneum.

Frankl, V. (1962). *Man's Search For Meaning*. New York: Touchstone.

Friedlander, A. (1968). *Leo Baeck*. New York: Holt, Rinehart and Winston.

Fuller, E., ed. (1980). *2,500 Anecdotes For All Occasions*. New York: Avenel.

Gersh, H. (1959). *These Are My People*. New York: Behrman House.

Gies, M., with Alison Leslie Gold. (1987) *Anne Frank Remembered*. New York: Simon & Schuster.

Gilbert, M. (1985). *The Holocaust*. New York: Holt, Rinehart and Winston.

_____ (1986). *Shcharansky: Hero of Our Time*. New York: Viking.

Golan, M. (1982). *Shimon Peres*. New York: St. Martin's Press.

Goldberg, M. H. (1986). *The Jewish You Wouldn't Believe it Book: The Jewish Connection*. New York: Steimatzsky/Shapolsky.

Golden, H. (1972). *The Golden Book of Jewish Humor*. New York: Putnam.

Grose, P. (1983). *Israel in the Mind of America*. New York: Knopf.

Gross, D. C. (1981). *The Jewish People's Almanac*. Garden City, NY: Doubleday.

Haber, J. (1956). *The Odyssey of an American Zionist*. New York: Twayne.

Halasz, N. (1955). *Captain Dreyfus*. New York: Simon & Schuster.

Hart, K. (1982). *Return to Auschwitz*. New York: Atheneum.

Hartman, G. (1960). *I Gave My Heart*. New York: Citadel.

Heschel, S., ed. (1983). *On Being a Jewish Feminist*. New York: Schocken.

Humes, J. C. (1978). *Speaker's Treasury of Anecdotes About the Famous*. New York: Harper & Row.

Jacobs, L. (1984). *The Book of Jewish Belief*. New York: Behrman House.

Javits, J. K., with R. Steinberg (1981). *Javits*. Boston: Houghton Mifflin.

Jones, E. (1953). *The Life and Work of Sigmund Freud*, vol. 1. New York: Basic Books.

Josephus (1972). *The Jewish War*. Middlesex, England: Penguin.

Kabakoff, J., ed. (1985). *Master of Hope: Selected Writings of Naphtali Herz Imber*. London: Associated University Presses.

Katz, S. (1968). *Days of Fire*. Jerusalem: Steimatzsky's Agency.

Keller, W. (1966). *Diaspora*. New York: Harcourt, Brace and World.

Knox, I. (1957). *Rabbi in America*. Boston: Little, Brown.

Koch, E. I., with W. Rauch. (1984). *Mayor: An Autobiography*. New York: Simon & Schuster.

Kohut, R. (1925). *My Portion*. New York: Thomas Seltzer.

Kurzman, D. (1978). *The Bravest Battle*. Los Angeles: Pinnacle Books.

_____ (1983). *Ben-Gurion: Prophet of Fire*. New York: Simon & Schuster.

Kurzweil, A. (1980). *From Generation to Generation: How to Trace Your Jewish Genealogy and Personal History*. New York: William Morrow.

Landau, R. (1984). *The Book of Jewish Lists*. New York: Stein & Day.

Levin, M. (1950). *In Search*. New York: Horizon Press.

_____ (1975). *Classic Hasidic Tales*. New York: Penguin.

Lindheim, I. L. (1962). *Parallel Quest*. New York: Thomas Yoseloff.

Mandel, M. (1974). *A Complete Treasury of Stories for Public Speakers*. Middle Village, NY: Jonathan David.

May, D. (1986). *Hannah Arendt*. Harmondsworth, England: Penguin Books.

Meir, G. (1976). *My Life*. New York: Dell.

Mendelsohn, S. F. (1935). *The Jew Laughs*. Chicago: L. M. Stein.

_____ (1942). *Let Laughter Ring*. Philadelphia: Jewish Publication Society.

Menuhin, Y. (1977). *Unfinished Journey*. New York: Knopf.

Milgrim, S. (1975). *Haym Salomon*. Philadelphia: Jewish Publication Society.

Mindel, N. (1969). *Rabbi Schneur Zalman*, vol. 1, *Biography*. Brooklyn, NY: Chabad Research Center.

Mortkowicz-Olczakowa, H. (1963). *The Massacre of European Jewry*. Kibbutz Merchavia, Israel: World Hashomer Hatzair.

Neches, S. M. (1938). *Humorous Tales of Latter-Day Rabbis*. New York: George Obsevage.

Netanyahu, B. (1972). *Don Isaac Abravanel*. Philadelphia: Jewish Publication Society.

Nordau, A., and Nordau, M. (1943). *Max Nordau*. New York: Nordau Committee.

Novak, W., and Waldoks, M., eds. (1981). *Big Book of Jewish Humor*. New York: Harper & Row.

Padover, S. K. (1980). *Karl Marx*. New York: New American Library.

Parzen, H. (1964). *Architects of Conservative Judaism*. New York: Jonathan David.

Perlmutter, Nathan. *A Bias of Reflections*. New Rochelle, NY: Arlington House, 1972.

Picon, M., with J. Berantini Grillo. (1980). *Molly*. New York: Simon & Schuster, 1980.

Polner, M. (1977). *Rabbi*. New York: Holt, Rinehart and Winston.

Priesand, S. (1975). *Judaism and the New Woman*. New York: Behrman House.

Ratner, J., ed. (1954). *The Philosophy of Spinoza*. New York: Modern Library.

Reader's Digest Treasury of Wit and Humor. (1958). Pleasantville, NY: Reader's Digest Association.

Reizenstein, J. (1921). *Rabbinic Wisdom*. Cincinnati: Union of American Hebrew Congregations.

Richman, J. (1926). *Laughs From Jewish Lore*. New York: Funk & Wagnalls.

_____ (1952). *Jewish Wit and Wisdom*. New York: Pardes.

Rosenstein, N. (1976). *The Unbroken Chain*. New York: Shengold.

Rosenzweig, F. (1972). *The Star of Redemption*. Boston: Beacon Press.

Rosten, L. (1970). *The Joys of Yiddish*. New York: Pocket Books.

Roth, C., and Wigoder, G., eds. (1972). *Encyclopaedia Judaica*. Jerusalem, Israel: Keter.

Roth, L. (1964). *Judaism: A Portrait*. New York: Viking.

Ruppin, A. (1971). *Arthur Ruppin*. New York: Herzl Press.

Rywell, M. (1960). *Laughing With Tears*. Harriman, TN: Pioneer Press.

Saint John, R. (1952). *Tongue of the Prophets*. Garden City, NY: Dolphin.

Samuel, M. (1966). *Blood Accusation*. New York: Knopf.

Schechtman, J. B. (1986). *The Life and Times of Vladimir Jabotinsky, Rebel and Statesman: The Early Years*. Silver Spring, MD: Eshel.

Schwarz, L. W. (1945). *Memoirs of My People Through a Thousand Years*. Philadelphia: Jewish Publication Society.

Senesh, H. (1972). *Her Life and Diary*. New York: Schocken.

Shahen, E. J., Jr. (1981). *Lionel Trilling*. New York: Frederick Ungar.

Shenker, I. (1985). *Coat of Many Colors*. Garden City, NY: Doubleday.

Siegel, R., and Rheins, C., eds. (1980). *The Jewish Almanac*. New York: Bantam.

Sills, B. (1976). *Bubbles*. Indianapolis: Bobbs-Merrill.

Silver, E. (1984). *Begin: The Haunted Prophet*. New York: Random House.

Silverberg, R. (1970). *If I Forget Thee O Jerusalem*. New York: Pyramid.

Simon, L. (1960). *Ahad Ha'am*. Philadelphia: Jewish Publication Society.

Slater, L. (1971). *The Pledge*. New York: Pocket Books.

Slater, R. (1971). *Rabin of Israel*. London: Robson Books.

Spaulding, H. D., ed. (1976). *A Treasure-Trove of American Jewish Humor*. Middle Village, NY: Jonathan David.

Steinberg, M. (1960). *Anatomy of Faith*, ed. A. A. Cohen. New York: Harcourt Brace.

Stevenson, W. (1976). *Ninety Minutes at Entebbe*. New York: Bantam.

Syrkin, M. (1961). *Nachman Syrkin: Socialist Zionist*. New York: Herzl Press and Sharon Books.

Teichmann, H. (1972). *George S. Kaufman*. New York: Atheneum.

Urofsky, M. I. (1976). *American Zionism From Herzl to the Holocaust*. Garden City, NY: Anchor Books.

Vorspan, A. (1960). *Giants of Justice*. New York: Union of American Hebrew Congregations.

Wallace, I., Wallechinsky, D., and Wallace, A. (1983). *Significa*. New York: Dutton.

Werbell, F. E., and Clarke, T. (1982). *Lost Hero: The Mystery of Raoul Wallenberg*. New York: McGraw-Hill.

Werblowsky, R. J. Z. (1962). *Joseph Karo*. New York: Oxford.

Wiener, N. (1953). *Ex-Prodigy*. New York: Simon & Schuster.

Wiesel, E. (1973). *Souls on Fire: Portraits and Legends of Hasidic Masters*. New York: Vintage Books.

_____ (1978). *Four Hasidic Masters and Their Struggle Against Melancholy*. Notre Dame, IN: University of Notre Dame Press.

Wigoder, D. (1966). *Hope is My House*. Englewood Cliffs, NJ: Prentice-Hall. 1966.

Yezierska, A. (1950). *Red Ribbon on a White Horse*. New York: Charles Scribner's Sons.

SUBJECT INDEX

Animals
  Akiba, (2) 10
  Ashi, 19–20
  Buber, (2) 44–45
  Chagall, 48–49
  Hesil, 99
  Moses, (2) 163–164
  Singer, (1) 213
  Talner, 225
Anti-Semitism (see also "Insults,
    Anti-Semitic")
  Abrabanel, 3
  Adler, H., 8
  Beilis, 29
  Breitbart, 43–44
  Dreyfus, 60–61
  Freud, (2) 81
  Hirsch, 101–102
  Hobson, 102
  Jacob David, 108
  Marx, H., 148–149
  Meir of Rothenberg, (1) 156–157;
    (2) 157–158
  Perlmutter, 179
  Philo, 179–181
  Rashi, 190–192
  Reuben ben Istrubli, 192
  Schreiber, 204
  Seligman, 204–206
  Straus, 221
  Trilling, 226
  Trotsky, 226
  Wise, S., (9) 242–243
  Wolfson, 243–244
Apostasy
  Asch, 18–19
  Baruch of Medzeboth, (1) 26
  Berlin, 37
  Gamaliel, (5) 84
  Heine, (2) 96
  Imber, 103–104
  Levi-Yitzhak, (1) 137–138
  Maimonides, (1) 143–144
  Meir, (1) 152
  Rashi, 190–192
  Spinoza, 219–220

Arabs
  Allon, 12–13
  Begin, (4) 28–29
  Blitzer, 40–41
  Cohen, E., 50–51
  Dayan, (1) 57–58
  Gebihah, (1) 84–85
  Kahane, 120
  Mansoor, 146
  Meir, G., (4) 155; (10) 156
  Montefiore, (4) 163
  Niles, 169–171
  Peres, 177–178
  Pool, 183
  Simeon ben Shetah, 212–213
  Sukenik, 221–222
  Trumpeldor, 227
Archeologists
  Sukenik, 221–222
  Yadin, 245–246
Art and Artists
  Chagall, 48–49
  Einstein, (8) 66–67
Auschwitz
  Hart, 93–94
Awards
  Agnon, 8–9
  Bialik, (3), 39–40
  Matlin, 150
  Singer, (6) 214
  Steinsaltz, (2) 221

Basel Program
  Herzl, (2) 97–98
Bible (see also "Torah")
  Abele, 2
  Elijah, 70
  Lindheim, 140
  Moses, (1) 163–164
  Rothschild, L., 194
Blessings
  Agnon, 8–9
  Akiba, (6) 11
  Twersky, 228
Brandeis University
  Baron, 25

Begin, 27–29
Ben-Gurion, 32–35
Ben-Zvi, 35–36
Blitzer, 40–41
Cohen, E., 50–51
Dayan, 57–59
Eban, 63–64
Einstein, (2) 65
Eshkol, 73–74
Herzl, 96–99
Jacobson, 109–111
Kahane, 120
Koch, 122–123
Kollek, 125
Kovner, 128
Marcus, 146–148
Meir, G., 153–156
Netanyahu, 168
Niles, 169–171
Nordau, 172–173
Peres, 177–178
Rabin, 187–188
Shamir, 207–208
Sharon, 208
Sills, 211–212
Sonneborn, 217–218
Weizmann, C., 231–233
Wise, S., (3) 241; (8) 242
Yadin, 245–247

Jerusalem
Akiba, (4) 10–11
Begin, (4) 28–29
Cresson, 53–54
Dayan, (3) 57–59
Salant, 198
Jewish Law
Isserles, 105
Landau, (1) 134
Yohanan ben Zakkai, 248–250
Jewish National Fund
Herzl, (4) 98–99
Job, Book of
Abele, 2
Journalists

Blitzer, 40–41
Cahan, 47–48
Koch, 122–123
Judaism
Ashi, 19–20
Brod, 44
Gordis, 87–88
Steinsaltz, (1) 221
Yohanan ben Zakkai, 248–250
Justice
Kovler, 127–128
Saadia, 197
Wolf, (1) 243

Kabbalah
Caro, 48
Kibbutz
Einstein, (4) 65–66
Kindness
Ben-Zvi, 35–36
Cohen, Henry, 51
Fox, 77
Hartman, 94
Luria, 141
Salanter, 198–200
Slonimsky, 214–215
Szold,(2) 223–224
Kosher Food
Bellow, 30–31
Berlin, 37

Lawyers
Adler, C., 7–8
Benjamin, 36
Brandeis, 41–43
Frankfurter, 78
Leadership
Abrabanel, 3
Ephraim ben Sancho, 72–73
Love
Baal Shem Tov, (3) 22; (4) 22–23
Ginzberg, 85–86
Gratz, 88
Lust
Amram, 15–16
Caro, 48